BREAKING IRAQ

BREAKING IRAQ

The Ten Mistakes
That Broke Iraq

**by Colonel Ted Spain, US Army (ret)
and Terry Turchie, Dep. Asst. Dir. FBI (ret)**

History Publishing Company
Palisades, New York

Copyright ©2013 by Terry Turchie and Ted Spain

Spain, Teddy R.

    Breaking Iraq : the ten mistakes that broke Iraq / by
Colonel Ted Spain and Terry Turchie ; foreword by Tom
Ricks. -- Palisades, NY : History Pub. Co., c2013.

      p. ; cm.

    ISBN: 978-1-933909-53-0 (hc) ; 1-933909-53-6 (hc
10-digit) ; 978-1-933909-57-8 (ebk.) ; 1-933909-57-9
(ebk. 10-digit)
    Includes bibliographical references and index.
    Summary: The unvarnished account of a brigade
commander's tour of duty in Baghdad during the first
chaotic year of the American occupation following the
2003 invasion. What went wrong and what was wrong with
the U.S. military is closely examined. The ten major
mistakes made in Washington and on the battlefield
are brought to light.--Publisher.

    1. Iraq War, 2003-2011. 2. United States--Armed
forces--Iraq. 3. United States--Politics and
government--21st century. 4. Iraq--Politics and
government, 2003- 5. Military assistance,
American--Iraq. 6. Deception--Political
aspects--United States. 7. Iraq--Armed
forces--Operational readiness. 8. Internal
security--Iraq. 9. Abu Ghraib Prison. 10. Prisoners
of war--Crimes against--Iraq. I. Turchie, Terry D.
II. Title.

DS79.76 .S63 2013   2013933037
956.7044/3--dc23   1303

LCCN # 2013933037

Published in the United States by
History Publishing Company LLC
Palisades, NY
www.historypublishingco.com

SAN: 850-5942

Dedication

Breaking Iraq is dedicated to the men and women of America's armed forces and to those thousands of civilians who have served on the domestic and international front lines of the war on terror. This book is especially devoted to the thirteen men and women I left behind in Iraq. They gave their lives in the early days of the fight to free Iraq from tyranny and protect America from further terror attacks. Not a day has gone by that I haven't thought of them. All of them are my heroes. May God forever be with them and the families they left behind.

SPC Narson Sullivan	411th MP Co.
SGT Travis Burkhardt	170th MP Co.
SPC Eric Hull	307th MP Co.
SSG Bobby Franklin	210th MP Co.
PFC Charles Sims	549th MP Co
LTC Kim Orlando	HHD, 716th MP Bn.
SSG Joseph Bellavia	194th MP Co.
CPL Sean Grilley	194th MP Co.
PFC Rachel Bosveld	527th MP Co.
SGT Aubrey Bell	214th MP Co.
SGT Nicholas Tomko	307th MP Co.
SSG Aaron Reese	135th MP Co.
SPC Todd Bates	135th MP Co.

Contents

Foreword

This is an important book, because it gives us the unvarnished account of one brigade commander's tour of duty in Baghdad during the tumultuous first year of the American occupation there. From it the reader will learn much about what went wrong in Iraq, and also what was wrong with the American military. There also are valuable lessons for anyone about command in any war.

Colonel Teddy Spain and his friend Terry Turchie here do what the U.S. Army should be doing: They soberly look back on what happened in Baghdad in 2003-04. This is a commander telling the truth as best he can about a tragedy he both witnessed and played a role in. Throughout, he conveys the nagging sense that it did not have to be this way. He tells the story of American soldiers who, like millions of Iraqis, suffered the consequences of poor decisions by the president of the United States and the generals he commanded.

As Colonel Spain shows, it was particularly frustrating for a military police officer, who—unlike the armor, infantry and artillery commanders to whom he reported—understood how to bring security and order to a civilian population. One of the most arresting moments in this account is when Spain listens to Brig. Gen. Robinson, acting commander of the 1st Armored Division, hold forth at great length of how to employ the MPs. Spain finally said, "Sir, I don't agree with anything you've said during the last thirty minutes. Where did you get your understanding of police work, from watching two episodes of 'Hill Street Blues'?" There is a smack of reality in that comment that brings me back for a moment to the agony of Baghdad in 2003, as it became clear that the people running the American military had no clue about what to do in the Iraqi capital. Or, as Colonel Spain puts it, "Our methods of trying to bring the rule of law to Iraq and establish law and order through trust and respect were shoved aside by military and civilian leaders who simply didn't know what they were doing and had no understanding of the role of law enforcement in a democracy." That sentence should be read and studied by our generals. Instead of doing what they needed to do, the Army's leaders in Iraq did what they knew how to do, the authors observe: They "focused on killing the bad guys because that was their comfort zone. They had trained their entire lives for that, and were good at it."

Likewise, the next time someone refers to "the coalition of the willing" that invaded Iraq, they should be reminded of Spain's observation that many of the troops sent by coalition nations were "largely irrelevant."

I have written two books about the Iraq war, and spent much time there between 2003 and 2008, but I still learned some very interesting things here. I wrote in my book *Fiasco*, for example, about the death of Lt. Colonel Kim Orlando, one of the highest ranking American officers lost in combat in Iraq. But I did not know that when he was attacked carrying out a mission to track Moqtada al-Sadr and be prepared to kill or capture that Shiite firebrand leader.

Nor did I know that in September 2003, just as the Iraqi insurgency began to take off, Spain's troops—and presumably those in other units—were told to turn in "special weapons" such as Stinger anti-aircraft missiles "because our government declared that combat operations were over." Among other things, that event shows how Washington's political rhetoric can become dangerous when it begins shaping how soldiers operate in a combat zone.

But the book is perhaps most memorable for its portraits of some key commanders in Iraq during that crucial first year of the war. The depiction here of Brigadier General Janis Karpinski, the American commander of the brutal jailers of Abu Ghraib, is likely to be definitive. Most striking of all, perhaps, is the profile that emerges of Lt. General Ricardo Sanchez as an inept leader, in over his head, and taking it out on his subordinates. Sanchez chewed out Spain after the killing of Lt. Colonel Orlando, even though Spain had no tactical control over what was happening. "It was probably the most indecent action by a leader that I've ever witnessed in my twenty years of service," Maj. Gillian Boice states in this book.

Sanchez was a remarkably uninspiring leader. Colonel Spain notes that he had his wife mail him a package of NoDoz because "I certainly didn't want Sanchez to make an example of me in front of the others if I nodded off while he was 'mentoring' us during his periodic marathon meetings."

It is a sign of the honesty of Spain that he does not excuse himself from scrutiny . Discussing the failure of the leaders of the American occupation force to protect the people, he confesses that, "Despite the misgivings I had and the thoughts I expressed to my commanding officers, I fell in line with the senior combat arms leaders." He adds that he, like many other American officials, "was dead wrong in my own assumptions."

The question remains: Will we benefit from the lessons that Colonel Spain and Terry Turchie provide here? They have done their part. They have spoken truth to power. It is now up to the to rest of us-and especially to the leaders of today's Army—to try to learn, and not forget.

—Thomas E. Ricks
August 2012

Preface

THOUGHTS ON COMMAND IN COMBAT

A commander is responsible for everything his unit does or fails to do. The army gave me the honor and the privilege of being a commander; then they asked me to lead thousands of soldiers in combat. As the commander of the 18th Military Police Brigade for the first year of Operation Iraqi Freedom, I only wanted two things; to accomplish all of our missions and see every soldier return home alive. From the initial invasion of Iraq in late March, until our one year deployment was over, we accomplished all of our missions. However, I failed to bring every soldier back home alive. I accept full responsibility for that.

The heroes who gave their lives in Iraq are not just names, but human beings who believed in something greater than themselves. How many Americans can say that about what they do everyday? They gave their lives to accomplish the mission we were given, which was to liberate the Iraqi people and help create a safe and secure environment in a country that had been oppressed by a brutal regime for thirty years. Regardless of what their duty position was, every day they went about accomplishing whatever mission they were given, regardless of the danger they faced. Today they are looking down on us, knowing they gave everything they had, so people they didn't even know would have an opportunity for a better life and a quality of life that is just a small percentage of what most Americans enjoy everyday. Our heroes must not have died in vain.

13

We gave each of our fallen comrades a fitting memorial and mourned their loss. Each time, I knew these heroes left wives, husbands, children and other loved ones behind. They were all volunteers and each had their reasons for joining the army and defending their country. They all had great plans for the future, but none of them had planned on dying in combat. These soldiers will never see their children graduate from high school, will never attend their weddings, and will never coach their little league baseball teams.

During our one year in combat, we had contact with the enemy 395 times and we awarded 180 purple hearts as a result of wounds received during these attacks. Some of the surviving soldiers will never be physically the same and none of us will ever be emotionally the same. Things that were real important before the war just don't seem important any more. In the movies, combat sometimes seems glamorous. But in the movies, after the cameras are turned off, the actors get up, wipe away the fake blood and go home. In real combat, slain soldiers do not get up and do not go home. I will never forget the soldiers who perished while under my command and our nation will never be able to pay them or their families the debt they are owed. We can only hope that the decisions that take our country to war in the future are based upon what we learned from our recent past in Iraq and on the battlefields of other wars that shaped our history as a nation.

It is the only way the men and women who perished in Iraq will be able to rest in Peace. Their sacrifice is our constant reminder that freedom has never been free.

—Colonel Teddy R. Spain—United States Army (retired)

Acknowledgments

We would like to acknowledge the following units that were assigned to the 18th Military Police Brigade at some point or the other during the first year of Operation Iraqi Freedom: 1/41 Infantry Battalion and their A, B, C Infantry Companies; Headquarters of the following Military Police Battalions: 709th; 720th; 519th; 211th; 503rd; 115th; 400th; 168th; 716th, the following Military Police Companies: 511th; 527th; 549th; 551st; 615th; 64th; 401st; 411th; 204th; 855th; 233rd; 65th; 108th; 978th; 143rd; 94th; 1139th; 186st; 812th; 307th; 170th; 72nd; 32nd; 443rd; 135th; 156th; 770th; 1165th; 214th; 2175th; 210th; 269th; 323rd; 442nd; 194th; 977th; 988th, the following Law and Order Detachments: 143rd; 382nd and the V Corps Band.

The brave men and women of these units answered their nation's call to service, and are part of the next greatest generation. We will let the historians sort out whether the politicians that decided to invade Iraq got it right or wrong. We know these brave soldiers got it right.

We would also like to thank Tom Ricks, who planted the original thought into Colonel Spain's head of writing a book about his experiences in Iraq, while he was interviewing him for his book, Fiasco. We are especially appreciative of him writing the forward.

We also want to thank our better halves, Joy Turchie and

R'ami Spain for their support and understanding during this very long process. And a special thanks to Chris and Josh Spain who shared their father, and R'ami shared her husband, with the soldiers in the units above, and the Iraqi people, just as thousands of other families have and are still doing.

Finally, we want to thank The US Army and the FBI, for being so good to us for over half a century. We are proud to have served in these two remarkable institutions.

Ted Spain
Terry Turchie

Introduction

"Breaking Iraq" is about ten critical decisions that broke Iraq and caused the war to be prolonged endlessly. Those decisions, made by high ranking military officers and political leaders in Washington, fell upon the U.S. military on the ground to carry them out unquestioningly.

With myopic focus, those decision makers caused severe, adverse ramifications to the U.S. military and the people of Iraq, many of which are present today. Some of the problems caused by those decisions, so lacking in foresight, were left to one particular army unit to resolve-the 18th Military Police Brigade. Some problems were resolved. Many were impossible to correct. As the commander of the 18th Military Police Brigade headquartered in Baghdad in 2003, I was in a unique position to personally witness the inherent difficulties caused by those ten decisions that virtually broke Iraq, and why we, the United States, were unable to make much progress in putting Iraq back together again during that first year.

I'd been told my entire military career that even the best of plans never survived their first contact with the enemy. I understood what that meant based on countless military exercises. However, I didn't understand that bad decisions, or decisions not made at all during the planning and execution of a war plan, created so many difficulties for a senior commander, such as myself, on the battlefield. Some of those bad decisions were made by me, but my soldiers and I inherited the vast majority of them. Even though I was helpless to prevent most, I should have seen some of them coming. I should have fought harder to prevent others. Regardless of the cause, things are what they are. Military commanders at all levels have to be flexible and adaptable to the situation. They must exercise great leadership to compensate for the negative effects of decisions beyond their control. The enemy gets a vote, the media gets a vote, and politicians surely get a vote, in decisions senior military commanders make on the battlefield. A commander can never underestimate the effects of any of these. This book is about the actions that my commanders, my soldiers and I took to overcome these decisions, or lack thereof, to try and accomplish our mission in Iraq.

The American led invasion of Iraq in March, 2003 had the effect of breaking the country's political, military, economic and industrial power base. Saddam Hussein, the glue that held Iraq's power centers together for decades, went from tyrannical dictator to fleeing felon. The result was a complete breakdown of order in Iraq's cities, towns and villages. The ensuing power vacuum was filled by multiple ethnic groups who had never gotten along; former soldiers from Saddam's recently disbanded army; violent criminals who were armed and released from prison by Saddam prior to the invasion; and outsiders who imported terrorism into the streets and directed it against the American "invaders."

General Colin Powell, who as Secretary of State went before the United Nations and pleaded America's case for invading Iraq, would later say:

"If you break it, you own it. We broke Iraq without any plan to fix it." [1]

In "A Conversation with Colin Powell," in *The Atlantic* magazine, in 2007, he explained what he meant:

"When you take out a regime and you bring down a government, you become the government. On the day that the statue came down and Saddam Hussein's regime ended, the United States was the occupying power. We might also have been the liberating power, and we were initially seen as liberators. But we were essentially the new government until a government could be put in place. And in the second phase of this conflict, which was beginning after the statue fell, we made serious mistakes in not acting like a government. One, maintaining order. Two, keeping people from destroying their own property. Three, not having in place security forces—either ours or theirs or a combination of the two to keep order. And in the absence of order, chaos ensues." [2]

I knew very well what my mission would be in Iraq. In the midst of an invasion of a nation and the ouster of a dictator, my soldiers and I would be largely responsible for replacing decades of tyranny with institutions, people, and philosophies that would provide a foundation in Iraq for the rule of law. To be successful, we would need support from senior American political and military leaders who understood the complexities of establishing law and order in Iraqi culture.

It didn't take long to realize that decisions made by high level political leaders at home and by some military leaders on the battlefield were placing the lives of soldiers unnecessarily at risk. Questioning those decisions based on our experience as to what worked and what didn't work, created conflict, expended energy we didn't have in the middle of a war, and discouraged good leaders from coming forward with alternate plans and strategies.

The ten key decisions or non-decisions discussed in this book actually complicated our efforts to establish law and order in Iraq. I am proud of the soldiers who served with me and tried to overcome the impact of those decisions. I couldn't have asked for a better set of battalion and company commanders to execute my decisions. But there's only one conclusion that I can reach from that first year on the ground. I ultimately failed in my mission to turn things around. No matter how hard I tried, I couldn't mitigate all of the impact of decisions where politics trumped tactics. I had been raised in the military to be a tactical leader. However, I learned to never under estimate the political or media impact on my decisions.

I quickly learned that the only possible strategy to try and overcome the effects of poor decisions was great leadership. The leaders in my brigade did the best they could. As I prepared to take the 18th Military Police Brigade into Iraq in March, 2003, leadership was foremost in my mind. Soldiers deserve great leadership. You give them leadership and they will perform miracles. We lost soldiers in Iraq and had others forever injured because they didn't have the right equipment, such as up-armored Humvees and the proper body armor. The least we could do was to give them great leadership.

On October 12, 2006 Gerald F. Burke, a retired Major in the Massachusetts State Police who was a member of a Department of Justice assessment team that traveled to Iraq in the spring of 2003 testified before the Senate Democratic Policy Committee Hearing:

> "First and foremost, I have nothing but praise for the military. Their war-making capabilities are simply awesome. In particular, I want to compliment the 18th Military Police Brigade and its commanding officer at the time, Colonel Teddy Spain. The 18th MP Brigade was the quickest to recognize the transition from war-fighters to stability and reconstruction operations." [3]

In the summer of 2009, I met Terry D. Turchie, a former FBI agent. He had spent 29 years in the Bureau before retiring as the Deputy Assistant Director of the Counterterrorism Division on April 1, 2001. Terry had been responsible for the FBI's Unabomb Task Force, the fugitive search for Olympic bomber Eric Robert Rudolph, and traveled with former FBI Director Louis Freeh in March, 2000 to Turkey, India, Pakistan and several former Soviet republics in an effort to secure cooperation from foreign governments to find al-Qaeda leader, Osama Bin Laden.

After leaving the FBI, Terry worked at the Lawrence Livermore National Weapons Lab, managed by the University of California for the Department of Energy. My younger brother Wes also worked at the lab and was aware of my feelings about the impact of good leadership on the outcome of events. Wes arranged for Terry and I to meet with each other. We quickly determined we had much in common, and in fact, it seemed like we had known one another for years. Terry traveled to my home in South Carolina and spent a week with my wife R'ami and I. We spoke for hours about leadership as a force for both good and bad. In our combined careers in government that totaled nearly sixty years, we had seen countless examples of the consequences of good and bad leadership.

Terry reminded me of Watergate, Ruby Ridge and Waco and the impact these events had on the image of the FBI and how they interfered with the trust between the FBI and the American public. Yet the decision by former FBI Director L. Patrick Gray to destroy White House documents related to the Watergate cover-up; the decision by a high level FBI official in Washington, D.C. to destroy a document concerning the FBI's strategy at Ruby Ridge and the assault on the compound at Waco were decisions made by individuals and not indicators of systemic problems within the FBI or its culture, as some politicians wanted the public to believe. Nonetheless, they had such a detrimental effect on the mission of the Bureau, the lessons they inspired, albeit negative, had to be studied and learned, if the same mistakes were to be prevented in the future. These were examples of bad leadership that threatened to undermine the entire institution if not heeded.

Of course, these were the same thoughts I had been having about my involvement in the invasion of Iraq and its aftermath. As the intensity and frequency of our conversations increased, Terry and I went through thousands of pages of my personal notes and other items that documented my time in Iraq and the decisions that were being made on a daily basis.

Terry interviewed many of the soldiers who served with me. Many wrote documents sharing their thoughts and conclusions in certain areas. We concluded that ten decisions made by high level military leaders and politicians, both in Washington, D.C. and on the ground in Iraq, had changed the course of the war and prolonged the conflict. Three years after first meeting one another, we incorporated our results into "Breaking Iraq." We hope that future leaders within government and private enterprise will learn from all that we learned in the government cultures where we spent our careers.

We know how important it is to speak the truth to power, regardless of the fear that might grip others in trying to face off with powerful and forceful people. We know that momentous historic events have sometimes been the result of bad decisions by people who simply did not understand how to think, recognize the difference between right and wrong, or were so weighted down by their own egos that they lost their way in life.

The results are usually tragic and in the calmness of hindsight and time, appear to have been preventable. In "Breaking Iraq," we have told the story accurately the way it was, and will remain, if we fail to learn from what happened there. Everything seems pretty clear in the blue sky of a decade later.

During my year in Iraq, the 18th MP Brigade conducted tens of thousands of combat patrols throughout Baghdad and across Iraq. The 18th personally apprehended thousands of Iraqis and others who intended to do us harm; held tens of thousands of detainees; and trained thousands of Iraqi police in the traditions of American law enforcement. The brigade helped rebuild or re-opened nearly one hundred Iraqi police stations, jails, prisons and other Iraqi police facilities. Thirteen soldiers under my command died on the battlefield during that first year to accomplish all of this.

I knew the day we entered Iraq that I wouldn't be able to bring all of my soldiers back home alive. My Deputy Commander, Lieutenant Colonel Tom Evans, could see the pain in my face as I came to grips with the thought.

"Damn sir, you're going to lose soldiers, this is a war," Evans told me.

Perhaps. But I'll never get over that some of my soldiers paid with their lives for decisions made far from the battlefield, where politics trumped tactics. It was the ultimate price of trying to put Iraq together again under the rule of law.

President Herbert Hoover once said, "older men declare war, but it is the youth that must fight and die." I hope American politicians understand the price we paid for Iraq's freedom. I hope the decisions they make about Iraq in the future continue to insure our soldiers did not die in vain.

INTRODUCTION: NOTES

1   The Atlantic, "A Conversation With Colin Powell," by David Samuels, April 18, 2007.

2   Ibid.

3   "An Oversight Hearing on the Planning and Conduct of the War in Iraq: When Will Iraqi Security Forces Be Able to 'Stand Up' So American Troops Can Begin to 'Stand Down?'" Transcript of Testimony Before Senate Democratic Policy Committee Hearing of Gerald F. Burke, former Major, Massachusetts State Police and former Senior Advisor, Iraqi Police, October 12, 2006.

THE MIDDLE EAST, MARCH, 2003

The invasion of the country began with a display of "shock and awe." The March 31, 2003 cover of *Newsweek* flashed the caption against the backdrop of an exploding Iraq. Thickened black smoke billowed across the city of Baghdad engulfed in yellow/orange flames that shot hundreds of feet into the night time sky. Saddam Hussein's fabled palaces, that hours earlier personified the tyrant's control and unending wealth, were visible only through the groaning sounds of their collapse and the smell of burning munitions and human flesh left in the wake of fast moving fires.

With the precision and choreography befitting a well rehearsed Broadway production, a stern voice shouted from the heavens:

> "What will follow will not be a repeat of any other conflict...it will be of a force and scope and scale that has been beyond what has been seen before... The Iraqi soldiers and officers must ask themselves whether they want to die fighting for a doomed regime." [1]

The narrator was Secretary of Defense Donald Rumsfeld.

During the first forty-eight hours of the massive attack, several thousand pounds of precision guided bombs fell onto priority targets, paving the way for the rapid advance of America's ground forces from the south, unleashed from their bases in Kuwait. The 101st Airborne Division and its Apache helicopters provided cover to the 3rd Infantry Division's M-1 tanks and Bradley fighting vehicles as they moved towards Baghdad. The 1st Marine Expeditionary used its F-18's and Cobra helicopter gun ships to soften up Iraqi troops before the arrival of ground forces. Flying into Iraq on C-130's, the 82nd Airborne went into action immediately, securing airfields and oil fields. Air Force B-52's, F-117 Nighthawk "stealth" fighters, and B-2 "stealth" bombers pounded Iraqi targets from south to north. And the hits kept coming, as the U.S.S. Kittyhawk, U.S.S. Abraham Lincoln, and U.S.S. Constellation supported the effort from the Arabian Sea.

Everything happened so fast, including the toppling of a statue of Saddam by Iraqi citizens that information from a senior U.S. government official months before the war, seemed an accurate reflection of the aftermath of the invasion.

"...the president...has been briefed about the need to have U.S. forces there for an extended period of time..." A couple of years is an extended period of time, and that we're prepared for." [2]

On May 1, President George W. Bush landed on the deck of the U.S.S. Abraham Lincoln, by that time steaming off the California coast.

"Major combat operations in Iraq have ended," he proclaimed. [3]

Just eleven days later, U.S. Ambassador L. Paul Bremer flew into Baghdad to coordinate the building of a post-invasion Iraq.

"We flew on a C-130 into Baghdad on May 12... The thing that was striking to us as we flew into Baghdad was that a lot of buildings were on fire. This was the looting that had started almost with the fall of Saddam's statue. It was to me a rather striking thing to see, both from the air and then driving into town, these buildings on fire and looting going on." [4]

The buildings burned at the hands of Iraqis, not American bombs. Controlling the ensuing criminal, terrorist, and insurgent activity would take years and result in thousands of American casualties. Iraq's cities, towns and villages broke into pieces, led by varieties of ethnic, religious, military and terrorist factions. Putting Iraq together again became the primary focus of America's military police. *Breaking Iraq* accompanies the 18th Military Police Brigade in Iraq to go inside the personalities, events and decisions in 2003 that turned "shock and awe," into "stop and stall." Hopefully, the lessons discussed in this book will help prevent the same result in our nation's future military endeavors.

NOTES:
1 Newsweek, March 31, 2003, "The War Begins," by Evan Thomas and Daniel Klaidman
2 U.S. News & World Report, December 2, 2002, "After the Fall," by Kevin Whitelaw.
3 Time, October 6, 2003, "So What Went Wrong?" by Michael Elliott.
4 Frontline, PBS, "The Lost Year in Iraq," June 26 and August 18, 2006 interviews of L. Paul Bremer.

CHAPTER ONE

WHERE ARE ALL THE MILITARY POLICE? THE FALLACY OF SECRETARY RUMSFELD'S DEPLOYMENT PLANS.

Combat arms soldiers were deployed to Iraq at the expense of the military police.

I assumed command of the 18th Military Police Brigade in Mannheim, Germanyin August, 2002. It took years of hard work with great mentors and soldiers to learn and polish the leadership skills the United States Army required to achieve the promotion to colonel. I was assigned the responsibility for two battalions of soldiers that made up the brigade, and any additional battalions, should we be deployed to combat. Not knowing what would lie ahead, I felt prepared to lead my soldiers into combat, but no one really knows how they will react during war, until tested in battle.

In previous assignments, I'd served as the Deputy Brigade Commander of the 16th MP Brigade, Airborne and Provost Marshal for the 82nd Airborne Division while stationed at Ft. Bragg, North Carolina seven years earlier; and commander of the 519th MP Battalion out of Ft. Polk, Louisiana. The 519th was later assigned to my brigade in Iraq. During the early 1990s, I was the Operations Officer for the 18th and Executive Officer for the 709th MP Battalion, one of the two battalions that made up the brigade I now commanded and would be taking to war.

The brigade was busy. The 709th MP Battalion was deployed on the peacekeeping mission to Kosovo and the 793rd MP

Battalion was preparing to take its place. The 18th also provided law enforcement services to United States Army military installations scattered throughout Germany. On top of everything else, my brigade was tasked to develop a contingency plan for the emergency deployment of an MP company to protect a Patriot air defense battery in the event of an Iraqi Scud attack on Israel.

I quickly learned that despite the training and experience I thought I had, the magnitude of this newest assignment was daunting. It became even more so when Lieutenant (Lt.) General William Wallace, the V Corps Commander, made a comment to me during one of our briefings.

"Colonel Spain, I predict that one day you'll be the Chief of Police of Baghdad, " he stated with confidence.

It wasn't long before his prediction came true. I went to Kuwait to participate in a four day planning conference in February of 2003. I was skeptical then that America would actually go to war with Iraq. I felt certain that I would soon return to Germany. Little did I know, I would be gone for a very long time. I was reminded of one of my favorite shows as a child, *Gilligan's Island*. In the show, Gilligan was the first mate on a cruise boat that gave groups of people three hour tours in the open ocean. A surprise storm whipped up during one of the trips and seven stranded castaways were ship wrecked on a tropical island for several television seasons. I left for a few days in Kuwait and returned a year later from war torn Iraq. Sadly, the year I was away was everything but funny.

I left the brigade in Germany in the capable hands of my Deputy Commander, Lt. Colonel Tom Evans, when I went to Kuwait. Evans was a close friend and confidant. We had known one another for years and I regarded him as a good old country-boy with lots of charisma. Being from North Carolina myself, we spoke the same language. Evans was born in Louisiana, raised in Mississippi, and joined the army so he could pay for his college education. He loved the army so much that after he paid back his loans he never left.

Evans knew that I worried constantly about a potential deployment to Iraq, the fate of my soldiers, and the need for precise and detailed readiness planning. He also knew I was a stickler for providing great leadership and training to soldiers. In fact, in the closing months of 2002 through my travel to Kuwait in early 2003, I shuttled from one army planning session to another, across Germany and the United States, working to prepare for war. In daily conversations with Lt. Colonel Evans I tried to keep my MP brigade in Germany updated on events.

Their scheduled deployment was still weeks away when I called him from Kuwait to let him know I probably wouldn't be returning. I told him things were moving more quickly than anticipated and I needed to get fifteen key personnel from my staff into Kuwait immediately. Evans worked out a plan to fly the soldiers I wanted ahead of their scheduled deployment by using spaces on commercial airliners out of Germany. By the time we were ordered to start the actual deployment of our brigade, Evans had been quietly securing spots on military flights leaving Germany to get additional staff members to join me whenever they had extra space. As a result, many of the 18th MP Brigade Headquarters was already in Kuwait by our deployment date.

The entire exercise was somewhat tricky. At the time, I still didn't know whether there would even be any invasion. In fact, my intelligence officer continued to predict that we would not invade Iraq before the fall of 2003. But I could tell from the first days of taking command of the brigade and then going on to Kuwait, that if there was any invasion, having sufficient MPs in the right places at the times I needed them was going to require as many bureaucratic skills as I could muster. Being bureaucratic was never my strongest suit.

We worked the "force flow" as hard as we could through military police channels while I was still in Germany. I contacted Forces Command out of Ft. McPherson, Georgia. They were responsible for controlling the deployment of MPs in the United States. I contacted the Department of the Army, headquartered at the Pentagon. They controlled all of the MPs in the Army, wherever they were based. Fortunately, Colonel Terry Carrico was the Provost Marshal for the Forces Command. He was one of the finest officers I ever served with in the Army. Terry and I had been friends since we first met as second lieutenants and he did everything he could to support us.

However, the most crucial decisions on MP force flow were made way above his level. Consequently, several months before leaving Germany for Kuwait, and until we initially entered Iraq, the Army kept changing the MP units available to me. Initially I had the 504th MP Battalion, commanded by Lt. Colonel Tom Tatum from Ft. Lewis, Washington. They were taken from me and given to the 220th MP Brigade, an Army reserve brigade commanded by Brigadier General Zachmerry, a U.S. Army reserve one star. I was told this was done to send a message to the army reserves that they could command and control an active duty battalion in combat. The politics had begun.

The 716th MP Battalion, commanded by Lt. Colonel Kim Orlando, was assigned to me initially, but then reassigned to the Marine Corps to support them for the ground war. I was told the Department of the Army wanted to send a message about the cooperation between the army and Marines, but they wanted to do it with an active duty battalion. The politics of war intensified. I found lots of irony in the concept that we were "one" Army-active, reserve, and National Guard, yet they wouldn't allow a reserveor National Guard MP Battalion to be assigned to the Marines. I was learning first hand there was a limit to the "one Army" concept.

Several reserve and National Guard MP battalions were listed as assigned to me, but taken away before my brigade ever left Germany. I was still responsible for briefing General Wallace on the readiness status of those units as the potential deployment date drew nearer. However, I had never seen or met them, and certainly had no influence ontheir combat readiness. This was clearly a political exercise to illustrate that the reserve and National Guard units were as ready as the active units of the Army. In most cases, it simply wasn't true, and many of those units were removed from the force flow and never deployed. The ones that did deploy, and served with me, were as good as my active duty units, if they had the right leadership, but that also applied to my active duty units. During my entire career I had heard about "good units," and "bad units," but my experience was that there was only good and bad leadership.

My beliefs about good versus bad leadership were confirmed in Iraq. Regardless of whether a unit was active, reserve, or National Guard, the quality of the unit depended upon the quality of its leaders. During one of my briefings to Wallace while we were still in Germany training for a possible invasion, he looked at the poor readiness of some of the reserve units on the briefing slides that were troop listed with me.

"What kind of brigade are you running Spain?" he jokingly asked me as he saw the poor readiness status of some of the units.

It was very frustrating that I was never allowed to contact any of these units to discuss their readiness. In some cases I wasn't even sure they knew they were being slated to deploy with me.

Evans was a tremendous help as we worked to get all of our plans implemented. Evans was a great planner in his own right, but always liked giving me credit for anticipating issues before they became problematic. He's one of the most driven people I've ever met when it comes to getting things done. Because of it, we formed a great team.

"Colonel, you're a great strategist, always thinking four steps ahead of everybody else. When we were thinking about the crossing into Iraq, you were already plotting what we'd be doing in Baghdad and where we should locate the headquarters company," he joked, as we put the finishing touches on the brigade's possible deployment.

But despite our best efforts to secure our own brigade's deployment to Iraq, the Army's overall war plan created significant manpower problems for us, and when time for the invasion came, MPs available to deploy were in short supply. There were several reasons this situation existed.

First, MPs were responsible for normal law enforcement missions at their home bases and couldn't just break away for deployment until they were replaced. Second, many of the reserve MPs were performing security missions in airports across the United States as part of a knee jerk reaction to the attacks of 9/11. Third, MPs were still deployed to peacekeeping assignments in Kosovo and Bosnia. Finally, the overall lack of MPs in the force structure was a direct result of President Bill Clinton's peace dividend after the Soviet Union fell apart, and following the drawdown from Operation Desert Storm, the first Gulf War. The U.S. Army had simply become too small to address all of the missions America's politicians were throwing its way.

From the very beginning of my taking command, the synchronization between the arrival of soldiers and their equipment was a significant problem. My first battle in the Iraq war was with the V Corps Army staff, as I tried to get adequate numbers of MPs in the Army's system for "time-phased force and deployment data maintenance." We referred to it using the military acronym, TPFDD. Given the mission assigned to us, to be effective doctrinally, we required fifty MP companies, but no commander ever thinks they have enough troops. When the war plan was published, the Army task organization before the invasion provided for just twenty companies, so we put together our war plan based on those twenty companies. By the time my brigade crossed into the Iraqi desert on the push to Baghdad, I had only three companies with all of their equipment, and sent another two platoons without equipment on helicopters to the first enemy prisoner of war holding area. Two thousand MPs had to be left in Kuwait, as they waited for their equipment to arrive from the states. Thousands more were back in the states with their equipment, waiting for transport to Kuwait. The situation was extremely frustrating, and the shortage of MPs potentially dangerous.

My MPs were never given any prioritization of space on the ships that carried troops into battle, rendering them almost irrelevant during the initial stages of the ground war. I was unable to send any MP assets to the combat arms divisions because of the extreme shortage of MPs. So, as the planning for an Iraqi ground war intensified, the arrival of MPs to the combat zone kept getting pushed back in the force flow. As if the lack of placement in the TPFFD wasn't bad enough, the Army created force packages, including some of my MP units, that would deploy with the major combat arms formations to the 101st and 82nd. The 101st and 82nd units arrived in time for the invasion, but my MPs were not with them.

I took another action to mitigate the shortage of MPs that will never make it into the history books. Back in Germany, General Wallace's band, the V Corps Band, was attached to me because we were collocated in Mannheim. I couldn't task them, but was responsible for their tactical training and supporting their administrative and logistical needs.

Once I realized there would be a shortage of MPs I decided to train the band members to conduct missions to control access to the Corps Rear Command Post, knowing that my limited number of MPs would be tagged with that mission. I also used them as opposing forces (OPFOR), against my MPs, who were training for the invasion. They performed magnificently while training.

They performed equally well providing security of the Corps Rear CP during the invasion, and until the CP was disbanded and moved to Baghdad.

Our experience was not isolated, but part of a larger pattern experienced by my commanders across the Army. As an example, Major John Bogdan, Operations Officer of the 720th MP Battalion fought countless battles with army leaders at his home base, Fort Hood, Texas. The 720th was not a division unit so they didn't have priority in getting access to the limited equipment available or training time. Stationed at the home of the 4th Infantry and the 1st Cavalry Divisions, the 720th was simply not a deployment priority.

In one instance we were able to secure enough pre-positioned equipment in Kuwait to outfit an entire MP company. I designated it for the 549th MP Company from Ft. Stewart, Georgia. They picked up the equipment, but found that it was substandard. I desperately needed those MPs, but when I personally inspected the equipment with them, I decided it was indeed of such poor quality that I couldn't risk sending the nearly 200 MPs of the 549th into Iraq with it. I pulled the 549th out of the invasion entirely at the last minute, pending the arrival of their own equipment from the states.

Everything came to a boiling point the first day of March, when I was summoned to a briefing at Camp Doha in Kuwait to discuss the Army's readiness status if the decision was made to launch the invasion on March 10. At the time we were being told that March 10 was a hypothetical date. I learned after I retired, it was the actual date the Pentagon had planned to launch the invasion, until it became obvious at the briefing we weren't even close to being ready. As I walked into a local gymnasium where the briefing was held, it was like attending a West Point graduation of all the Army's top officers rolled into one class.

It was at the briefing that I first became acquainted with

Major General James Thurman, the Operations Officer for the Coalition Forces Land Component Command (CFLCC) for Operation Iraqi Freedom. Some people referred to the general as the "Thermonator." Thurman was one of the senior leaders at the briefing. A large map of Iraq was drawn on the gym floor. We used it to conduct war gaming. Each division commander and separate brigade commander, meaning they were not assigned to a division, took turns discussing the readiness status of their units with the assembled generals. Then, almost as if it were a high school or college class where role was being taken, each of the division commanders in the room gave an assessment of his readiness status.

"I have everything I need and will be ready to go on March 10," was the word from Major General Buford Blount, III, commanding the 3rd Infantry Division.

Major General David Petraeus, Commanding General of the 101st Airborne, said his soldiers weren't ready and was unable to commit to a March 10 invasion date.

"The 82nd won't be ready for an invasion on the 10th," Charles Swannack, Commanding General of the 82nd echoed the words of Petraeus.

I was surprised when they called me out to be the first of the non-division commanders to brief. I faced Lt. General Wallace, who was the commander of the V Corps and Lt. General David McKiernan, commander of the allied ground forces, who were sitting side by side. They were the key Army commanders involved in the invasion.

"If we invade on March 10, it will just be me, my operations officer and a rental car. I will call the rental company to see whether or not I can take the car to Baghdad."

At the time of the brief, the only vehicle I had in Kuwait was a rental car that had been picked up at the Kuwait City Airport. I wasn't trying to be disrespectful, but was extremely frustrated with the force flow that we had been fighting for weeks and figured the commanding generals needed to hear the truth, whether they wanted to or not.

Everybody but Wallace laughed. McKiernan could see that Wallace didn't think my comments were very funny and leaned over towards him.

"Scott, you know I had to take a risk with the MPs."

McKiernan and Wallace both knew that the MPs were pushed back in the force flow to get in all the combat arms.

"I hope you didn't take too much fucking risk," Wallace shot back at McKiernan. Although McKiernan was the ranking officer to Wallace, the latter wasn't at all shy about expressing that he failed to find anything about the situation funny. I just stood there looking very solemn because I didn't know whether Wallace would turn his anger towards me or not. Fortunately, he never did.

McKiernan sensed the frustration. He told Wallace he would look at diverting the 551st MP Company to Kuwait. They were already in the process of leaving Jubuiti after a six month deployment to return to Ft. Campbell Kentucky. They could be easily redeployed in our direction.

At a break in the meeting, General Thurman approached me and introduced himself, extending his hand in my direction.

"Colonel, you're crazy as hell. The rental car line was hilarious!" It was a key connection that would pay off for us in the days ahead.

Watching General Petraeus in action during the meeting made me think about the wisdom he always seemed to possess. Petraeus and I had known each other since the mid-1990s. We served in the 82nd Airborne Division when Petraeus was a brigade commander and I was the Provost Marshal.

Just days before the invasion was underway, I witnessed General Petraeus' intelligence and foresight yet again. None of us present at the time fully realized how much his wisdom would impact the battlefields of Iraq and Afghanistan in the coming years. Wallace had called all of his division and brigade commanders together to discuss the current war plan. During the discussion, Wallace dropped a bomb shell on us. President George W. Bush and Secretary of Defense Donald Rumsfeld were considering calling for a "strategic pause" in Iraq as the invasion progressed. I had never heard of such a thing. Saddam would have one more chance to leave Iraq or surrender since such a pause would amount to a break in the fighting. It was going to be timed to occur prior to the battle for Baghdad, and after the taking of Tallil by the Army and, An Nassariah, by the Marines.

Wallace, along with all of us, knew this was a dumb military tactic that could put our soldiers' lives at even more risk. But all professional military leaders understand, we all worked for and were subservient to civilian leadership. I personally thought it was insane to consider a "pause" during the ground war to allow Saddam to hit us with his chemical weapons. I absolutely believed he had them and would not hesitate to use them. Wallace went around the room to ask us our thoughts regarding the proposed "strategic pause."

When it was my turn to talk, I offered my assessment to the group. "If I was an enemy soldier and hadn't had a chance to surrender during the air campaign and our 'shock and awe' armored assault, this pause would give me an opportunity to find the closest soldier and surrender. If that happens, my estimated number of enemy prisoners of war could significantly increase, and quickly exceed my capabilities."

"I disagree. If I was an enemy soldier, I would just take off my uniform and blend into the local village so I could come back and fight another day," Petraeus interrupted me and was very confident in his assessment.

Petraeus' judgment turned out to be one hundred percent correct. Although there was never any strategic pause, this is exactly the action that some of Saddam's soldiers took, as they faced certain death at the oncoming American blitzkrieg.

Not long after our gathering about the strategic pause, Wallace summoned us for what turned out to be the final time in Kuwait, and offered another display of his outstanding leadership ability. It was one of the most emotional experiences in my military career. He had asked to see his Division and Brigade Commanders only. We all gathered and anxiously awaited his arrival. We chatted among ourselves about what he could possibly want to discuss. I personally thought it was going to be a butt chewing because several soldiers in the Corps had been hurt by vehicle accidents and a couple of accidental shootings. Fortunately, none belonged to me.

"Is everyone in here a commander?" Wallace asked when he walked into the room.

About four Colonels raised their hands, indicating that were staff officers, not commanders. He told them to leave. Now I really was curious about what was about to happen.

After they left he told us that President Bush was going to go on TV the next night to give Saddam 48 hours to leave Iraq. He said he figured we only had about 48 hours left in Kuwait. He told us we were the right commanders to do the job, and that probably the next time we would all be together would be in Baghdad. As usual, he turned out to be right. He then said he felt he should be giving us a "win one for the gipper" speech, but he just didn't have one in him, because not everyone was going to make it to Baghdad. The emotion in the room was overwhelming. I was in the midst of some of the toughest SOBs in our Army, but there wasn't a dry eye in the room. We knew what he meant.

When the meeting was over, I immediately returned to my headquarters at Camp Virginia and gathered my key staff to let them know we were about to launch. I gave them their guidance on how best to use our final hours. I then went to visit all the soldiers I had in Kuwait, whether they had their equipment or not. Since I knew I would be seeing some of them for the last time, I thought it was important for me to look them in their face and share my final thoughts about what was about to happen.

As I met with each company I told them I knew we didn't have the equipment we needed but we had to go with what we had. I told them we would win the war, and the world would be a safer place for their kids and grand kids because of what they were about to do. I asked them to watch out for each other, maintain their situational awareness, and always remember safety. I ended by telling them how proud I was of them and how proud I was to lead them into combat. Seeing the faces of those soldiers as I spoke to them for the final time reminded me of how much they were counting on me. It is an image I'll never forget, and portrayed to me the heavy burden of commanding soldiers in combat, which is leadership at the highest level.

Not too long after the earlier briefing at Camp Doha, Wallace told me he knew I didn't have enough MPs to perform all of my assigned missions. He asked me to make two things a priority. First, he wanted me to assure him that the enemy prisoners taken during the ground war wouldn't be allowed to slow down the 3rd Infantry's march to Baghdad. Secondly, he wanted me to do everything I could to ensure the fuel convoys made it to their destination. The Abrams tanks and Bradley fighting vehicles of the 3rd Infantry would need to rely on fuel that would be desperately needed to quench their energy thirst. We had to keep these fighting machines moving rapidly on the war's front line as they made their way toward the Iraqi capital, as part of one of the longest ground assaults in the history of modern warfare.

"Just get them there Ted. The tanks will need that fuel!" he directed me.

There was no better example of meeting General Wallace's intent to get the fuel to his fighting vehicles than my early bizarre decision to use only my Brigade Headquarters Company, along with my personnel security detail, to escort a fuel convoy ourselves. There wasn't anything written anywhere in Army doctrine that supported such a decision, but it was one of the first two major impacts of not having enough MPs. I was certainly never taught the concept by any of the great Army mentors I had, or in any of the numerous military schools I had attended.

The night before we left Kuwait to cross into Iraq with my Headquarters Company, a fellow army colonel whose last name was Brown and whom I had never met, found me in my make shift headquarters. He asked me for MPs to escort one of his companies and their fuel trucks into Iraq. I explained to him that the only MPs I had with all of their equipment had already entered Iraq that morning. He emphasized to me the criticality of getting the fuel into Iraq. It was then that I recalled the look on General Wallace's face when he explained to me days earlier how important the fuel trucks were to him. During that conversation Wallace said he had enough ammunition to kill everyone in Iraq, but if he didn't have the fuel to get his vehicles in the fight it wouldn't do him any good.

After a short argument with myself, including thoughts like, "What in the hell are you thinking?" I told Colonel Brown we would escort his fuel company. I just didn't tell him that I would do it with my Brigade's Headquarters Company and my personal security detail. I searched the camp and located Evans. I wanted to fill him in on the plan.

"Colonel Spain, you've lost your mind!" Another reason I thought so highly of Evans was he never held back on what he really thought.

Evans had a point, but I kept my word to Lt. General Wallace. At the same time, escorting fifty-five fuel trucks carrying over two hundred fifty-thousand gallons of fuel across 147 miles of enemy controlled desert seemed like a suicide mission. Without sufficient weapons capabilities and with so few soldiers, we were carrying enough fuel to light up the Iraqi sky from north to south if the enemy fired on us.

But with the decision final and Evans made aware, Colonel Brown and I walked across our encampment where he introduced me to Captain Emily Holcomb, the commander of the 515th Transportation Company. Holcomb, who went by the radio code name, "High-Roller 6," arrived at the invasion launch site with some of the tankers and fuel that I knew General Wallace desperately needed. With a handshake and a nod, I formalized the commitment I had made to Wallace, agreeing to escort the "Convoy from Hell" across the Iraqi desert.

To this day, many of my army buddies still think I was insane to accept the mission. At that time and on that day, we were the only option. My Headquarters' Company Commander, Captain Dereck Bellows, went by the radio call sign "Stallion 6." While I silently ran through a mental checklist that would power our Headquarters Brigade into Iraq, "Stallion 6" coordinated the fuel truck escort with Holcomb.

"I don't have any guns, I have fuel. If we get hit, we're screwed!" Standing barely 5'3", Holcomb, who struck me as being as tough as woodpecker lips, climbed on top of a Humvee to capture the attention of the 130 men and women who would follow her into war.

"We're not going to be supported by tanks. And there aren't going to be any "halts." Just stay on the road and you'll be fine," she told her assembled soldiers. She could feel their anxiety under the stifling sun. Holcomb dared not say the escort would be an MP Brigade Headquarters. They didn't need to know.

Just as I found out with my MP battalions, Commander Holcomb had her orders made up on the run. The 515th arrived in Kuwait in mid-March without the benefit of a battalion headquarters. There were no maps available, so she brought with her a tourist map of Iraq, printed in Canada. Heading directly to the port city of Arifjan, the company downloaded their equipment, sixty-one retail like fuel tankers, eighteen wheelers that could also be used to fuel airplanes.

The tankers were M-969 vintage, manufactured in the late 1980's. Each carried five thousand gallons of fuel and had a pony engine filter that allowed retail and bulk operation. The tankers were pulled by M-931 tractors, weighing five tons and built in the 1981-1982 timeframe. Traveling at speeds of fifteen to twenty miles per hour on sand and forty-five to fifty miles per hour on the pavement, the tankers performed well, but frequently blew seals because they were working so hard to pull their load through the desert grit.

After picking up their equipment, the 515th drove from the port city directly to Camp Virginia. They drove in the dark, without headlights and with no maintenance support. The orders Holcomb received from Brown, her commanding officer, were simple: be at the forward invasion assembly area on the border at 11:30 am and the MPs will take you to your designated location in Iraq that has the codename "Kenworth."

By the time our convoy pulled out of Kuwait for Iraq, Holcomb's 515th contributed fifty-five of the sixty-one tankers it started with, three Humvees and two support vehicles to our numbers. Our assembly point was a large area of sand surrounded by a manmade berm. There was a delay on the border as our convoy waited its turn to begin the journey into Iraq, following long columns of soldiers and equipment from other units comprising the force flow.

The delay gave Holcomb additional time to worry about the state of her equipment. Her four-door M-998 Humvee was not "armored up." The plastic doors were covered with a canvas top and the surface undercarriage was metal. The vehicle was painted in the camouflage green of Germany, not the desert sand of Iraq. A transistor radio enabled her crew to hear the British

Broadcasting Company. The speaker on her field radio didn't work so she had to hold it to her ear to hear it and be heard if she wanted to communicate with other units in her part of the convoy. Everyone agreed that four-way flashers would be a sign of trouble because no one expected much from the radios. In fact, her convoy should have had twenty-seven radios, but had only four. The containers with the radios were on a ship that had not arrived at port in time for her company's departure. Without maps and reliable means of communication, it was always a relief for all of us to travel with light from the morning sun.

Even tents remained in duffel bags at Kuwaiti port cities, having arrived too late for Holcomb's company to pick them up. As her convoy of soldiers and equipment finally had the green light to disappear over the border with us into hostile territory, whatever "life support" equipment Holcomb's company had with them, was tied to the tops of the vehicles.

Looking like *The Beverly Hillbillies*, another of my favorite television shows as a child, we all clumsily treaded across the indented tracks made by the first invaders to snake their way into Iraq. Mobile kitchens, tables, chairs, generators, light sets, camouflage netting, any extra ammunition, and a water buffalo, a two hundred fifty gallon trailer of precious liquid, pulled by another of the convoy's vehicles, rounded out the necessary creature comforts of this modern day wagon train.

At first, the sand was like baking powder. The heavy tanks that preceded us rendered the already fine sand, even finer. There weren't any roads. There were only the tracks made by vehicles from the earlier crossings. During darkness there was a complete ban on lights of any kind, so the twenty-seven hours it took for our six mile long convoy to travel one hundred forty-seven miles was made as dangerous by nature, as it was by the enemy. Having the benefit of the "Plugger," the U.S. Army version of the GPS, our columns moved across terrain that never changed.

Hour after hour, only the sensation of forward motion gave

any hint that we weren't traveling in circles. Sometimes, the night sky was so dark or the blowing sand so thick that soldiers in lead vehicles had to stick their head out of windows to tell the troops behind them to turn left or right. At one point during the night my vehicle lost sight of the convoy ahead. I had my radio operator call Evans' radio operator to let him know we were separated. Evans told his solider to tell my soldier how to catch up with them. I made it very clear I would not go any further, knowing there were many vehicles behind me, until Evans sent someone to link up with us and get us back together. To this day, Evans jokes with me about not trying to "catch up" with him. I had no way of knowing at the time that getting lost on the battlefield, as we were about to do, would lead to the death of so many fellow soldiers.

When one vehicle broke down, all of the vehicles along the six mile route stopped and formed a perimeter while a fix was invented. Signal lights were used to communicate that repairs were being made and almost always involved a story of creativity under duress. Holcomb gave her maintenance officer, whose last name was Patterson, a special commendation after the desert crossing for his efforts to keep vehicles moving. On one occasion he used a shoe lace to repair a broken belt so that a truck could keep running. He took parts from several vehicles that had to be left behind so that they could be used in other repairs. Whenever a vehicle did have to be left stranded, Patterson removed the oil so that it could be used again later.

Despite the hardships, our convoy moved along throughout the day, into the night and the next morning, following hand written road signs left by the Army at critical junctures. Every convoy had to cross its fingers and pray that the signs were where they needed to be and wouldn't be overlooked or obscured by the Iraqi weather and sandstorms.

Our "Convoy from Hell," finally reached a paved highway about the width of a golf cart path that took us to our targeted destination, code named "Kenworth." Colonel Brown caught up with us. Learning Holcomb was without a map of Iraq, he gave her the only one he had.

The truth is, there were never enough military police in Iraq in the early days of the war, to accomplish all the missions we were tasked to perform. Making matters even worse, some of the MPs assigned to Iraq were improperly used and given missions other than military police work. I was peripherally aware of discussions taking place among higher level civilian and military leaders that would result in decisions that had the effect of undercutting the military police role in the initial stages of the invasion of Iraq. Unfortunately, I had no avenue of on going communications with higher level authorities to influence their decisions and neither did any of my peers.

Secretary of Defense Donald Rumsfeld focused on getting combat arms soldiers to Iraq first to ensure a quick victory on the ground. Rumsfeld tried to maintain as much strategic surprise as possible to protect oil fields, keep Saddam off balance and to minimize casualties. He wanted to launch the invasion of Iraq before getting very far along into April when the weather would get so hot that it would be as big of an enemy as Iraq's vaunted Republican Guard. There was only one suitable seaport in Kuwait to bring in ships carrying the vast array of military equipment and supplies that would be necessary to support the invasion force. The arrival of military police in the theater was therefore pushed back to make room for the combat arms and their logistical requirements.

I understood some of the reasons for bringing combat arms soldiers into Iraq first. But I believe the Army had learned enough from previous deployments to countries like Panama, Kosovo, Bosnia, and Haiti that better planning would have created a more proper balance of combat arms and MPs at the outset of the invasion. As it turned out, the impact of higher level decisions to hold

off on the deployment of additional MP companies arguably prolonged the beginning of proper post hostility operations, possibly
increasing casualties because of the Jessica Lynch fiasco. This
may have assisted in the growth of a multi-dimensional insurgency which led to even more casualties, and perhaps most dam-
aging of all it could have undercut confidence in America's political leadership among American and Iraqi citizens. By the time
the invasion was ordered, even the credibility of former Secretary
of State Colin Powell's presentation on Iraq before the United
Nations was in doubt.

I saw the negative effects of insufficient numbers of military
police in the early stages of the invasion manifested in several significant areas.

First, we were unable to properly secure invasion and supply
routes. Ambush and tragedy in an Iraqi city was the immediate
result. The 507th Maintenance Company carrying Army Private
Jessica Lynch veered in the wrong direction at a critical juncture
on the invasion route and ended up in enemy territory in the middle of An Nasiriya. Someone had missed the handwritten signs at
points along the way and the ill fated convoy found itself trapped
in the midst of a raging battle.

The eighteen vehicles of the 507th were mostly slow moving
cargo trucks—easy targets as they turned in the direction of An
Nasiriya and away from the road to Tallil AirBase. Ambushed by
the Iraqis, the 507th saw eleven of its soldiers killed, nine wounded,
and seven, including Private Jessica Lynch, captured. Some of the
dead soldiers' bodies showed signs of extreme torture. I quickly
learned we were not facing an enemy that cared about the Geneva
Hague Conventions. Nonetheless, during our massive responsibilities for thousands of detainees over the coming months, myself
and my commanders never lost sight of the obligation we had to
abide by the Conventions, despite the brutality of the enemy.

Had there been significant numbers of MPs and had they

been used as their doctrinal mission dictated, they would have controlled those points along the invasion route to ensure that the seventeen thousand vehicles carrying soldiers and supplies into Iraq remained on the safest course. The lack of MPs in the force flow when the invasion began prevented us from directing convoys at critical junctures. There just weren't enough MPs to take on so many missions.

The lack of MPs during the ground war severely hampered the Provost Marshals of the 3rd, 101st, and 82nd. The three MP Division Provost Marshals were unable to adequately support their division commanders, because I could not adequately support them by providing them their requisite number of MPs. I had been a division Provost Marshal seven years earlier and clearly understood what they were up against. It made me sick to my stomach that I couldn't support them the way I was supposed to.

Major Steve Smith, the Provost Marshal of the 101st Airborne and senior MP for Major General David Petraeus compensated for not receiving additional MPs from me by using every military policeman in the 101st to run escort missions. The division was conducting operations to the south of Baghdad initially and later up north in Mosul. They became a reactive unit when it came to supporting their own division.

Lt. Colonel Jerry Stevenson was the Provost Marshal for the 82nd Airborne Division, the very job I had in 1996-1997, and the senior MP for Major General Swanock. Jerry and I had served together years earlier at Ft. Bragg, but despite our long standing relationship, I couldn't support him. His division was conducting combat operations in Al-Samawah and An-Najaf and were in dire need of an MP company, but I simply couldn't provide one to assist him.

Without the company, there were four missions his division couldn't perform. First, they were unable to increase the security of the division main headquarters detachment. Having more MPs would have permitted area security patrolling and given the access control team a more sustainable battle rhythm. Second, they would have been able to evacuate enemy prisoners of war and establish a Division Central Collection Point. Third, MP resources would have been available to re-form the Iraqi police in Al Samawah and An Najaf. Finally, the 4th Infantry Division would have received more support when it passed through the territory held by the 101st on the way north to Tikrit.

Lt. Colonel Mack Huey wore two hats. He was the commander of the 3rd MP Battalion and the Provost Marshal for the 3rd Infantry Division. But in Iraq, he was a battalion commander with no MP companies, other than the one company organic to the 3rd Infantry Division. After my retirement, Huey was blunt with me about the impact of not having an additional MP company when he crossed into Iraq:

"We were only capable of conducting one of our five primary battlefield functions, causing the division planners to question our capability and value added to the fight. Enemy prisoner of war operations took one hundred percent of our assets with no flexibility or capability to do any other MP missions. We ended up pretty much being aone trick pony."

Within days of my arrival at Tallil Air Base, I got a call from Major General Walter Wojdakowski, Deputy Commanding General, V Corps. At the time, there were very few V Corps units at Tallil, and I just happened to be the senior commander from V Corps. It was my first hint that something tragic had happened in the early days of the invasion.

"I've got a mission for you. This is really, really important Ted, I'm sending a tank company your way. I want you to give them anything they need—fuel, food, a place to camp." His tone was solemn.

"Yes, sir," I responded to him. Although the details were slim, I could tell from Wojdakowski's voice that something serious was about to happen, or already had. I didn't waste any time asking further questions of him if he didn't want to volunteer anymore information.

"Really important, Ted, you're the only SOB I can trust up there," Wojdakowski added, as if his colorful words could explain it all.

Later, Major James Wilson, my Assistant Operations Officer, gave me a closure report on a special mission involving an Army rescue operation. I subsequently learned this was the rescue mission mounted for the 507th and Army Private Jessica Lynch.

"Colonel Spain, I just spoke with the tank company commander and Army colonel encamped here at Tallil with a Special Forces and Army Ranger unit. They have come off an all night fire fight in one of the nearby towns in support of a rescue mission. They took some casualties. The soldiers are sleeping all over the ground in personal pup tents, poncho field expedient shelters, mini tents and ponchos. They have no overhead cover."

It would take more time for me to learn exactly what happened on that night in Iraq down the road from Tallil. But I already had a terrible feeling that whatever happened might have been prevented had there been enough MPs stationed along the supply and invasion routes to keep all the rumbling convoys on the right road to Baghdad.

Another result of the lack of MPs was that the army placed the 1st Battalion, 41st Mechanized Infantry Division (1-41) under my command so it could be used to clear supply routes. To my knowledge, this had never been done before in the history of the army. Had enough MPs been available, the 1-41 could have been freed up for combat usein the invasion force.

Originally, during the planning back in Germany, the 1-41 was under the command of a combat arms staff officer, even though they would be operating in the same area as my MPs. I was very concerned about fratricide, the killing of one friendly force by another friendly force. I approached Major General Wojdakowski to express my concern and recommended that he put the infantry battalion under my command. I assured him that if he did, I could coordinate the operations between them and my MPs, accomplish more missions, and all but eliminate the likelihood of fratricide. He said he had to think about it, but I could tell he wasn't initially wild about an MP Brigade commander having command and control over an infantry battalion. In fact, this was the same type of battalion he had commanded during Desert Storm. I'm sure he wouldn't have been happy working for an MP Brigade commander.

The next day he agreed, and the 1-41 mechanized infantry battalion later invaded Iraq as part of an MP Brigade, but you won't ever see that in the history books. It would be too embarrassing. Without enough MPs and proper equipment, I had to make some tough leadership decisions that created additional risks to soldiers performingtheir missions.

For example, I needed MPs to take over the enemy prisoner of war camp outside of Tallil Air Base. MPs assigned to the 3rd Infantry Division had established the camp in the first hours of the invasion. They needed to be freed up to continue moving forward with the rest of the 3rd Infantry. On March 22, the 709th Military Police Battalion Headquarters, along with the 527th, 615th, and 551st MP companies joined over seven hundred soldiers of the 1-41 and entered Iraq. The 1-41 had mortars and Bradley Fighting vehicles to insure they could clear key supply routes.

I decided to send two platoons of the 511th MP Company, out of Ft. Drum, New York, then part of the 709th MP Battalion, into Iraq on helicopters, because their vehicles hadn't arrived before the invasion started. To neutralize the substantial risks connected to this plan, Lt. Colonel Rich Vanderlinden, Commander of the 709th assigned Major Gillian Boice, his Executive Officer, to lead the platoons. Boice later described to me what it was like to tackle the assignment:

"Since the MP flow was late, we had units in our formation that had no fighting platforms or vehicles to take to the fight. We improvised. We were all dismounted, carrying all of our basic loads of water, ammunition, and support on our backs into Iraq. We were combat loaded into 101st AA UH-60 Blackhawk helicopters from Camp New York, flown across the border and air inserted into Tallil Air Base. It was a wild ride. All of the seats of the UH-60s were stripped out and we basically loaded in stacked like cord wood with soldiers, weapons, backpacks and gear. Each copter was at maximum capacity.

I was the senior leader and mission commander so I was packed in last to be the first off. I was lying on top of several soldiers, head rubbing against the roof of the helicopter and just able to peer out of the window as we flew 10-20 feet off the ground of the desert. The pilot and I did coordination by headset."

My Brigade Headquarters Company entered Iraq the day after Boice, the 709th, and the 1-41, planning to connect with them near Tallil Air Base. My company was without any heavy weapons or combat arms soldiers. My decision to send Boice and the 709th into Iraq on March 22, fulfilled the other promise I made to Lt. General Wallace before the war began—to ensure the 3rd Infantry's advance to Baghdad wasn't slowed down by enemy prisoners of war.

The final negative result of not having sufficient MPs at the outset of the invasion was a growing chaos in Iraq that impacted the establishment of law and order after the ground war. There was a substantial delay in standing up the Iraqi police to bring law and order back to the country. Shortages of both MPs and civilian police advisors, combined with the lack of emphasis placed on the role Iraqi police should have played in providing security to local populations became some of the building blocks for insurrection and terrorism.

We had been in Baghdad for nearly ten weeks by the time I had received all of my units. We had assumed so many responsibilities inside Iraq, we were over-extended. The nearly 7000 MPs under my command were managing detainees in numerous locations, running Iraqi police stations, conducting joint patrols with the Iraqi Police, conducting combat patrols and raids on their own, and standing up the police academy. They were also performing combat operations in support of the combat arms brigades. Managing Camp Cropper, the High Value Detainee Site, Abu Ghraib Prison, 34 police stations and four regional jails in Baghdad landed me in the middle of one political dispute after another. On top of all of this, Major General Wodjakowski approached me one day to give me a heads up.

"Lt. General Sanchez is going to ask you to be his Provost Marshal when he stands up the combined joint task force," he told me.

"Well, I can be a brigade commander or a Provost Marshal, but not both." I knew I was on thin ice, but decided I might pay a heavier price if I wasn't candid.

I also recommended he get someone else to serve as Sanchez' Provost Marshal. I told him it was critical for me to focus on the Iraqi Police if he ever wanted to have aviable police academy, police stations, and Iraqi police who would uphold the rule of law. This was a critical conversation for another reason. It was during this conversation that I told him about the soon to be promoted Brigadier General Janis Karpinski, of the now infamous Abu Ghraib Prison abuse scandal. She was assuming command of the 800th Enemy Prisoner of War Brigade and I recommended to General Wojdakowski that she be brought up to Baghdad and take Abu Ghraib Prison, Camp Cropper, and the four regional jails from me. I told him that I would give her the two internment/resettlement battalions I had, that I was currently using to run these facilities.

When I left him, I wasn't sure what his position was, but since he didn't immediately dismiss my idea, I thought it might have a chance. I assumed Wodjakowski would return and discuss it with Sanchez.

My reluctance to take the Provost Marshal position had started weeks earlier during a transition brief. Lt. Generals McKiernan and Wallace were already preparing to leave Iraq, and the soon to be named Lt. General Sanchez was preparing to stand up Combined Joint Task Force 7 (CJTF7). Two senior MP colonels, who I had served with earlier in my career, Colonel Dave Treuting, and Colonel Della Jaccono pressured me to take the dual mission of brigade commander and Provost Marshal. They honestly thought it was the best way to operate. I made it clear to them that I didn't want to do it because I honestly felt the mission of standing up the police would suffer. They seemed adamant about their positions. Prior to our briefing on the issue, I discussed my reasoning with Wallace. He supported me. Yet later, when one of the briefing slides appeared, it had me listed as the Provost Marshal. Someone had done an end run on me. When Wallace saw my name on the slide, he looked at me as if to ask, "Did you change your mind?" I'm sure the look on my face showed total surprise. Wallace then looked at McKiernan.

"Damn it, Dave, Spain isn't going to be the Provost Marshal."

Although my name was on the slide, I prevailed in my bid to stay away from the assignment. Somehow I had succeeded in convincing the powers to be that it was best for my brigade and best for our overall mission accomplishment in Iraq for my brigade to get the local jails in order, train the Iraqi police and conduct joint policing operations with them.

Tom Evans was familiar with the ongoing battle with the army brass involving MP assignments. After my retirement he said, "We entered Iraq with a few hundred soldiers under Colonel Spain's command. Within weeks, he was responsible for nearly 7,000 troops. But senior officers wanted the military police attached to their individual divisions. Outside of Baghdad, that's what happened. The colonel had responsibility for many of the MPs in the theater but many of them were later assigned to other commanders, especially those north of Baghdad. We never really had enough military police companies to take on all our responsibilities—jails, prisons, police training and patrols. It remained that way throughout our year in Iraq."

The Army we had at the time included sufficient numbers of MPs to make a difference, but because of the decisions of Rumsfeld and those advising him, thousands of MPs were left at bases in America, in Kuwait or on ships at sea waiting for their equipment and trying to catch a ride to the war front any way they could. It didn't have to happen that way.

After we reached Baghdad, it didn't take long for the lack of MPs or the improper use of MPs we did have, to become a substantial problem that could no longer be ignored. Varying elements of the Army started fighting with each other over the MP issue. Former United States Ambassador L. Paul Bremer, who headed the Coalition Provisional Authority (CPA) in Iraq, said later in his 2006 book, "My Year In Iraq," that he had requested additional military police be deployed to Iraq when Baghdad started burning. During a 2006 interview with *Frontline*, called "The Lost Year in Iraq," Bremer was asked what he did when he flew into Baghdad in 2003 and saw buildings burning and rampant looting.

"I asked General Abizad if he could send us some more American MPs (military police) to try to bring some order to Baghdad." [1]

It all came to a head with an April 23 email from Stephen Curry, Brigadier General and Commandant of the MP School to Colonel Dave Treuting and I. The email titled, "What's Up," had me so steamed that I waited five days before sending a response. Curry was a former commander of the 18th MP Brigade, and had taken it to Bosnia in the mid-1990s. I worked for him from the summer of 1994 until the summer of 1995 as his operations officer. He was a great commander, and a great tactician, but I knew that as the Commandant he was probably fielding a lot of questions from the Army and the media about the MPs in Iraq.

In his email, Curry said he was getting phone calls from other officers asking where the MPs were in Iraq and why they were never seen on TV doing policing, peacekeeping or anything else. One of the officers who contacted Curry was in a northern suburb of Baghdad doing one such mission. He complained that the MPs should be doing the job and posed the question, "Where in the Hell are the MPs?"

Curry tried to make the message more palatable by telling us he understood the "gun battle" within the Army about the relevance of the Army's combat formations. He wanted to know if the Army was keeping the MPs under wraps and getting the combat-arms in the forefront.

My response to Curry, written during extreme fatigue and frustration, started with the cautionary note that I knew my email was "politically incorrect." Then, I got to the heart of the problem. I explained that because the force flow was so "dicked" up, it forced V Corps to give security missions to combat arms units. I told him they started doing this after the loss of the 507th Maintenance Company. At first, the Army used the 101st and 82nd Airborne for these missions. The combat arms were not doing a lot of route security. Instead, they hung out in the big cities killing people. The MPs did the best they could to secure routes, escort convoys, deal with enemy prisoners of war, and report massive amounts of abandoned equipment and soldiers all across the desert. I explained we were conducting checkpoint operations capturing Iraqis in possession of arms and weapons. We were clearing out several small villages, working with the village people, who were providing important intelligence to us on the location of arms caches and Ba'ath party members.

I was aware that the media was not providing much coverage of us. The embedded media traveled mainly with the combat arms and didn't choose to report on some of the mundane sounding, but important jobs, being done by the MPs. I reminded Curry of our lack of MPs when we crossed over into Iraq. Instead of the twenty companies we were promised, we joined the invasion force with only eleven platoons with equipment and the two platoons without any equipment that I decided to air mobile into Iraq.

I let Curry know that the guys calling about us and asking what we were doing were free to join us in Iraq. I told him none of my soldiers had enjoyed a hot meal or shower in over six weeks. We were working hard and doing the best we could do. I commented that had the armchair quarterbacks in the Pentagon and elsewhere weighed in or listened to us as they designed the force flow before the invasion, perhaps thing swould have turned out differently. Then, I ended my email as curtly as I started it:

"Unfortunately, we didn't have any say so on the force flow, but we damn sure paid the price for it!"

Of course, all of this could have been changed had we adapted to the situation we faced later on in Iraq. I subsequently provided input to Lt. General Ricardo Sanchez that gave him the opportunity to make decisions about MP manpower issues that could have lessened the impact of the shortage of MPs during the second year of the occupation. He failed to pay attention to my suggestions.

CHAPTER ONE: NOTES
1   PBS Frontline, "The Lost Year in Iraq," transcript of two interviews of L. Paul Bremer, June 26 and August 18, 2006.

Chapter Two

LAW AND ORDER IN THE REAR VIEW MIRROR

Pre-war planning failed to address the security needs of everyday Iraqi citizens.

Regardless of the extreme shortage of MPs when the war began, we had to play the hand that was dealt us. As the saying goes, when you're given a bunch of lemons, you make lemonade. Based on my years of experience as an MP, I knew that once we occupied Iraq, establishing law and order would be critical, if we ever hoped to hand control of Iraq back over to its citizens. In America, we turn to the local police when we want protection. They are the first responders. They are the key to separating order from chaos. But even in our own country, we've experienced chaos from time to time when a natural or man-made event, disrupts the rule of law.

In New Orleans, Louisiana, after Hurricane Katrina, a massive disruption of police services led to panic, extensive looting of downtown businesses, and even corrupt actions, by some of the police themselves. In Los Angeles, California, after the Rodney King verdict, mayhem erupted in the streets as people didn't feel that justice had been served. When I first witnessed the looting in Baghdad, it reminded me of the images I had seen on television twenty years ago during those riots in Los Angeles. The point is that no matter where they live, people will have the same reaction to extremely stressful events. While still at Tallil, I quickly learned that the war was all too real for Iraqi people whose basic needs were no longer being met. My soldiers and I experienced shortages of necessary food and water for just short periods and it certainly got our attention. But for some Iraqis, the same necessities of life were going to be missing for a long time. I hadn't given it any thought before the invasion, but now, knee deep in the middle of Iraq, my foremost thoughts were centered around one question—how could we win hearts and minds over starving people, when the starvation was brought on by our own invasion. It wasn't anything we had drilled or trained for before the war started, but answering that question became my primary focus in the early days of the invasion and its aftermath. Resolving the issue would mean the difference between success and failure, far exceeding the value and impact of "shock and awe." The 527th MP Company, part of the 709th MP Battalion, had been conducting reconnaissance missions after entering Iraq, providing security escorts for transportation elements and working to gain the trust of villagers. One of the local villages was having an especially difficult time so the company commander, Captain Mike Johns invited me to a meeting with the local cleric. Mike escorted my security detail and I through the winding, narrow streets of the small village outside of Talill. There was barely enough room for our Army combat vehicles to grind their way through the narrow passage ways that substituted for roads. Staff Sergeant Jordan, who was the head of my personal security detail, was especially alert. As the lead "eye," his obligation was to instinctively sense every danger and take whatever actions necessary to protect me. The job was almost impossible since each step we took in Iraq was dangerous. Around every turn in the road and from every window in each of the buildings of the small village, an ambush could await our snaking column.

In the village, the small, tan-colored buildings of stucco and sand looked more like sets of squares and rectangles interspersed on an open field. As our convoy pulled to a stop in front of the religious hall, groups of armed men stood guard at its entrance, staring intently at the soldiers from the U.S. Army. There was only one way in and one way out of the building. I took immediate notice of the weapons I knew could be turned and pointed at us in an instant. I looked at Jordan, and without saying a word, gave every impression that his security detail should defend itself in the event of any disturbance. They didn't have to wait on me to give them the word. Their instincts would tell them all they needed to know and was good enough for me.

The village cleric greeted me at the door and we all walked into the religious hall. The room was carpeted but sparsely furnished, nothing more than a concrete block that looked more on the inside like a stand-alone trailer. Before we entered, my Kuwaiti translator relayed a request from one of the Iraqis that my soldiers and I remove our boots out of respect for religious custom and the sanctity of the hall. "We're not taking our boots off," I shot back at the translator, as if I was speaking directly to the Iraqis.

Although security details for Captain Johns and I were present, I was acutely aware of the danger we faced in the small village surrounded by armed Iraqis who were withholding their fire only because of their allegiance to the village cleric. Conditions could deteriorate without notice and the meeting could become another Somalia. I didn't plan on staying long and certainly had no intentions of removing my boots even if I did. The cleric defused the situation immediately, overriding the request, and motioning to me that we could enter the religious temple, boots and all.

The cleric sat on the carpeted floor at one end of the room. Captain Johns, my translator and I sat on the opposite side facing him. I accepted the offer of a cigarette even though I didn't smoke. I was provided with hot tea and decided that I would drink it, although concerned about the possibility that it could be drugged. I drew the line when offered food. My translator explained to me that the smoking, drinking and eating were all customs in the village before getting down to business, but I had made my mind up—insult or not there would be no eating by me or my soldiers. The cleric, sensing the time to talk business was upon us, got to the point. "We don't have enough food or water," he started. Saddam had controlled the villages and their people by providing them food and water; significant life necessities where most of them lived. When the U.S. military invasion was launched, Saddam and the powerful men who supported his government went into hiding. The system collapsed and villages throughout the country were left helpless. The villagers turned to U.S. Army commanders on the ground to help them. I realized the importance of being sympathetic to their concerns, but at the same time, I had no means to come up with an answer to the cleric's problems. I had enough problems making certain that my own soldiers had enough food and water to sustain them while we were at war. The cleric continued talking to me and patiently waited for the Kuwaiti translator to convey his words. I was trying to appear at ease, but the tension I felt was related to my own survival instincts. I knew we were in a Shiite village and there was no love among the people for Saddam, but still this was a war zone. Terrorists, revolutionary guard elements, and a variety of common criminals and Iraqi regular soldiers could turn the cordial meeting into a free for all fire-zone. My eyes continued to move from the cleric to the entrance way and around the room searching for any sign of trouble.

When an unknown disturbance outside disrupted the meeting, I halted the cleric's plea and turned to my translator. "Tell him it's very important for his security people not to point any weapons at me or my soldiers or they will kill his people and I will personally kill him."

"Sir, you can't do that," the translator protested, "It would be really offensive."

"No, you tell him just like that, he's got to clearly understand."

I was conflicted. I knew I had to be careful about what I promised the villagers. I didn't want to offend them because we would need their help gathering intelligence to identify and capture the remnants of Saddam's army. But the security of my soldiers trumped every other issue.

From the beginning of the invasion, the military police I commanded realized the significance of building relationships with the Iraqi population if we were to begin the process of establishing law and order in Iraq. We got that! But I drew the line when it came to protecting my soldiers. I had decided all else would be secondary.

As the Kuwaiti reluctantly translated my message to the cleric, he and I followed the conversation while watching each other's eyes. When the translator emphasized that I would personally kill the cleric, a startled expression emerged from the religious leader's face. I looked sternly in his direction and patted the military pistol on my right side, to confirm that the translation was not misunderstood. The cleric nodded that he clearly received the message and our meeting continued. I promised I would do all I could to help the villagers with their needs. In reality, I was a failure at getting them any additional food or water. We were short ourselves, and before long, we moved on, heading towards Baghdad. Nothing in my extensive Army training had prepared me for that moment with the cleric. But the tension in the room and the anxiety that impacted all of us in the meeting reminded me more of a policing situation in the states than it did my vision of a military invasion with a clear cut enemy. The danger of the unknown seemed to have no border. I quickly understood how a small misunderstanding, in a country where we didn't understand the language, the culture, or the customs, and no one understood us, could turn deadly.

The experience with the villagers took me back to college and the lessons I learned from the work of psychologist Abraham Maslow. In a 1943 paper, "A Theory of Human Motivation," he described a human's hierarchy of needs. Viewed as a pyramid, Maslow said that people were motivated to fulfill basic needs at the lower end of the pyramid before moving on to fulfill others. At the lowest rung of the pyramid, people required food, water, sleep and warmth. As they fulfilled those needs, they went to the next level of the pyramid in search of safety and security. As they progressed higher on the pyramid, their needs were psychological and social, until they achieved a certain self-esteem and self-actualization, which involved growing and developing one's individual potential. This hierarchy of needs stayed with me my entire time in Iraq, especially as I argued with senior civilian and military leaders about the importance of Iraqi citizens feeling secure in their homes and neighborhoods. I was frustrated constantly whenever politicians asked me what I thought the Iraqi police should look like in forty years, when we had daily chaos on the streets. I never had an Iraqi citizen ask me about my thoughts on Iraq forty years out. They were striving for daily survival, just like my soldiers and I. I tried to leave the deep thinking to those who worked in the safety of the Green Zone, in Kuwait, and at the Pentagon. It didn't take too long for me to realize there weren't very many deep thinkers in any of those exalted places. And usually the deeper they thought, the more we got into trouble.

It all sounded so amazingly simple when applied to the meeting with the village cleric. After decades of depending on Saddam for their basic needs of food and water, now the common Iraqi had to depend upon the U.S. military. In reaching out, they were acknowledging that the American government was now in control of their fate.

"How could we have missed such a basic point in our training for this invasion?" I thought to myself.

"For crying out loud, this was introductory psychology!" I found myself almost cursing at our lack of understanding of something so basic.

The answer would take on new dimensions as Iraqis moved from the lower level of the pyramid and started searching for security, safety, and a regaining of their national and individual self-esteem. The only way they would move up Maslow's hierarchy was through the development in Iraq of the rule of law. For that, the civilian leaders in America and the Army that trained my soldiers had developed not a single plan.

Our journey to gain the trust and respect of Iraqis began with developing confidence in ourselves and one another. For me, that started days after our arrival at Tallil Air Base. While my MPs were gaining the upper hand in managing enemy prisoner of war problems, I lost interest in sitting around Tallil dealing with detainees. I felt I needed to experience first hand what the soldiers were experiencing, as well as see how the ordinary Iraqi citizen was reacting to our occupation. In order to do this, it was time to insert the group into every day Iraq. I went to Staff Sgt. Jordan. "Get your guys ready, sergeant, we're doing some checkpoints." Jordan assumed that I was interested in visiting Army units out in the battlefield engaged in manning critical locations. Assessing their effectiveness and gathering firsthand intelligence would come in handy as the war continued.

I had a different idea. Staff Sgt. Jordan and my security detail had performed well as we entered Iraq. It was time for us to learn how to operate in the midst of a society at war. Leading by example would be the best way to establish law and order in Iraq. Leaving the gated security of Tallil, our small convoy journeyed back to the six lane highway that had brought us there days earlier.

"Hey, Staff Sgt. Jordan, let's set up a checkpoint here," I reached out to Jordan over the radio, prompting our group of army vehicles to create a formation that offered some degree of protection to one another and at the same time allowed us to stop traffic on the highway. Now, we would be face to face talking with real Iraqis only days after invading their country.

The assignment was dangerous. No one knew who might be driving any particular car. Iraq was an armed camp of differing factions holding grudges against another faction. With Saddam in hiding, Iraqi police forces non-existent, and no controlling figure to hold the country together, we would be viewed by some as liberators and others as foreign invaders who needed to be killed. Car stops were always dangerous in America. They were even more perilous in Iraq.

During the car stops, my MPs were outfitted with inadequate flak vests, that wouldn't have even stopped a bullet from an AK-47 rifle. These were the same vests they had been wearing during the initial invasion. But now we had to be ready for the uncertainties of Saddam's next step. War planning and operations were driven by intelligence and the perceived mix of threats the Army might face at any time on the battlefield. The planning process was driven by the perceived threat and the types of weapons Saddam might use against his invaders. Primary among threats to America's soldiers were the use of chemical weapons.

No matter where we were in Iraq, we had to be prepared for chemical weapons attacks against both front line troops and those of us moving up from behind the lines. Although we made it to Tallil without experiencing chemical weapons attacks, the conventional wisdom held that once Saddam realized we were advancing onto Baghdad, the weapons would be deployed in one final attempt to defend Iraq. We had prepared for any possible contingencies by taking numerous anthrax and small pox shots, as well as consuming malaria pills. The combat arms soldiers on the battlefield wore their chemical suit "tops and bottoms" underneath the Kevlar protective armor and other load bearing equipment necessitated by war. The MPs had only their flak vests at the outset of the war, although several months later had been equipped with the Kevlar armor. One of the soldiers described the feeling as "similar to wearing a snowsuit on a desert hike in 100 degree heat."

The temperature was ramped up several degrees by the stress of the battlefield and the mystery associated with each car stop. While manning the checkpoint on the highway, my soldiers stayed in stages one and two of the protocol for wearing the chemical suits. Stage 1 meant that they had to wear the pants. Stage 2 mandated the jackets be worn. Had conditions changed to where an attack was underway, they would have needed to move immediately to Stage 3, donning the boots and gloves to Stage 4, the protective masks. They found out quickly that the suits and flak vests were great for winters in Germany, but not so pleasant during late spring and summer in Iraq.

Staff Sgt. Jordan recalled the results of the first round of highway stops wearing the flak vests and chemical weapons suits.

"We ended up searching a lot of tomato trucks and a couple of cars before I think the colonel got bored because we didn't find anything and so he said, Let's go!"

While at Tallil, we drilled over and over again in the art of the highway stop. Crossing from Kuwait into Iraq and coming to grips with the noises, smells, and sights of war, we had to learn quickly that everything we did had to be done as if all of our lives depended upon the results, because they did. We were experienced in conducting vehicle stops and running checkpoint operations back at our home stations in either Germany or the United States, but once inside Iraq, everything was different. Every vehicle was a potential car bomb. Every item held in the driver or occupant's hand was a potential triggering device. My MPs had only a split second to decide whether the failure of an Iraqi citizen to follow our instructions was a threat to us, or a lack of understanding of our language or culture. When we were training back in Germany I told my soldiers they may find themselves in a situation where they had a fraction of a second to decide if the Iraqi teenager standing in front of them was handing them a gift or a hand grenade. Faced later with the exact situation in Iraq, their understanding of the minimum use of force, combined with honed instincts for survival, paid huge dividends. During the time we spent at Tallil, my personal security detail became more familiar with Iraq and more comfortable working in the midst of combat operations. Although they were trained as military policemen with a unique role in the America narmed forces, they were also more than capable of supporting combat arms operations when called upon. They worked hard while we were in Tallil preparing them for what they would face in the weeks to come. As we went on numerous "checkpoint" missions, patrolled around the perimeter of the base, dealt with the security of detainees and the special problems of Iraqi citizens and villages, they learned to function together as a team. Each of their lives was in the hands of the family member standing next to them. When I heard on the nightly update that Saddam International Airport in Baghdad had fallen to the 3rd Infantry Division, I summoned Staff Sgt. Jordan.

"We've taken Baghdad airport," I told him. "Let's go check it out."

Baghdad was at least one hundred miles from Tallil. Jordan went to our brigade's Tactical Operations Center. He retrieved maps of Iraq and Baghdad. The walls in the room were eight feet high, so he hung the first one as close to the ceiling as he could. After he laid out the route he planned on taking, he taped additional map sheets down the wall and across the room. He found two pieces of particle board to mount the maps on until they were needed. He later said it was one of the most stressful assignments he had in Iraq. He would need to navigate the trip using only the map sheets and the Army "Plugger." There was no way to determine whether the maps were accurate or how many armed Iraqis might intercept our group while we were on the road. But Jordan's planning was flawless and on the day of the trip, our little convoy made it all the way to Baghdad without any incidents.

"Sir, you want to go back the same way, right?" Jordan asked me after visiting the airport.

"No, let's go back a different way, I want to get as close to downtown as possible," I told Jordan, wanting to see first hand the chaos, looting and more importantly, how the Iraqi people in this huge city were reacting to our occupation.

"Ok, roger that sir, I just need to check the map first," Jordan realized he had made a big mistake as he turned and headed back to his Humvee.

"We're going back a different way," he regrettably told his guys, all the while cursing through the makeshift guide maps to find a suitable route back to Tallil.

The route he settled on led out of the airport and in the direction of Baghdad proper. The highway was good until we came upon American M1 Abrams tanks sitting adjacent to concertina wire strung across the road. We had reached the outer limits of the perimeter the Third Infantry Division had established. Jordan jumped out of the truck and approached the soldiers standing near the tanks.

"Hey, what's up the road?" he inquired.

"Nothing, we're the last American troops. There are no more friendly soldiers in front of us," came a response that Jordan didn't want to hear. He returned to my vehicle and briefed me on the situation.

"Okay, I want to go there anyway," I smiled as Jordan returned to his Humvee.

Our truck convoy continued down the empty three lane highway, which quickly turned into a narrow one lane road, packed on both sides by crowds of rowdy people. Piles of rotting garbage, miscellaneous junk and growing crowds of people slowed our small army convoy down to a crawl. Iraqis cautiously kept an eye on us and at the same time went about looting anything that wasn't bolted in place and even somethings that were. The highway guardrails were even being detached and carried away. Cars were dragging big generators down the road behind them. Jordan kept thinking that we were only in Humvees, not Abrams tanks like the soldiers we had just passed. Now, it really mattered, we were wearing Vietnam era flak vests, not the body armor of the soldiers of the Third Infantry. He was quietly pondering the same thing as I was—we were screwed if anyone started shooting. The crowds kept growing larger and it was obvious they were suspicious of the Americans in their midst. Still, I kept thinking if we just left them alone, they would leave us alone. Through the trash and tons of people, everyone's blood pressure and security instincts was heightened, until we finally intercepted the route we had traveled on earlier in the day. We had come twenty miles through a no man's land formed by the invasion and its aftermath and breathed a collective sigh of relief as we turned onto the familiar road and headed back to Tallil without any more scares.

I visited Baghdad and the 720th MP Battalion I had stationed outside the city a few more times. We increased the number of our patrols to Baghdad as the brigade headquarters neared its permanent move to Iraq's prize city. With the travel between Tallil and Baghdad came more adventures.

In ongoing efforts to pinpoint the exact location of American units fighting on the battlefield, we set out across the vast desert between Baghdad and Tallil Air Base to coordinate with other commanders and the Division Provost Marshals to determine where each of the units was conducting operations. The work was painstaking and needed to be done with precision. If the American combat forces didn't constantly update information on where varying units were engaged in combat, they could easily mistake each other for the enemy on the vast spaces they needed to maneuver. The result was that they could start directing fire at each other. Preventing "fratricide," was one of my key concerns. My MPs and I took it seriously. The trips between Baghdad and Tallil became the next logical phase to help us fulfill our many obligations. On one such trip during the middle of April, my personal detail's three vehicle convoy was accompanied by Command Sergeant Major Charles Guyette and his two security vehicles. We were returning to Tallil in the afternoon when Guyette's Humvee was halted by a flat tire. Across the brigade, we had a shortage of spare tires for our Humvees. We found ourselves without a spare to fix our tire. As the sun was fading, we realized we were in the middle of a desert ground war with darkness closing in on us. It would take at least four hours to travel to Tallil, retrieve a spare tire and return. I was worried that Guyette and his team might not be safe if left that long in the desert. But the only other option was to destroy the vehicle on the spot. Guyette and I discussed the situation and quickly decided that I would take my security detail and make a run for Tallil to get a spare. We simply couldn't afford to destroy the vehicle. I bid my good friend a temporary farewell.

About thirty minutes down the road we came across a group of Marines stealing parts off of an abandoned U.S. Army vehicle. Apparently, my brigade wasn't the only unit without spare parts. As they saw an Army colonel climb out of the Humvee and walk in their direction, they started fumbling for a reason to justify their actions.

"Sir, this is an abandoned vehicle," several stammered in unison.

"Certainly it is," I responded in my firmest and most serious voice, as my eyes scanned their Humvees. "Which of you is the senior Marine?" I asked. "I am, sir," one of the Marines stepped up, about to offer more reasons as to why he and his men were removing parts from the army vehicle left abandoned on the side of the road. I couldn't have cared less about them stripping the vehicle, but let them think I did.

"Do you guys have a need for that spare tire?" I pointed to an extra Hummer wheel strapped on the back of one of their vehicles.

"No, sir," the Marine cleared his throat, eager to surrender one of his unit's tires to us, if it would make me go away. His men immediately removed the tire and tied it to the back of my security vehicle. The Marines were more than pleased to help us get back on the road.

Command Sergeant Major Guyette was shocked when I returned with the security detail and the spare tire in less than an hour. The flat tire was changed and we made it back to Tallil without any problems.

Even in the middle of the battlefield, the soldiers tried hard to maintain their sense of humor, something especially important when seeing the irony of war up close everyday. Our small personal security detail was returning to Tallil one afternoon following a visit with the 720th MP Battalion encamped at the logistical support area designated "Bushmaster," not far outside of Baghdad. On a stretch of road that was being routinely patrolled by the MPs of the 720th known as "ASR Miami," which was Iraq's Highway 9 between As Samawah and An Najaf, my personal security detail ran into elements of the mighty 2nd Armored Calvary Regiment (2ACR), the longest serving regiment in the U.S. Army. The 2ACR had been working with the 82nd Airborne Division to destroy Saddam's Fedayeen forces and ensure that lines of supply and communications we reopened and maintained, connecting American forces in Baghdad with those in southern Iraq. Facing off with my unit's Hummers on the desert road, the Stryker Light Armored Vehicles manned by the 2ACR looked like Goliath squaring off with David. I was delighted at the time we were all on the same team.

M11126 Infantry Carriers were armed with M2 50 caliber machine guns or MK1940mm grenade launchers. M1128 Mobile Gun Systems carried 105mm cannons, M2 50 caliber machine guns, and M6 smoke grenade launchers. The 23 foot-long weapons platforms each weighed around 38,000 pounds, were covered with 14.5mm armor protection and equipped to survive RPG-7 attacks. They had a crew of two and could carry an infantry squad of nine soldiers.

"Colonel, what are you doing on this route?" the startled squad leader looked atthe small group of military cops in amazement. The enemy was everywhere and he couldn't believe our group had traveled the road without encountering disaster.

"Well, let me ask you, what are you doing?" I answered, while staring at the cannons pointed in our direction.

"Sir, we were given the mission of clearing ASR Miami and opening lines of supply between Baghdad and Kuwait. We're here to clear this route so that it's safe to pass and free from enemy control," the squad leader stared back at the military cops with our pathetic looking Hummers in comparison to the light weapons systems arrayed behind him.

"It's already cleared because we just came down it. The MPs have been patrolling this route for some time now," I countered rather indignantly.

I realized then that the next phase of our mission would be the most difficult of all—getting the combat arms leaders to understand the capabilities and importance of the MPs in a post combat environment in Iraq, when citizens would want to talk to policemen, not the soldiers who had been shooting at them the day before, who had such a different outlook, shaped by their differing purpose.

"I'll guarantee you one thing," I looked at my driver, Sergeant

Loren Buchmeier as we drove away. "When you read the history books someday, you'll see that the 2ACR cleared ASR Miami, and you won't see anything about the 720th MP Battalion."

I wasn't mad, just a little frustrated at the thought that my military police had been doing so much, with so little, for which they would get little credit. I would grow used to it in the coming months.

Later, after our arrival in Baghdad, and our work began with the Iraqi police, establishing a solid bond with the Iraqi police would be important. If the Iraqi people were ever to start having any faith in what life would look like after the invasion, we had to demonstrate that American police behaved differently than what they were used to. So I decided to expedite getting my MPs involved in law enforcement type interactions with the Iraqis. It would be good for both sides.

All of my staff worked double duty to get our brigade relocated from Tallil so that we could devote our time and attention in Baghdad to the true doctrinal missions of the MP Corps. Nothing came easy. During move week, Staff Sgt. Jordan and his entire team came down with food poisoning and had to stay behind at Tallil and receive IVs. Schedules were altered so that other teams could fill in on the rotation. After the entire brigade headquarters staff was successfully relocated to Camp Victory, named after V Corps, "Victory Corps," patrol missions began immediately. It was time to let the everyday Iraqi citizen meet the American military policeman. Our days in Iraq settled into a predictable pattern after the patrols began. Camp Victory was on the outskirts of downtown Baghdad. Each night, Staff Sgt. Jordan was briefed on my plans for the next day. Sometimes I'd travel for meetings with one of my battalion or company commanders. Other times I visited the police academy, some of the police generals, one of our detention facilities, or one of our Iraqi police stations. On some occasions, I wanted to patrol in a certain part of the city. Every day and every night, it seemed like Sgt. Jordan and I had the same conversation.

"How long will it take to get to where we're going tomorrow, Sgt. Jordan?"

"About 15 minutes, sir," was almost always the answer.

"Okay, I'll be ready, don't be late now." Sgt. Jordan was never late. He would make certain that his teams were awake on time, had studied the routes, and were ready and waiting for me to come out from the palace at the agreed upon time to begin the patrol. I was never on time. Finally, I'd come charging out of the door, already ten minutes late, hastily looking at Jordan.

"Sgt. Jordan, can you get me there in time?" I asked, jumping into the waiting Hummer.

Jordan laughed inside, always with the secret voice that told him, "Hell no," while outwardly smiling at me saying, "I'll do my best, sir." And he always did.

We never knew what to expect when we left the security of Camp Victory and headed for the streets and alley ways of Baghdad. We didn't always end up in the safest parts of town because we were military police and our job was to encourage local citizens to help make their neighborhoods safer. We weren't needed in areas that were safe. We were desperately wanted where order had been replaced by crime, looting, random killings and rampant intimidation of Iraqi citizens by other Iraqis. Where at Tallil we saw the faces of enemy prisoners of war, out on the streets of Baghdad we saw the true victims of war. During the march to Baghdad, our team came across twenty-two members of one Iraqi family living beside a temple. Their home had been destroyed during the fighting. It was the first of many encounters with innocent Iraqi civilians, victims of a war who couldn't move for fear of being killed by the Americans, and at the same time needing to depend on the same Americans for food and water and clothing.

I recalled one of the predictions Lt. General Wallace made back in Germany before we ever left for Kuwait.

"I predict that part of your brigade will be involved in combat operations, while another part of your brigade will be involved in stability and support operations."

As usual, Lt. General Wallace was right. The displaced family reminded me of his prediction. Americans hate to see suffering and are deeply touched by any show of emotion and kindness. America's soldiers have always been a reflection of that quality. On one patrol shortly after the fall of Baghdad, I got out of my Humvee and was approached by a young Iraqi child who handed me his only possession, a homemade cross made out of beads. He came at me so rapidly one of my security team members nearly tackled him. He was yelling at me in Arabic. My interpreter at the time told me he was trying to thank me. I told my security team to let him go, so I could talk to him.

I wanted to give the cross back, because I didn't want to take his only possession. My interpreter quickly backed me away from that thought. "He gave it to you to say thank you for his freedom," he explained.

My eyes were quick to water and I understood how much I had to be thankful for each day of my life. To this day, I still look at that cross and wonder what happened to that child. I wonder if he is still alive. I wonder if the ensuing years of chaos turned him against us. I had believed that fighting in Iraq might cause me to question that supposition. Instead, it was reinforced daily by countless acts of kindness and heroism under pressure demonstrated by Iraqi citizens and the men and women of my brigade.

The patrols galvanized my security team and I like no other aspect of our mission. If we wanted to return safely each night to the palace, we needed to meld our individual wills into a collective instinct that would get us back home. We learned the importance of the strength of our relationships with each other and realized how connected we had become in war.

Rebuilding the Iraqi police was a difficult task. We had to depend upon support from senior American military and civilian leaders if we were to have any luck at all. Some understood the importance of the Iraqi police in putting the country back togetheragain. Sadly, others were clueless.

But rebuilding the police paled in its complexity when compared with the problem of how to best replace Saddam's dictatorship with the rule of law. This became the job that was nearly impossible. We could rebuild Iraqi police stations. We could teach effective law enforcement techniques such as patrol and crime scene investigations. We could provide training in crime scene forensics and the importance of applying science to solve crimes like murder, assaults, bombings and robberies. We could emphasize the importance of securing the trust of Iraqi citizens. There was no way to underestimate the significance of the Iraqi police circulating among the towns and villages, getting acquainted with the citizens for whom they served. All of this was new to Iraqi police and citizens, but over time they understood that everyone had to work together to tame post invasion Iraq and bring security and safety to the places they lived and worked. Eventually, they began to see the tangible results, new police facilities, improved relationships between police and citizens, and greater success in solving crimes against persons. Establishing law and order in Iraq under a system of justice and the rule of law was a far greater task. Intangible, invisible, and inviolable, many Iraqis didn't understand it and there were some who didn't want it.

Long protected in political and military positions bestowed upon them by Saddam, the rule of law held little appeal for Iraq's power elite. They didn't need the American Army to tell them they were no longer aspecial and cherished class. They had little interest in being exempted from their corrupt practices and tyrannical cronyism.

As important as the rule of law was to the successful outcome of rebuilding a post-invasion Iraq, I was involved in little to no discussion before the war on exactly how we were going to accomplish the task. I believe I was negligent in not pushing the issue harder. Like others, I was consumed by the Iraq invasion planning and made a terrible assumption that the Iraqis would quickly reopen their country under new management. As I learned the hard way, it just doesn't work that way. The failure to have a plan and a consistent philosophical message to educate Iraqis on what the rule of law was and why it was vital to a democratic Iraq, substantially delayed our progress in the country. This was manifested in a number of ways.

First, decades of Saddam's rule had so frightened some of Iraq's policing officials that they were reluctant to embrace a thought process that placed the law above powerful political personalities. For the longest time, it always appeared that some of these officials were afraid to be seen with U.S. Army officers and soldiers should Saddam suddenly reappear. In fact, many of the Iraqi Police Generals thought Saddam would some day return. It was not until his capture that they finally started to believe his fate was sealed. We had to figure out how to overcome their fears, change their behavior, and convince these officers that the law of the land would be supreme and beyond the power of personality. It wasn't an easy sell.

Second, average Iraqi citizens had to understand that although their country had been invaded, there was a new sheriff in town. Somehow, we had to illustrate to them that we could protect them at the same time we were desirous of searching their cars and, occasionally even their homes. In Saddam's Iraq, these kinds of interactions could end with brutal consequences. The Iraqi police had to understand that they were responsible for helping people, insuring their safety, and protecting their rights and liberties. But it wasn't easy talking about liberty and rights with people who never had any. They had only the movement and freedom allowed them at any particular time by their government. The common Iraqi citizen saw the police as responsible for keeping Saddam's government in power with all its tyrannical practices. We had to illustrate to the police and Iraqi citizens through our own example that policing could be both intrusive and protective and that through policing actions, the police still had to abide by the law. The police had to maintain a demeanor and civility that allowed them to do their job while keeping the rights of citizens paramount. Third, in the middle of a war zone, my own MPs had to realize that we were there to police Iraq. The invasion was one thing, but soldiers can't kill Iraqis one day and then police them the next. We had to have the courage of our own upbringing and remain convinced that we were, in fact, the sacred bridge between the road to war and the road to peace. Establishing law and order in Iraq was only possible if we believed in it, practiced it, and made it happen. We had to remind ourselves of that every day, as we interacted with Iraqi police and citizens, and in the way we treated and took care of each other.

I decided the only successful path to such an outcome was to throw my MPs into everyday life in Iraq. For every Iraqi who got to know us and every Iraqi policeman who watched us at work, we would try to convey the difference between America's rule of law and Saddam's dictatorship. We would try to show, by our example, the foundation for the rule of law was equality and respect. We would show them that no man or woman was above the law of the land. Specialist Michael Prokop, my communications expert, recalled how our normal days in Iraq began to take shape.

"Colonel Spain would come running out of his palace, jump into the Humvee and look over at Staff Sgt. Jordan with the same greeting every morning, 'Sorry, I'm a little behind. Okay, let's go patrol the city.'"

Prokop was right about my eagerness to get started in the mornings. I knew the Iraqi police were supposed to be on patrol across Baghdad, but I wanted to find out for myself if they were doing the job. My small security convoy sometimes left Camp Victory near the airport and turned onto the highway headed for a traffic circle in the direction of the Green Zone. Once there, we crossed the 14th of July Bridge, and drove by a monument which was the Iraqi equivalent to the Tomb of the Unknown Soldier at Arlington Cemetery in Washington, D.C. We passed by massive "cross swords," rising into the air, the location of the parade grounds for Saddam's army. Prokop, who had become our internal historian, was always impressed by the swords and wondered how, "something so beautiful could represent something so evil." After passing a gate near Saddam's palaces, our convoy turned right and crossed a bridge designated the 3rd ID Bridge for the infantry division that manned it. Driving across the bridge, we saw Baghdad spread out beyond us. Where color and lush landscape painted the areas where Saddam's palaces were located, Baghdad was bland and boring. It was like driving from Oz into Kansas. Our convoy slowed for increasing numbers of traffic lights, was frequently stopped by tangles of people and cars, and was cautiously wary as we passed by outdoor markets where throngs gathered to find whatever food was available on a given day. It seemed to take forever to travel two miles. It was during these journeys that we found the answer to the challenge of establishing law and order in Iraq. Again, I believe Michael Prokop said it best, describing one of our outings:

"Our patrol was on its way to a particular part of town when somebody spotted what appeared to be a house on fire off in the distance. Colonel Spain noticed the fire and diverted our convoy towards the location. When we got closer we could see a crowd- of people, young children and what appeared to be a husband and wife standing helpless by the flames. There was actually a shed on fire in the back of their home and it was threatening to catch the house on fire too. They had tried to pump water out of a nearby well to put out the fire but had no luck. Iraqi firemen came but had to leave to go find water since they had none in their truck. The place was barren with no plants and no green vegetation anywhere to be seen. Garbage of sewage, rotting plants and dead animals covered the ground while cattle wandered within and ate from the trash. Children ran through the same garbage. The smell was enough to make any of us gag. But Colonel Spain told the people we would stay and help them put out the fire. And that is what we did and it saved their house. All of the people were very grateful and couldn't seem to thank us enough."

The Iraqis kept waving and smiling to us as we drove away. I watched the reaction from my MPs. They all got it. We had spent weeks talking about self discipline and how we needed to take care of one another. Some of my own MPs might have thought I was too harsh on soldiers who didn't fasten the chin straps on their helmets and failed to take proper care of their equipment. But it was all about keeping them alive.

The way we learned to treat and watch out for each other was the best indicator of how we would treat conquered Iraqi citizens. In the same fashion, the act of kindness we demonstrated by putting out the fire transcended language barriers and cultures. This was the only formula the 18th MP Brigade would have to develop trusting relationships with Iraqi citizens. This was how we would help establish law and order,and show the decency of democracy to war torn Iraq, since we were the ones who broke it to start with.

I began to feel pretty certain that the lack of pre-war decisions about how we planned to transition Iraq to a country bound by the rule of law had to do more with the enormous complexity of the concept and not from a devious and uncaring conspiracy. We would have needed to evaluate heritage, tradition, cultures, relationships, caste systems, religious values and the impact of fear in figuring out how to insert America's very soul into Iraq's new foundation. Not even the Pentagon had the thinkers to conceive such a design. So instead of anticipating the issues and creating solutions for what we would face in Iraq after the invasion, they made a conscious effort to avoid making any decisions at all.

It was left up to us to move through Iraq one day at a time and figure it out town by town. No wonder a rapid invasion turned into a long and costly stall. Establishing law and order in a country with Iraq's past, was akin to the symbolism of its geography and weather that greeted at us at Iraq's back door when we entered through Kuwait.

The sand frequently blew into our faces, causing our eyes to water and close. Our breathing almost stopped as we tried to keep our mouths clamped so as not to taste the thickened sand. Our noses had already shut down automatically like filters clogged with so much dirt they simply stopped working. But we had to constantly keep moving to avoid detection and maintain the forward momentum of our columns. The soldiers had nothing to rely on but their trust and faith in each other if we were to achieve a peaceful end to every day. I felt the heavy weight of combat on my shoulders daily. I knew we were setting the stage for years to come.

I know that Prokop worried at times about me and the decisions I made after we entered Iraq. He told me so later on.

"You were going to be one of the guys who was going to be partly responsible for the future of Iraq," was his first impression, as he watched me lead us into action.

I was certainly never any hero. I didn't realize that my personal security detail, the soldiers who lived with me twenty-four hours a day, seven days a week, were watching my every move and analyzing my every decision. They got to know me better than anyone. But it didn't take long for the soldiers who got to know me best to realize my only two priorities were to accomplish all of our missions and make sure we all got back home alive. My

"inner circle," including Prokop, realized I took personal responsibility for their well-being and would never have considered any
decision foolishly placing us in harm's way. However, if we were
to see everyday life in Iraq theway Iraqi citizens were seeing it, we
needed to be on the streets with them.

My Humvee driver, Sgt. Loren Buchmeier would later explain it this way as he came to know and understand me better
than just about anyone, other than Evans and Guyette:

"Colonel Spain had genuine concern and compassion for his
soldiers. Nearly everyday he spent time on patrol. It wasn't
because he was cavalier or just looking for trouble. He just wanted to be out in the streets doing what the soldiers in his brigade
were doing. The colonel took us out to dangerous places, often
making it hard for us to keep him alive. But all of us would have
gladly followed him into any hell in the world."

Through our experiences together, my MPs started to learn
how we could establish law and order and bring the rule of law to
Iraq. But some of the combat arms leaders never got it. After Lt.
General Sanchez was promoted and assumed command of
CJTF7, and before the arrival of Major General Martin Demp-
sey, Brigadier General Robinson was the acting 1st Armored
Division Commander, and one of my several bosses.

During one of my first conversations with General Robinson,
I told him that if I had 20,000 more MPs we wouldn't need the
1st Armored Division, which consisted ofnearly 20,000 soldiers.

"I hope you're going to explain that comment, Colonel," he
said to me at the time.

I went on to explain myself by saying that a lot of what was
going on in Baghdad was an MP mission, not combat arms. I
suggested that instead of focusing on taking MPs from me and
putting them in the infantry and armor units, I thought he should
be giving me infantry and armor companies to put in my MP
Battalions. I went on to say that during the raids on the homes

of the Iraqis I thought the first people through the door should be the Iraqi police, supported by my MPs. I told him that I could use some heavier firepower from the infantry and armor, to serve as a quick reaction force, should my MPs get overwhelmed by the enemy. He obviously didn't listen to anything I said. I was summoned to his Headquarters across the city for a strategy meeting one day. I took Majors Gillian Boice and Tom Blair with me to the meeting. For thirty minutes we sat in front of Robinson while he lectured us on his vast knowledge of law enforcement and where we needed to be going with the Iraqi Police, and how to establishlaw and order.

As we watched the expressions on the faces of Robinson's own officers sitting around the conference table, it was obvious that he had failed to take the advice of even his own experts. Robinson did not like "non-doctrinal" missions, was close minded to the manner in which the military police had to work, and held countless poorly conceived ideas about policing operations. The longer he spoke, the more obvious it became to us that he had little idea what he was talking about. On more than one occasion, I attempted to react to Robinson's comments, only to see the Brigadier General continue talking, and paying little attention to my efforts to educate him to the realities of the conflict we were engaged in. I grew more and more impatient, with the incompetence of Robinson's understanding of our mission, as well as resentful that Robinson hadn't even been in Iraq during the invasion and arrived only after combat operations had been declared over.

Finally, as his thirty minute lecture came to a close, Robinson looked over at me, awaiting approval and support for his position. He asked me what I thought about his ideas.

I had heard enough and let my disdain for the senior officer show with a somewhat belligerent response.

"Sir, I don't agree with anything you've said during the last thirty minutes. Where did you get your understanding of police work, from watching two episodes of *Hill Street Blues*?"

The room went silent. Robinson's staff looked down at the notes in front of them, as my staff did the same. Robinson glared at me and I glared back. I knew I was out of line but felt better for having taken a stance in front of this senior officer. I had little to lose. Following Robinson's directions would delay the implementation of our plan at least a month. That's when he was scheduled to be replaced by Major General Dempsey. It was an eternity in the ongoing struggle to establish law and order in Iraq. The meeting ended abruptly with no further words spoken. I expected to be held after class and dressed down by the Brigadier General. Instead, I had very little contact with him before Robinson departed the war zone a month later. Robinson's own brigade commanders didn't think much of him, but Lt. General Sanchez loved him and that's all Robinson cared about.

"I don't much care for Colonel Teddy Spain," Robinson commented to one of his friends as he departed Iraq. I was happy and grateful that he was gone.

Once we were established in Baghdad, it was time to turn our attention to the Iraqi police. They had to put their fear of Saddam behind them and I felt we could play a role in speeding up the process. By the time my brigade headquarters arrived in Baghdad, Command Sergeant Major Guyette had identified a suitable place for us to locate. Guyette found me at Camp Dogwood, outside of Baghdad, visiting the 720th MP Battalion. A few days earlier he had departed our location to link up with the V Corps Command Sergeant Major, and future Sergeant Major of the Army, Command Sergeant Major Preston. The group of Command Sergeant Majors were going to conduct a recon of Baghdad to determine where the Corps Headquarters would be established.

"You had better get us a palace," I jokingly told Guyette. He took me seriously and had great news when he returned.

"Sir, we got us a palace. It's got a big hole in the back of it. Command Sgt. Major Preston told us we could have it because they don't want it because of all of the damage. Even though they aren't even in Baghdad yet, they said they don't want any palace with the back blown out."

The palace was situated in an area later designated as Camp Victory. Surrounding a large man-made lake, it was in the vicinity of several other presidential palaces built by Saddam Hussein using money that came from the United Nations "oil for food" program after Desert Storm, the first Gulf War. The entire water complex was beautiful. It had sustained some damage from the air war and during its capture by the Third Infantry Division. The largest building at Camp Victory became the Headquarters for General Wallace and several other generals and was commonly called the water palace.

Sergeant Major Guyette selected a specific palace complex for us, and started to patch up the holes and clean it up. The back of the palace was blown out by a cruise missile during the first night of the two day air campaign, a casualty of the "shock and awe" phase of the war. All of the windows had been blown out and there was glass and lots of rubble covering the otherwise ornate floors. But there was a great view of the lake, so we decided to call it home. We went to work on our own version of "flip that house." The soldiers cleaned up the debris, repaired the holes, replaced the windows, and made the place our home away from home.

Even though Guyette had described the palace, the first day I saw it for myself was April 25. I had left Lt. Colonel Dave Poirer, and the 720th MP had been there earlier that morning and taken the relatively short drive to link up with Guyette and my "new home." When we rolled up, Guyette was waiting outside with a big smile on his face. He was so proud of himself for getting us that palace. It was beautiful. He was almost giddy as he nearly jerked me out of my vehicle, anxious to show me around. He quickly saw I was depressed, but didn't understand why. He asked me if I was okay. I fought back tears as I told him we had just lost our first soldier hours before, SPC Narson Sullivan. Later that night, as I prepared to sleep in my new home, I was able to get a satellite signal on a phone and call my wife in Germany for the first time since leaving Kuwait. She had been watching the war on TV, without a clue as to my whereabouts for over five weeks. When she heard my voice for the first time she was fighting back her own tears. I was so happy to hear her voice, and anxious to let her know that I was alright, but couldn't hold back what had been on my mind all day.

"Honey, I just lost my first soldier," then I broke down and cried for the first time in combat.

I didn't want to admit it to myself then, but there would be more tears. As hard as we tried to avoid it, we would lose more soldiers in Iraq during our one year deployment. Even harder to admit is that the attitude expressed by leaders like Brigadier General Robinson prevailed in Iraq during that first year. Our methods of trying to bring the rule of law to Iraq and establish law and order through trust and respect was shoved aside by military and civilian leaders who simply didn't know what they were doing and had no understanding of the role of law enforcement in a democracy. My soldiers and I worked hard to fight for our philosophy, but as it faded in influence, Iraq collapsed into near civil war and open insurrection. Conditions only worsened until General David Petraeus assumed command of all coalition forces in Iraq in February of 2007 and adopted our philosophy of interacting with the Iraqi people and rebuilding the Iraqi police. Sadly, the intervening years turned the successful invasion into four years of significant bloodshed for American and coalition troops. And I am certain that on quiet nights in private moments with their wives or husbands, other military commanders shared tears with their loved ones for the fallen soldiers that had stood by their side.

CHAPTER THREE

ENEMY, TERRORIST, OR CRIMINAL?

**Pre-war planners failed to define differences between
enemies, terrorists and criminals.**

Eventually, our column left the rut-filled desert road, departing
Camp Adder, and headed towards Tallil Air Base to join up with
the 709th MP Battalion and the 1/41 Infantry Battalion. Turning
onto a major Iraqi highway, Staff Sergeant Jordan, in the lead
Humvee, practiced the role he played for the next year during
combat and police work in Baghdad. Turning his head from side
to side, staring at the roadway beyond him, all in one constant
motion, he was on the lookout for anything that that could pose
a danger to the soldiers in the vehicles lumbering down the road
behind him. Nothing he ever dreamed of in the states prepared
him for the responsibility of protecting the soldiers of the
brigade who would become his extended family. And that
included me.

The Humvees that carried my personal security detail served
a trio of purposes, part transportation system, part weapons system, and part mobile home for the thousands of hours we spent
riding throughout Iraq's most dangerous zones. Most hummers
carried three soldiers, two up front and one standing up behind
either a mounted MK19 (a weapon that rapidly fired the equivalent of grenades), 50 caliber machine gun or a squad automat-

ic weapon (SAW). My hummer was driven by Sergeant Loren Buchmeier. I sat in the front right seat. Specialist Prokop my communications expert, and my interpreter, of which I had several until I met Bennie, sat in the two rear seats.

Jordan later wrote about the Iraq expanding in front of him:

"It suddenly looked like we were in downtown New York. This was a six lane highway, full on both sides. There were tanks, armored personnel carriers, and every other vehicle that the Department of Defense has, sitting there in a traffic jam. After moving along at a snail's pace for about an hour, the highway finally cleared out and we moved to our first stop to refuel. Then, we moved near Tallil Air Base."

I was proud of Sgt. Jordan and all of the men and women who endured the convoy from Hell. All of us were exhausted from our day and a half drive through enemy territory. We'd inhaled enough desert sand to last the entire war. I was gratified and relieved my small brigade headquarters contingent had accomplished its first mission of Operation Iraqi Freedom, although the invasion hadn't been so designated at the time. We had thrown the dice and won. We delivered the fuel trucks and "High-Roller Six" to their destination and every soldier was safe. There wasn't any time to savor the moment. Based on General Wallace's guidance, I was focused on preventing the Iraqi detainees from slowing down the 3rd Infantry Division, and helping them get whatever they needed. Now that we were inside Iraq, I soon found myself having to figure out how to deal with problems connected to the capture of Iraqi soldiers, detainees and other prisoners in the army's custody because they happened to live in the small villages and towns that hugged the invasion route. Nothing in our pre-war planning prepared my soldiers and I for the task of dealing with the multiple problems and issues related to the variety of prisoners we inherited.

I wanted to take a breath and tell my soldiers to relax. But relaxing in the middle of a war could get us all killed. I kept thinking about the motto of the 18th Military Police Brigade, "Ever Vigilant." The motto that I was so proud of, and that had been used by tens of thousands of soldiers since Vietnam, was now taking on a whole new meaning forme personally. The lives of my soldiers depended on all of us remaining "Ever Vigilant." We were determined to live up to the meaning of these carefully chosen words.

As our convoy maneuvered closer to its destination, near Iraq's Tallil Air Base, I couldn't help but recall the other words Lt. General Wallace had said to me as we were leaving the relative safety of Kuwait.

"The next time I see you, we'll be in Baghdad."

The war was real now. During the twice daily updates on the radio, while I was waiting my turn to brief, I heard the Third Infantry Division Commander, Major General Blount, as he reported his successes, but more tragically, his casualties. He was briefing for the first time about Americans who gave their lives. I was fearful of the days ahead of me where I would be giving similar briefs. Now that we were inside Iraq, the only way out was to fight. There was no turning back. The eyes of the world were looking at us through the non-stop media coverage reporting from the battlefield. I knew we were making history that would be studied for years to come.

The stop at Tallil, however long, was temporary at best. For the 18th Military Police Brigade, the stop would be the beginning of our next mission, the responsibility for enemy prisoners. As the Third Infantry Division swept quickly north towards Baghdad, I was reminded of the Union General Tecumseh Sherman driving through the south to Atlanta in the American Civil War. Being a Southern boy from North Carolina, I was no fan of General Sherman, but I was getting a first-hand taste of what it might have felt like to have been a part of that historic movement. The pace was almost numbing as the Army herded mounting numbers of enemy prisoners to the rear so the rapid advance could continue.

We had little time for celebration upon our arrival. The pre-war intelligence and satellite images had been used by Army planners from the Third Infantry Division to select an area just outside of Tallil Air Base for the first holding area for enemy prisoners of war. Their Provost Marshal, Lt. Colonel Mack Huey, an old friend of mine, had shown me the satellite imagery in a meeting while we were still in Kuwait. The pictures looked okay, but if a picture is worth a thousand words, the words I was thinking of when we arrived at the location included some words that aren't in the dictionary. The high tech satellites and billions spent on intelligence gathering sometimes don't work near as well as one highly placed insider riding a top a camel through the desert to get a first hand glimpse of things. As I surveyed the area after climbing out of my Humvee, I could see we were encamped near one of Saddam's ammunition dumps. As I scanned the geography, my soldiers were thinking the same thing I was, and watching for my reaction. I just shook my head and looked at them without saying aword. I just couldn't believe that we had been encamped near an ammo dump. Deep inside, I reminded myself of my own leadership principles in tough times. Don't sweat the small stuff seemed appropriate for the situation—at least as long as none of the ammo started exploding.

The Third Infantry Division had already detained over fifty Iraqi prisoners. They placed them in an open field, not far from the ammo dump. The prisoners were surrounded by a hastily constructed fence composed of a single strand of concertina wire. They were guarded by MPs from the 709th Battalion. These were the same soldiers that went ahead in the helicopters with Major Boice and who had arrived at the location shortly after the invasion of Iraq began. As I was still thinking about a better solution than to have our encampment near the ammo dump, a soldier approached one of the officers I was talking with.

"Sir, we've got a dead enemy prisoner, what do you want us to do with him?"

I overheard the comments and after a second of deliberation, I felt I had the right answer. "Give him to the medical folks," seemed the proper response.

"Sir, we already tried that. Even though he died under their care, they said we have to take him now."

None of my previous twenty-five years in the Army prepared me for this moment. I had assumed that if a prisoner was dead my responsibilities were through. I believed that the medical people could deal with the dead bodies. I went over to argue my position with the chief medical officer, but to no avail. "Ok, I need to get some legal guidance from V Corps as to what my legal obligations are."

Before I had time to think about it, another soldier offered a potential solution, "We could bury him where we buried the other two."

I almost catapulted at the messenger when I heard the words, "the other two." Now all of this was starting to sound like much more than small stuff. And I did want to sweat. "What other two?" I glared, waiting for an explanation.

"Before your arrival, we buried two other enemy prisoners a little beyond where we're standing now." I asked where, and the soldier said about two hundred meters from where we were standing, so I told him to take me there. We walked several hundred meters to where I saw what appeared to be freshly dug gravesites. I went back to my hastily erected headquarters and called Colonel Marc Warren, the chief military lawyer, assigned to General Wallace's staff.

"Marc, what are my obligations?" I asked, knowing that I had more than one dead Iraqi prisoner on my hands, and assumed there would be more, given the number of severely wounded enemy in the medical facility. I wanted to ensure I was complying with the Geneva Conventions.

"Just bury them, and report a ten digit numerical grid to us so that we know the location," was his advice to me. In less than 24 hours I received a call from someone on the Corps staff asking me if we had buried them facing Mecca.

"The last time I saw them their ass was facing up, so if I need to report that they were facing Mecca, then they are facing Mecca," was my unpolished response.

How in the hell was I supposed to know which way was Mecca, in the middle of the desert? I thought to myself. It sure would have been nice to know what to do about dead Iraqis before we left Kuwait, or at least during my first conversation with the Corps staff. I really didn't appreciate some staff officer, sitting back in Kuwait, eating hot chow, and relieving himself in a real bathroom, second guessing me. There was much more of that to come.

Before we departed Tallil, and headed towards Baghdad, we ended up burying a total of seven enemy soldiers in a location that my Deputy Commander Tom Evans affectionately named, "Spain's Cemetery." I reminded him that he was a real wise ass and told him to knock the crap off. All that I could think of was that the term would be used as part of a Red Cross investigation into my care of enemy soldiers. It was the last thing I needed to worry about. Little did I know at the time it was just a small preview of what was to come.

I could never have dreamed we were only a year away from pictures appearing in the media about detainee abuse at Abu Ghraib prison. I would eventually become responsible for opening Abu Ghraib to house Iraqi prisoners. I would turn the responsibility for managing the prison over to General Janis Karpinski. Even before she took over, I would have my hands full with allegations of detainee abuse at yet another detainee/prisoner facility for which I was responsible—Camp Cropper. I divided Camp Cropper into two sections. In one section I housed the high value detainees. In the other section, I co-located the regular detainees.

In one incident, some of my MPs had been attacked by some of the regular prisoners, resulting in one prisoner's death and the shooting of others. One of my MPs was stabbed severely in the attack In the other incident, a prisoner had escaped. In both cases I directed what we called a "15-6" investigation. The investigations cleared my soldiers of any wrong doings. I also personally walked the ground with Lt. Colonel Ron Chew, the battalion commander responsible for Camp Cropper so that I could see firsthand what happened and, more importantly, to see what corrective action the battalion commander had taken to ensure it didn't happen again. I then personally briefed General Sanchez, who was the 1st Armored Division commander at the time, even though I had approved the findings in the investigation. We had nothing to hide. After my retirement, someone took one of the "15-6" investigations and put in on the Internet. I believe this was a clear ethics violation, if not an outright criminal violation. When a formal investigation of the allegations of prisoner abuse was opened over the Abu Ghraib prison affair and supervised by General Taguba, he reinvestigated the Camp Cropper incidents and they became the first of many investigations under the umbrella of the enlarged detainee abuse scandal which subsequently engulfed the Bush Administration and ended the military careers of Generals Sanchez and Karpinski.

While still located at the initial enemy prisoner of war holding area, my personal security detail and I made several trips onto Tallil so that I could talk with Brigadier General Jack Stultz, the leader of the 143rd Transportation Command. Stultz was responsible for the establishment of the first forward logistical base at Tallil in support of Operation Iraqi Freedom. A couple of years after my retirement he was promoted to three star general, and became head of the entire Army Reserve. He was a good guy, trying to make the best of a bad situation, just like we all were.

On the first evening we talked together, we sat on the front porch of Brigadier General Stultz' temporary battlefield residence. While Stultz was smoking a cigar, I noticed several strands of concertina wire lying on the ground by the porch. We desperately needed the wire to reinforce, and expand, our prisoner holding area because supplies simply were not making it into Iraq. I asked if I could have the wire but Stultz told me the wire was needed for other purposes. About 24 hours later, I found myself in the same situation as the night before. Stultz and I were sitting on the porch while Stultz enjoyed another cigar. The concertina wire was still lying on the ground in the same place it was the night before, so I decided to try another run at it. "Sir, the concertina wire is still here so you must not need it bad enough, can I take it back with me?" As I waited for an answer, Stultz made a face at me. It was the kind of face that was telling me I had really become a pest.

"Go ahead and take it," Stultz shot back.

"Okay, load it up boys," I gave the order to my security detail to load up the wire before Stultz had any time to change his mind.

Having been successful getting Stultz to break lose with the concertina wire, I thought it time to raise the other issues bothering me. I explained to Stultz the many reasons I wanted permission to move my soldiers and the enemy prisoners of war onto the base. They would be more secure. It would free up my soldiers for other duties. I was looking for better accommodations for the detainees than the open area where we had them detained. This was during the time of the now infamous Iraqi "Shamal," where it was impossible to see an outstretched hand, let alone maintain security over the prisoners. I had been to the edge of the concertina wire surrounding the enemy and couldn't see to the other side of the wire, only about thirty yards away. Detainees were standing there looking at me, covered in the blankets we had looted from a warehouse. The looks on the faces of a couple of them were saying, "just shoot me." I felt sorry for them, and really didn't want my soldiers to have to shoot any of them for attempting to escape, which wouldn't have been very difficult given the lack of wire and visibility. The issue of moving the soldiers and prisoners onto the base wasn't as easily resolved as getting concertina wire. Stultz was reluctant to give the go ahead to move the brigade and the enemy prisoners onto Tallil. When I met with Stultz the second time on this subject, he said his lawyer recommended that he not give permission because of the Geneva Hague conventions. His lawyer believed this was tantamount to moving prisoners onto a likely enemy target, thus placing them in greater jeopardy. When I discussed this with my lawyer, Captain Mike Banks, he believed just the opposite, that moving the prisoners onto the base would be more in compliance with the Geneva conventions because the prisoners could be better protected and secured. I had spent my entire military career dealing with military lawyers, and this was not the first time I had dealt with exact opposite military legal opinions.

The concept of providing more security to the enemy prisoners was a no brainer for me. I was concerned there would be a counter attack to free them and simply didn't have enough MPs to fight off even a minimal attacking force. I also was concerned that the minimal concertina wire would perhaps even encourage an escape attempt, forcing us to kill them, or allowing them to get away and fight another day. All of my assets were being used securing these detainees, and even though that was one of the two main missions General Wallace asked me to do, I knew I could do this with fewer assets, if I could move them onto to Tallil into some type of building. I could provide them better accommodations, get them out of the harsh weather, secure them better, and free up some of my MPs to do proactive patrolling around the perimeter of Tallil, hoping to prevent attacks, and any enemy attempt to free the detainees. But Stultz wouldn't budge on the matter.

"Sir, I mean no disrespect, but who do you work for?" I asked him as we continued our discussion about moving the enemy prisoners of war onto the base.

"I work for Major General Thurman," he proudly told me.

It was the very same General Thurman who had approached me during our briefings at Doha, Kuwait to tell me how crazy I was to make my rental car comment. I immediately concluded that I might have an outside chance of convincing Thurman, if only I could get Stultz to call him. "Sir, please call General Thurman and tell him Colonel Spain is here and is asking to move the prisoners onto Tallil because he thinks that is best. If he says no, can I please talk to him sir?"

I thought I had about a fifty-fifty chance of Stultz calling him. To Stultz' credit, he stood up, went over to the phone and called Thurman. I could only hear half of the conversation, but Stultz did a great job of explaining his position, as well as mine. I was leaning forward and ready to get on the phone if Stultz told me that Thurman said no.

"Yes, sir," were the final words I heard Stultz say.

When he hung up the phone, he told me I could move my soldiers, and the prisoners onto Tallil. I told him we would come up with a quick plan on where to put them, so as to not interfere with his logistical operations, yet provide them with the best protection in accordance with his concerns, and my concerns, over the Geneva conventions. I then shook his hand, thanked him, and then hauled my ass out of his office, before he could put any further constraints on me.

I went back through enemy territory, which we called "Indian country," to my brigade headquarters and told my staff, and Lt. Colonel Rich Vanderlinden, the 709th commander, that we needed to find suitable accommodations on Tallil as soon as possible. I already knew that some of his senior non-commissioned officers, and my command sergeant major, Charles Guyette had been scouting Tallil, in case we were allowed to occupy it.

After having spent three nights outside of Tallil, our brigade headquarters, along with the 709th headquarters and their companies, finally moved inside, establishing a camp at the far end of one of the two runways on the air base. We set up shop inside a building that only days before our arrival had been an Iraqi Officer's Club. Stinking from the smell of rotting chickens inside a refrigerator that had been without power for a few days the location wasn't perfect, but we would clean it up and be happy to have it. Prokop and Buchmeier slept in a small garage, shooing away stray dogs so they wouldn't have their boots stolen at night. The electricity had been cut off by the invasion force moving north. The dead chickens cooking under Iraq's 115 degree desert sun didn't do much for their appetites, even though they were hungry for real food and already tired of meals ready to eat.

Yet, the move onto Tallil was almost like trading a campground for the luxury of a roadside motel. Only several days into war, we realized how much we had taken for granted back at home. At Tallil, I was so excited when Sergeant First Class Brown, from my logistical staff, built our first "slit" latrine, a big hole in the ground covered with a handmade toilet seat. My maintenance warrant officer, Chief Ward, jump started an abandoned Iraqi hole digger and dug the hole. It was a big deal after we had been crapping on the ground in front of each other and then covering it up.

While he was digging the hole, Chief Ward asked me if I wanted to climb up on the hole digger and operate the stolen, I mean, borrowed Iraqi "caterpillar." I said I did. I climbed on board and he showed me how to operate it. After less than a minute, I nearly turned it over. He asked me to get down, and never allowed me to operate anymore Iraqi earth moving equipment.

Months later, in Baghdad, the first sergeant of the 170th MP Company asked me if I wanted to drive a captured Iraqi armored personnel carrier in their motor pool. I said I did. I climbed on board and he showed me how to operate it. After about a minute, I nearly ran it over two of our hummers. He asked me to get out, and never allowed me to operate any more captured Iraqi military equipment. All of my soldiers saw the trend. They all thanked God that the army was paying me to lead soldiers and not operate captured Iraqi equipment.

Only in the fantasies brought on by the stress of the mission did we picture the running water of hot showers and the smells of home cooked meals streaming from the kitchens back home. So it was no surprise—three weeks after moving onto Tallil, we were ecstatic to eat our first hot T-rations meal, even if it was the same breakfast meal every night. Back at home, during routine training exercises, it would have been awful, but in the desert, in the middle of war, it was like dining in a five star restaurant on New York's Park Avenue. Even without saying it to each other, one by one, minute by minute, the war was changing our perspective of life and living, things we took advantage of before the war became the things we longed for after the war was over. The common thoughts about simple pleasures bound us even closer together—forging families out of strangers. To this day, there are simple pleasures in life I no longer take for granted. I appreciate my hot shower every morning.

Rich Vanderlinden's soldiers did a great job in converting an abandoned gymnasium on the base to a holding area for the enemy prisoners of war, by now increasing in number each day. An Iraqi prisoner, a Brigadier General, and former Iraqi commander of the Tallil Air Base told the MPs where they could find blankets inside a base warehouse that had been used by Iraqi army units. The blankets were given to the detainees. My soldiers took the pork out of their meals ready to eat and gave the remaining parts of the meals to their prisoners. They learned quickly that the keys to success were creativity, frugality and kindness.

But planning was the backbone of everything we did.

Nowhere did planning become more vital than in dealing with the prisoners. Before we left Germany, I put out the word that I was in dire need of a Judge Advocate General or "JAG." In the army, the role was filled by a military lawyer who became the principle adviser to army officers on the administration of army law. I lobbied Colonel Warren to have a lawyer assigned to me, given my upcoming responsibilities for thousands of enemy prisoners, but more importantly my concerns that I comply with all my legal obligations in accordance with the Geneva Hague Conventions.

At the same time I was looking for a lawyer, Captain Michael Banks, assigned to V Corps in Heidelberg, Germany had let his commanding officers know that he wanted to be deployed. Banks had arrived in Germany during the summer of 2002. He had graduated from law school, was "up to his ears," in student loan debt and eager to start repaying the money he owed. He spent three years as a military interrogator before taking on his first assignment as a JAG in Japan, where he focused on administrative, operational and international issues. Knowing of his desire to be deployed, Colonel Marc Warren told him the 18th MP Brigade was looking for a good lawyer.

Banks first met me and my crew in December of 2002 at an Army training base in Germany. I spoke with him at length about the MP mission, the importance of professionalism, the need to properly address the issues related to the enemy prisoners once the fighting began and my worry about following the law. Captain Banks later let me know that while I was assessing him, he was deciding whether he wanted to work for me. He said he made up his mind from a single comment in our entire discussion.

"Your job is to keep me and my soldiers out of jail!" he recalled me telling him.

Banks decided I was ready and willing to listen to him and he returned to Heidelberg, Germany with his mind made up that he

would become the JAG for the 18th MP Brigade. He read everything he could get his hands on that reviewed MP doctrine and
the mission of military police. With Colonel Warren and other
operational law personnel he discussed detention operations.
Colonel Warren arranged for a Lieutenant Colonel from the
Israeli Defense Forces to come to Germany and provide training
on occupation law. Banks kept in constant touch with the Brigade
and later returned to Mannheim, Germany, boarded the bus with
my staff, and left for Kuwait, assuming full time responsibility as
the 18th MP JAG.

I could never have been more pleased with the choice. Banks'
work began immediately. The 3rd Brigade of the 3rd Infantry
Division charged across the Kuwaiti border with Iraq, picking up
detainees early after the invasion started. To continue their move
north, they requested assistance. MPs from the 709th were placed
on helicopters and sent ahead to assume responsibility for the
detainees.

When Banks arrived with our brigade headquarters, there was
already a group of detainees at the compound at Tallil. Some were
Iraqi soldiers. They were easy to categorize as combatants who
had surrendered, fitting nicely within the Geneva Conventions.
Some were civilian-non-combatants, who also fell easily within
other articles of the Geneva Convention.

Some of the prisoners were not Iraqi soldiers or civilians.
Rounded up early in the fighting, these were al-Qaeda members
in Iraq. President Bush had already determined that the Geneva
Conventions did not "apply" to members of al-Qaeda. But army
lawyers held key discussions on the issue of "status," versus
"treatment." Everyone agreed that the Geneva Conventions provided no category of "unlawful enemy combatant," a description
that best matched the al-Qaeda in Iraq members. But the Geneva
Conventions provided a clear framework for "treatment," that
needed to be followed without exception. The final guidance on

al-Qaeda members were that they should be considered unlawful enemy combatants, not covered by the Geneva Conventions, but still to be treated humanely in accordance with those Conventions. The army interpreted the guidance to mean that all of the basic human rights issues, such as food, water, medical treatment, shelter and religious practices were to be followed.

As the weeks went by, the Army found itself dealing with a different type of fighter, the Fedayeen soldiers of Saddam Hussein's displaced army, now employing terrorist tactics against the Americans and Iraqi civilians. Trained and called upon to fight-like terrorists, these individuals could not be given status under the Geneva Conventions as regular combatants since they were not visibly complying with the Laws of War. Under international law, there is a distinction between "international armed conflict," and "internal armed conflict," or "non-international armed conflict." The Geneva Conventions applies to "international armed conflict," but not to "internal armed conflict," which encompasses insurgencies against a functioning government.

The original invasion was an international armed conflict in the beginning. But as soon as the Iraqi government became non-functioning, with the United States effectively governing Iraq, the situation looked more like the Israeli occupied territories. It was more than an internal armed conflict, but something less than an international one. Suddenly, Iraq looked and acted more like Afghanistan than a state in the mid east. It was easy to label the Fedayeen, terrorists, and other groups using similar tactics as unlawful enemy combatants.

But the problem for me and the MPs was that these types of enemy prisoners did not meet the standard definitions within the Geneva Conventions for combatants or EPWs; retained personnel such as physicians or chaplains; or civilian detainees. We needed strict legal authority to detain someone, had to label them properly under the Geneva Conventions, and then treat them appropriately. It would have been accurate to use the word insurgent to deal with this category of individual. Captain Banks defined an insurgent as, "an individual who is from a given State and who is fighting against the government that currently controls that State." The word "insurgent" was never mentioned around me during my year in Iraq. The term that finally stuck as a description for these types of detainees was unlawful enemy combatant. The final issue for us became treatment of this category of individual. How were we to treat an unlawful enemy combatant who fell outside of all of our previous experience? Captain Banks provided the legal advice that my soldiers and I would followto the letter during our days in Iraq:

"The bottom line is that there are certain behaviors that are fundamental to who we are and how we treat people. We provide food, shelter, medical care, water, and clothing to detainees— those circumstances where that does not happen are almost always inexcusable, unless food is so short that everyone, detainee and guard alike, are on short rations." This was the actual state of affairs for about twenty-four hours. Before we moved the enemy prisoners onto Tallil, we ran out of water, and my soldiers who were guarding prisoners, only ate the pork products that had been removed from the MREs. I was quite upset when I heard about this, and made it clear that if we got to the point that either my soldiers went hungry, or the enemy prisoners went hungry, then we were just going to have some hungry enemy prisoners. Fortunately we were able to quickly establish our supply lines back to Kuwait.

The struggle to classify my detainees continued from our move onto Tallil AirBase, until I handed over my part of the detainee mission to General Karpinski in June. My worries over detainee conditions and the Red Cross is reflected in my brief during my nightly update to General Wallace on May 24:

"Red Cross showed up late today and looked at some paperwork and left for the day, they will return tomorrow. We are prepared to move 70 detainees to the new jail tomorrow in Zone 1, they will be held for the Iraqi courts. We are also prepared to move 200 detainees tomorrow to Camp Vigilant in the old Abu Ghraib prison if we overcome a small sewage issue, because slit latrines will not work. These detainees are being held, not being sent to court."

The note illustrates my concern about the impact the Red Cross could have on my operations, and was my first attempt to classify detainees on my own, absent any guidance or support from my higher headquarters. I was trying to use the four regional jails as pre-trial holding facilities. My thought process was to have the jails in close proximity to the courts. I knew taking detainees back and forth would be a nightmare. We already had attempted escapes during earlier transport.

Camp Vigilant, located inside the walls of the old Abu Ghraib prison, would then be used to hold those that had intelligence value. I guess these are the ones that are called insurgents today. I called them enemy prisoners of war back then. All I received was conflicting guidance about their legal status. Some guidance said everyone we were holding was subject to the Geneva Conventions. Some said it was only the combatants. There was no way for me to sort this out.

There was little to no interest from my superiors towards holding what they considered criminals. However, Iraqi citizens were most interested in and afraid of the criminals. Early on, they were not concerned about those who attacked the coalition, aslong as they themselves were not targeted. I realized this was human nature. In June, after we had established Camp Cropper and Camp Vigilant at Abu Ghraib Prison, we attempted to segregate the detainees based on where they were from or what they had done. Absence any guidance from the Army, I decided to create three categories of detainees. The first category I called the enemy. These were the former members of Saddam's military. The second category I called the terrorists. These were the outsiders who entered Iraq just to create chaos and kill Americans. The final category were the criminals, who were Iraqis taking advantage of the chaos created by the invasion for personal profit. I was making this up as I went along. I frequently spoke with Captain Banks about the protection these categories of detainees should be afforded. I was very concerned about the intermixing of these three groups, even though we never did a good job of separating them. The one exception was the high value detainees, primarily the individuals from the "Deck of 55," Saddam's inner circle. I kept them in a location we had the engineers build, as a part of Camp Cropper. I ensured there was no way for them to physically intermix with the "common detainees." We put the likes of Tariq Aziz, Chemical Allie and many others there. That's also where Saddam was housed when he was captured.

Whether it involved the humane treatment of enemy prisoners or building relationships with local Iraqis, my men and women soon found validation for what we already believed. the only way to insure success of the MP mission was to treat everyone with respect. This was something that had been beat in my MPs heads since their initial training at the MP School. Just as we expect to be treated by the local police with dignity and respect back at home, so did I expect my MPs to treat the detainees, and the Iraqi people with dignity and respect. Unfortunately not everyone in the Army shared my philosophy. Even though we were concerned about how we would be treated if captured, we knew the United States had to practice our own principles in Iraq. In a land where potential danger hid behind every earthen wall, balancing safety with dignity was always a tenuous task, just as it was for fellow police officers on the streets of America. We had to practice what we believed every day in Iraq, often under conditions that were very dangerous and resembled policework on the streets in the states, more than war in Iraq.

The detainees and prisoners were important to us, since some of the Iraqis we had incarcerated early in the invasion were influential citizens in their communities. As we gathered intelligence inside Iraq, we sometimes found a need to free people from jail so they could help us get to know other influential villagers. A good example was a situation that developed with General Petraeus. I was contacted by Petraeus, who was grappling with this issue and needed a favor. One of the village leaders in his area of operations north of Baghdad had been picked up by his soldiers and taken to Abu Ghraib prison. Petraeus asked me if I could find the individual and get him released so he could return to his village. By this time I had already transferred Abu Ghraib over to General Karpinski, so I called her deputy, Colonel Al Ecke, and asked him if he could find the detainee that Petraeus wanted. A few hours later, Al called me back and said they had already evacuated the detainee to Basra, in Southern Iraq. I asked him to coordinate with the commander in Basra to get the detainee released. Al was a good guy and immediately helped me out.

I coordinated with General Petraeus. He sent one of his majors and two helicopters to Basra, picked up the village leader, and returned him to his village. Clearly, Petraeus knew, and I was quickly learning, how the pre-war planning void could only be filled by leadership and doing what had to be done to build trust with Iraqis.

Dealing with the detainees was indeed a challenge. We had issues before Karpinski came into the picture. There were issues long after she left Iraq. Detainees tried to escape from everywhere. They did anything possible to gain their freedom to fight again, including jumping from the back of fast moving trucks, even while flexi-cuffed.

The timing of release approval was important. If a detainee was released too early, it was unlikely they would be convicted in a court and they'd be back on the street to cause more problems. If they were released too late, the result was overcrowding in the jails. The problem of when to release detainees was never completely resolved.

Transporting detainees to and from court required extensive assets. Using MPs for this role stretched our capabilities significantly. Army Divisions outside Baghdad wanted to bring their detainees who had no intelligence value to the jails, but usually didn't have the proper documentation to allow us to hold them. It took precious time and effort to sort these issues, tying up the few MPs available.

Iraqi guards were constantly involved in bribery scandals. For example, they released prisoners routinely in exchange for favors and money. Before I handed the mission over to Karpinski, I was visiting a jail we were standing up across the street from the Police Academy It was common practice for family members to bring food to their loved ones who were being detained. After my unannounced check of the jail, I was departing through the front and saw a lady, with her two children, handing a bag of food to an Iraqi police guard. The scene looked wrong. I sensed something was unusual. I asked one of the MPs on my personal security detail to take the bag from the guard and inspect it. The guard reluctantly handed it over. My soldier emptied out the bag. At the bottom of the bag, under the food, was a roll of Iraqi money. She was bribing the guard to release her husband. When I questioned the supervisor of the guard I was told that they really did not have enough evidence to hold the detainee. I went back into the jail and had my interpreter review the paper work with me and the jail commander.

Afterwards, I made a decision on the spot that we shouldn't have been holding the detainee at all. I released him to his family. I fired the guard who accepted the bribe and returned the money to his wife. I have no way of knowing whatever happened to that detainee. I could have made a mistake. I do know, for at least some period of time,we won the "heart and mind" of that particular family.

It was always impossible to differentiate between short and long term detainees. We always had to ensure that we knew how many detainees we had and which category they fell into, since the Coalition Provisional Authority (CPA) asked us lots of questions. I briefed the number of detainees, by location, every night on my nightly update to the commanding general. My questions were always the same. The answers were always confusing because of the lack of consistency and pre-war planning. What was the status of a detainee? Are they enemy prisoners of war? Are they criminals? Are they protected under the Geneva Convention? Do they have rights? The only way we had of overcoming the lack of pre-war planning and finding answers to these questions as they pertained to each individual Iraqi prisoner was to ensure we were closely involved in and monitoring all the activity at each prison facility. Karpinski's failure to recognize this led to her downfall amid the torture and abuse scandals after I left Iraq.

Another potential conflict we always had to address with the detainees was the intense media interest in who we had in our prisons. The embedded media that accompanied the invasion force, as well as "visiting" media that were frequently present in some form or another, relished stories about Iraqi prisoners and detainees. They had a particularly strong appetite for the high-value detainees. We were confronted almost daily with media attempts to gain access to our prisoners. I'd never seen such creativity than some of the ideas the media came up with to secure interviews and glimpses of the Iraqis we had detained as prisoners of war. I had never been involved in discussions, nor had anytraining, regarding how best to handle such situations. Dealing with the media was hard enough. Securing and handling prisoners was difficult and demanding. Trying to prevent the media from having contact with the prisoners was a nightmare.

I constantly had to take on media types or make decisions against media representatives when it came to access to my prisoners. It seemed like we were always one step ahead of some sort of problem that could have been caused by media efforts to get near our various holding areas.

On one occasion, an Iraqi television crew interviewed several Iraqi police officers conducting joint patrols with us in Baghdad. Questions were asked about the jails, prisoners and detainees. Everyone understood the nature of the problems the army was dealing with and one sided assessments by random Iraqi police giving their opinions stirred controversy.

In another instance, an army unit from outside Baghdad brought three enemy prisoners of war to the holding area at Camp Cropper by ambulance. When everyone climbed out of the ambulance there was a reporter from *Newsweek* accompanying the group. We immediately escorted the reporter out of our detention facility. We'd developed some clear guidelines— reporters were not allowed access to our jails and holding locations unless by some prior agreement.

An Iraqi reporter entered the American police station in what was called Zone 7 in Baghdad and asked to see the detention cell. The reporter had another male with her. She and her friend were immediately escorted away from the station and never allowed back.

An Al Jazeera news crew drove up to the al Khadra Police Station in Baghdad's Zone 54 and started videotaping. The Iraqi police approached them and asked that they stop filming in front of the location. One of my brigade lieutenants went outside to meet with them. He determined they had no press badges or any type of clearances. They were asked to leave and complied with our orders.

One of the more humorous stories, even though not funny at the time, involved the collision of the media with prisoner issues and happened to me when I decided to take a news crew to one of my jails.

They had seen Ambassador Bremer, Bernie Kerik, and myself conducting a sham ribbon cutting on national TV, marking the opening of my first regional jail in Baghdad, so they asked to visit it. I agreed to take them there, but it turned out to be a very bad idea. A crew from the television news show, *60 Minutes* was spending the day with my MPs and I. They were interested in filming jails and police stations. Things had been going well, but I let my guard down. I took them to one of the newest jails to open in Baghdad.

Since the jail was newly renovated, I thought it would make a great choice. There were approximately a hundred Iraqis incarcerated there awaiting court appearances. The jail was being run by a reserve MP unit. The senior MP at the jail at the time of our arrival was a Hispanic buck sergeant who struggled to speak English. Combined with my own hearing problem, communications were extremely difficult as the news crew looked on with the camera running. The group I was escorting was separated from the main part of the jail by a door with a see-through glass. This was the same jail where Bremer had done the "sham" ribbon cutting." I thought it to be in pretty good shape or I would never have brought the *60 Minutes* delegation on the tour. All of the prisoners were supposed to be housed in individual rooms with locked doors segregating them from a larger open area.

Working hard to understand what I was being told by the buck sergeant, I was looking past his shoulder and into the open area where I saw many of the detainees wandering around unsecured out in the hallways.

"Sergeant, why are so many of the detainees out of their rooms and roaming around in the hallway and open area?" I inquired of the senior MP in charge of the buck sergeant.

"Oh, we're having a riot," was his calm and casual response.

With *60 Minutes* rolling their cameras and microphones and catching all of the activity, I realized I would have to think fast.

"So, the disturbance just happened and you have additional MPs on the way to quell the uprising?" I looked for clarification from the sergeant.

"No, sir, this has been going on for about the last 24 hours."

Getting one of those feelings inside, I instantly regretted bringing the *60 Minutes* crew to the jail. Now I had to engage in serious damage control.

"Sergeant, I'll have a response force sent immediately to take back control of the jail." I made certain the news crew could hear my commands.

Meanwhile, I could see that the detainees had ripped the doors off of their individual rooms and were having free run of the facility. Fortunately for the seven or eight female detainees, they were still locked up and protected from the male rioters. Followed by the *60 Minutes* news crew, I went out to my vehicle, contacted the Tactical Operations Center and asked for reinforcements. When I got off of the radio, *60 Minutes* wanted to return to the jail and do more filming. When I told them it wouldn't be safe because we would probably have to use force, they asked if they could wait for the MP response team. Again, I told them no. As everyone was preparing to depart, the news team went over to an outside window and filmed one more time the chaos inside.

It wasn't my best day in Iraq. But it was yet another indicator of the chaos created by the Department of Defense decisions early in the pre-war planning to ignore the best ways to address the myriad issues pertaining to Iraqi enemy prisoners of war, terrorists, and common criminals.

CHAPTER FOUR

DETAINEES AND INTELLIGENCE COLLECTION

**Interrogators started making their own playbook for Iraq
before the war even started.**

I fully understood from years of tactical military experience that
intelligence drives combat operations. Combat operations are
based on the gathering of intelligence about what the enemy is
doing, or planning to do. Intelligence gathering is absolutely
critical to planning and conducting successful combat operations.
Even though I understood this before Iraq, I didn't understand
how the methods of gathering that intelligence could impact us
so severely. Military and civilian interrogators gather the intelligence, but military police commanders like me, are responsible
for the health and well being of the detainees. It is not a responsibility that can be abrogated, regardless of the circumstances. I
viewed the situation as pretty simple—either I was responsible for
the detainees or I wasn't. I refused to be responsible only when
something went wrong. The Abu Ghraib prison scandal is a perfect example of what happens when interrogators control the
detainees. If some military leaders had issues with Karpinski's
administration of the prisons, they should have helped her
improve, or removed her from her position, instead of giving
more control of some of her detainees to the interrogators.

The conflict between interrogating and managing the detainees in Iraq began long before the invasion. My first unpleasant
encounter with the intelligence community occurred during a
planning conference at Third Army Headquarters at Ft.

McPherson, Georgia. About four months before I deployed to Kuwait. A U. S. Army Lt. Colonel assigned to military intelligence provided us a briefing on how they would conduct their interrogations. Their plan involved me being responsible for setting up special locations,and escorting the prisoners to interrogators at those locations. I told the officer that I would establish a separate location inside my perimeter and that they could pick up the detainee, and interrogate them at that location. The Lt. Colonel countered that's not how it would work and again told me what I would do. As we sparred back and forth over the issue, I started getting pissed off. Since we were discussing what I thought would be a hypothetical situation, and since I had never seen the officer before, and would never see her again, I abruptly ended the discussion. "Don't tell me what to do. If I run the camp, I'll do what I want."

I had an eagle on my collar and she didn't, so she made a face and moved on to the next subject. I couldn't imagine at the time how the relationship between the military police and military intelligence would play such an important role at Abu Ghraib Prison just two years down the road, putting the Army in the middle of a Constitutional crisis and undercutting the war effort.

Military intelligence personnel were focused on acquiring intelligence from prisoners. I knew all along that another great source of intelligence would be the Iraqi police themselves. Ironically, I was at a conference at the Military Police School, in Ft. McClellan Alabama in the mid-1990s when the concept of police intelligence operations was first born. That concept was created from the lessons we had learned in Panama and Haiti. My predecessors in those countries gathered important intelligence information from the host nation police.

Countless times in Iraq, my battalion commanders conducted combat operations based on intelligence they gathered from the Iraqi police. I had several military intelligence personnel praise my MPs for the amount of intelligence they were providing, much of it coming from the Iraqi police. In fact, the birth of the Major Crimes Unit we subsequently stood up in Baghdad, was the result of an Iraqi police major who convinced me it would work, based on the large amount of intelligence he had collected. I was so impressed I authorized him to establish the unit.

Initially, I limited their size to fifty people. I tasked my 168th MP Battalion to provide them oversight. The Major Crime Unit eventually grew to a staff of nearly five hundred before I departed Iraq. I allowed them to grow in increments, as they produced results.

Unfortunately, ten days after I departed Iraq in 2004, the Iraqi police major that had been so helpful and creative in building the unit was murdered. I assume the individuals responsible waited until we left to viciously murder the officer in front of his family. They knew we would certainly come after them if they had murdered him while I was still there. The crime was not uncommon in Iraqi culture and was intended to send a clear message to other potential supporters of the United States. There is nothing so intimidating to a citizen than to see criminal and terrorist groups get away with murdering the very policemen who are supposed to defend the rest of the population from the same type of activity.

In Iraq, the American military and civilian agencies involved in intelligence collection from the detainees and high value prisoners failed to follow through with a carefully thought out plan of action. Instead, they became locked in conflict and bureaucratic battles with the military police chain of command, which contributed to the torture and abuse of prisoners at Abu Ghraib.

Years after the events that gave America a black eye around the world and didn't serve our country well, I wasn't surprised to find out that the CIA destroyed records related to the torture of suspected terrorists early in the war on terror. In 2005, then CIA Director Michael Hayden confirmed that his agency had destroyed videotapes of the harsh interrogations of two terrorism suspects at Guantanamo Bay. In 2007, Hayden told employees of the CIA that he supported the decision to destroy the tapes, although that decision had actually been made by his predecessor, Porter Goss.

"There are other people at the agency who know about this far better than I," Hayden said after answering questions posed by the Senate Intelligence Committee. [1]

Mr. Hayden was being modest. He had succeeded Porter Goss as the Director of the CIA. Goss had succeeded George Tenent. Goss was the CIA Director from September 24, 2004 until May 5, 2006. The dates are crucial to an understanding of what was likely going on in Iraq under the nose of U. S. Army General Janis Karpinski, but far beyond her ability to influence.

Goss himself came from a long career in the U. S. intelligence community. He was a graduate of Yale University. At Yale, he belonged to the same fraternity as an uncle of former President George W. Bush and John Negropointe. Negropointe went on to serve as the U.S. Ambassador to the United Nations, the head of the CPA in Iraq in June, 2004 after Paul Bremer and Director of National Intelligence. During the 1980s Negropointe was working in Honduras at the same time as the Iran Contra affair.

Goss was a CIA officer assigned to clandestine services during the 1960s. He was subsequently elected to the House of Representatives. He was the chairman of the House Intelligence Committee from 1997 until his appointment as Director of the CIA in September, 2004. In 2005, after the fact, Goss approved of the destruction of the CIA's videotapes of the interrogations of two terrorism related detainees. The actual decision to destroy dozens of tapes had been made by the head of the CIA's clandestine service, Jose A. Rodriquez, Jr. In October of 2004, Goss appointed Kyle "Dusty" Foggo as the CIA's Executive Director. The job is the third highest position in the agency. After the 9/11 terrorist attacks, Foggo was in charge of the CIA's office in Frankfurt, Germany. According to an article in the August 13, 2009 *New York Times*, Foggo played a key role in the CIA's detainee interrogation process.

"Mr. Foggo oversaw the construction of three detention centers, each built to house about a half-dozen detainees. The C.I.A. prisons would become one of the Bush administration's most extraordinary counterterrorism programs."[2]

In June, 2005, as a result of an FBI investigation, a Federal Grand Jury indicted Foggo and a San Diego defense contractor, Brent Roger Wilkes, for fraud and corruption in connection with the awarding of U. S. government contractors. Foggo left the CIA inearly May, 2006, shortly after FBI agents searched his home. Goss followed him out the door. Additional indictments followed in 2007 charging Foggo with fraud, conspiracy and money laundering. In September, 2008, Foggo pleaded guilty to a single charge and was sentenced to 37 months in prison. Foggo was the highest ranking CIA official ever to be convicted of a crime. An article in the August 12, 2009 *New York Times* described Foggo's clandestine prison system:

> "Eventually, the agency's network would encompass at least eight detention centers, including one in the Middle East, one each in Iraq and Afghanistan and a maximum-security long-term site at Guantánamo Bay, Cuba, that was dubbed Strawberry Fields, officials said. (It was named after a Beatles song after C.I.A. officials joked that the detainees would be held there, as the lyric put it, "forever.")
>
> The CIA has never officially disclosed the exact number of prisoners it once held, but top officials have put the figure at fewer than 100.
>
> At the detention centers Mr. Foggo helped build, sev-

eral former intelligence officials said the jails were small, and though they were built to house about a half-dozen detainees they rarely held more than four.

...The detainees, held in cells far enough apart to prevent communication with one another, were kept in solitary confinement 23 hours a day. For their one hour of daily exercise, they were taken out of their cells by CIA. security officers wearing black ski masks to hide their identities and to intimidate the detainees, according to the intelligence officials.

...CIA. analysts served 90-day tours at the prison sites to assist the interrogations. But by the time the new prisons were built in mid, 2003 or later, the harshest CIA. interrogation practices—including water boarding —had been discontinued."[3]

Everything that happened in Iraq during 2003 and early 2004 and with certain people in the CPA started coming back to me when I learned of these events and patterns of behavior. My own experiences with Camp Cropper and civilian interrogators in Iraq indicated the same patterns were developing in Iraq early in the war.

My brigade had been inside Iraq for only a few days when I had my first suspicious run-in with unknown civilian interrogators who were in the country under the guise of a "non-government agency." While visiting my enemy prisoner of war holding area on Tallil Air Base I came upon two men conducting interrogations of some of our Iraqi detainees. I confronted them in the upstairs gym on the base which we had converted into a secure jail facility. The civilian interrogator who seemed to be in charge asked me to leave immediately.

"What are you guys doing?" I probed for answers.

"It's none of your business; you need to leave," the two men gave every indication I had no authority over them or their activities.

"No, these are my prisoners and you either tell me what you're doing or you're leaving. In fact, I'll have you taken out of here." I was adamant.

"You can't talk to us that way—we don't like your attitude," was their return verbal assault.

"Bullshit, I run this place. These are my detainees." My tone and heightened posture let them know I was ready for a fight. Of course it helped having some of the members of my personal security detail standing with me.

"We're with the U.S. government. We're just interrogating the folks." Their demeanor quickly changed as they saw that I had no intention of backing down.

I made certain the two interrogators understood the rules of the road and that I was responsible for the holding area at Tallil. They would need to abide by my rules. I later reminded Lt. Colonel Rich Vanderlinden, the battalion commander responsible for that holding area, he was responsible for what happened there and that anyone allowed entry, especially to interrogate detainees, would follow our rules. I knew I didn't have to worry about anyone pushing Rich around.

It was not the only time I confronted interrogators, who when challenged, readily asserted their authority as representatives of the U. S. government. The second occasion was at Camp Cropper before the prison was turned over to Karpinski. One of my battalion commanders, Lt. Colonel Ron Chew, Commander of the 115th MP Battalion, was responsible for Camp Cropper at the time. Chew expressed concern to me about an Army colonel wearing the uniform of military intelligence who was busy at the camp interrogating high value detainees like "Chemical" Ally and Tariq Aziz. Chew was worried that the military intelligence colonel and his staff were taking some of the detainees out during the day and not bringing them back for many hours. The MPs also noticed that sometimes the detainees were not returned to the camp in the same condition in which they left. Chew told me the military intelligence interrogators were housed about a half mile away in a building near a jail where we had once held Abu Abbas following his arrest in Iraq. Dressed in full uniform, I paid a visit to discuss the ground rules for interrogations and access to my prisoners. I found the military intelligence colonel in his office. He didn't know who I was until the introductions.

"I understand you're a colonel but I need to be able to control access to these detainees," I began the conversation after an initial greeting.

"Colonel," the military intelligence commander shot back, "my men are conducting interrogations of these detainees and they will come and go as they please with these prisoners. And they will not be identifying who they are."

"Well, then," I responded, "you will not be interrogating anybody because these detainees are my responsibility and unless I know who has access to my detainees, then you won't have any access at all."

"Colonel Spain, you won't be getting any access roster from us," the colonel from military intelligence was cordial, but stood his ground.

"Well, Colonel, then you won't be getting access," I was equally firm as I turned and walked away.

I went back to Chew's office and gave him the order to keep military intelligence away from the detainees.

"As of right now they have no access to these people. If they show up you turn them around. Until I know more and unless they comply with my rules, they will not be allowed to see these detainees and take them from these premises under any circumstance."

Within 24 hours I received a call questioning my authority to proffer such a position. I made it clear to the caller that I was responsible for the detainees. They were not going to be removed from the camp and any access to them would need to be supported by an access roster. Lt. Colonel Chew and his soldiers would know who was allowed to see the high value detainees. Many of the detainees on the "Deck of 55" were there. Any harm to them had the potential to create an international incident, that would surely play out poorly for those of us caught in the middle.

The next day, I received the roster I requested and from that time until we turned Camp Cropper over to Karpinski, I had no problems with the military intelligence interrogators. Without question, the situation made me uncomfortable and reiterated in my mind the importance of following and maintaining a clear cut line of authority and responsibility.

My confrontations with the military intelligence interrogators and their chain of command happened before any allegations of torture and abuse of detainees had ever been made. Major General Geoff Miller had not yet visited Iraq and Lt. General Sanchez had not issued his memos with guidelines for interrogations of prisoners, be they detainees or otherwise. But I was already having problems with civilian and military interrogators and was concerned about their conduct and treatment of my detainees long before the discovery of prisoner abuse. After the run-ins I became convinced the military intelligence types, fortified by mysterious higher level civilian connections in the U. S. government, would stop at nothing in their interrogation methods. I was genuinely worried that one or more of our detainees could be abused. I made up my mind, regardless of the consequences, I would not allow military intelligence to come between me and the detainees who were my responsibility. I really felt that these guys would take some of our high value detainees out from the prison and from under our care and use abusive tactics to secure admissions. I believed that to be a real possibility.

But my concern about intelligence gathering and the treatment of detainees was not just with those of us from the United

States. I was also concerned about how the Iraqi police gained some of their intelligence, and how they treated some of their detainees before they turned them over to us. I maintained detention cells in each of my 34 police stations in Baghdad, and occasionally the number of detainees would reach a total of nearly 2000. Every time I would do an unannounced check on a police station, which was several times a week, I would always check the detention cell and talk to the detainees. I would do it without the police present, and they hated that. Many of my detention cells were overcrowded and borderline inhumane by any standards, but we were all doing the best we could.

The police frequently complained to me that we were moving the detainees out to other prisons before they could complete their investigations, and in some cases that was true. But there was always a fine line and a delicate balance between keeping them there long enough, but not too long. The longer they were there, the greater chance of corruption, overcrowding, and abuse. The Iraqi police culture also had a very unusual custom, compared to our Western culture. In a couple of rare cases I personally saw criminals and their victims in the same jail. This was bizarre to me, but when I questioned it they would say that if they didn't hold the victim, they couldn't ensure he would appear in court. One day I asked a detainee why he was being held, which was standard practice for me, and was shocked when he pointed to another detainee and told my interpreter he was there for robbing the person he was pointing at.

On another occasion, I made an unannounced check on a police station and when I walked in the front door behind my security detail, I thought it strange that a policeman walked over to the front of the steps that led upstairs. There was just something different about the way he was standing and looking at me. I decided to walk upstairs, but the policeman moved in front of me. I told my security to move him, so they pushed him aside and I rapidly walked the remaining distance to the top of the stairs. I heard some noise in a room behind a closed door. When I opened the door, I saw an individual sitting in a chair, with his arms tied behind his back and blood running down his face. He had obviously been beaten. When I asked the police what was going on, they told me the Iraqi in the chair had been accused of killing a police officer and they were "interrogating" him. There's no doubt in my mind if I had not stopped at the police station, they would have killed him. We called for an MP patrol to come over, get the detainee medical treatment, then take him to Abu Ghraib prison. The commander of the Iraqi police station was upset that I was sending the person to the prison, and complained that he would just be released later on. I told my MPs to give me the paperwork that they would be leaving at Abu Ghraib when they dropped off the prisoner. When they did, I wrote a note on it that the guy was a suspected cop killer and that if they felt they had to release him, to contact me. I put my name and phone number on the paper. I left the police station once my MPs took control of the bloodied detainee.

I was appalled at what I had seen. It was a reminder to me that we would never be able to stop such practices and start the process of re-training the Iraqi police under the rule of law, if we overlooked the same type of conduct in our own army. It didn't much matter what part of the army it was. The eventual exposure of torture and prisoner abuse contributed to the setbacks we began to suffer in 2004 because it interfered with our ability to trust and be trusted by the Iraqi population. Lt. General Sanchez' decision to allow interrogators to be in charge of some of the detainees at Abu Ghraib prison didn't help us. The subsequent disclosures of our own conduct as it related to Iraqi prisoners and detainees simply set us up to look hypocritical and lacking in integrity and discipline. No army can be sustained for long under such conditions. Our civilian and military leaders should have known that from the beginning.

CHAPTER FOUR: NOTES

1 Public Statement of General Michael V. Hayden, Director of the CIA, after classified testimony before the Senate Intelligence Committee, December 11, 2007.
2 New York Times, "A Window Into CIA's Embrace of Secret Jails," by David Johnston and Mark Mazzetti, August 13, 2009 update of an August 12, 2009 article.
3 Ibid, original article of August 12, 2009.

CHAPTER FIVE

JANIS KARPINSKI, WARDEN OF ABU GHRAIB

Brigadier General Janis Karpinski controlled the prison, but not her soldiers.

Based on a previous conversation I had with Major General Walter Wojdakowski, I had no one to blame but myself for Brigadier General Karpinski moving to Baghdad and taking responsibility for the regional jails, Camp Cropper, and Abu Ghraib Prison from me. But the road that ended with the Abu Ghraib Prison scandal started way before my conversation with Wojdakowski. Shortly after our arrival in Baghdad, I could see that I would soon be overrun by the massive numbers of detainees. I asked all the battalions to check their area of operations for any facilities that would be suitable to hold prisoners. A few days later, my Command Sergeant Major, Charles Guyette, who shared an office with Lt. Colonel Evans and I, told me he had seen a huge prison earlier that day while out on patrol. It was located outside of Baghdad but had great potential to be a long term prison. He agreed to take me there the next day. I was amazed when I saw Abu Ghraib Prison for the first time. As we drove through one of the gates, we saw two looters begin running from us. We drove in their direction. We gave chase and captured them. They obviously thought we would kill them, and were very frightened. I could have cared less as they rattled off in Arabic to my interpreter as to why they were there. Instead, I wanted to know the background of the huge complex I was standing in. They explained to us they had been prisoners at Abu

Ghraib at some point, and offered to show us around. I accepted their offer and they took us on a tour of every part of the prison, including Saddam's execution chamber. The chamber was used to execute two people at a time. One executioner would stand on a platform and pull a lever with his left hand, and another lever with his right. These levers controlled the floor that the two condemned people stood on, with a noose around their neck. This method was eventually used to send Saddam to his death. There were some shackles on the walls and what appeared to be electric cables. I could only assume they were used to torture the prisoners before they were hung. Our two escorts also told us of rumors of Americans being buried in the vicinity, but they didn't know the exact location, and didn't know if the rumors were even true. At the time, we were all looking for evidence of the presence of Scott Speicher, the U. S. Navy pilot still missing from Desert Storm, so I reported this information up through my operations and intelligence channels. After we had seen the entire prison, our two guests assumed they would become our prisoners, but that had never been my intent. I was so grateful for the information they provided, we gave them some food and then let them go. They walked away with a huge smile on their face. At least for a little while, we had won their "heart and mind."

On May 8, as a part of my nightly update to General Wallace, I briefed the following:

> "I visited a huge prison about ten kilometers outside of Baghdad. With a lot of work it will be perfect for a prison to put long term inmates that have been convicted. However it is too far away to be practical for capturing units to drop off pre-trial detainees. We will keep them as enemy prisoners of war for now." Opening Abu Ghraib didn't turn out to be as simple as it had seemed on May 8. On May 14, I briefed that construction material had arrived

to construct Camp Cropper:

> "We have identified our requirements to temporarily detain 4000 personnel at the prison outside of Baghdad. It will take us 72-96 hours to get it operational with Division engineer support."

On May 17, I briefed that my most immediate issue was engineer support for my temporary 4000 man facility at Abu Ghraib. Two days later I was able to report that the 94th Engineers began work at Abu Ghraib. But after about a week, the engineers stopped working on the prison. I already had several hundred detainees out there being controlled by two of the main walls, triple strand concertina wire, and my heavily armed MPs in the towers and outside the wire. Just hours before the engineers ceased working, ironically General Wallace received his final brief from me the day before he left Iraq. My notes summarized our problems that day at the prison:

> "We just had a disturbance at the confinement facility at Abu Ghraib—numerous detainees charged my guards and several have been shot. Medevac has just landed and I have no other information currently except so far I have one dead prisoner and seven in critical condition.

The crisis at Abu Ghraib had just begun and was bad enough, but then the politics kicked in. During my nightly update on June 15, I briefed my superiors on the issues we were having as we tried to re-open the prison:

> "We've been given a heads up we may have to provide information to CPA tonight for a point paper from Ambassador Bremer to Secretary Rumsfeld on why

wehave to re-open Abu Ghraib prison. We are currently putting the paper together."

We wrote and re-wrote the paper until all the political language was just right. But the bottom line was that we concluded we didn't have a choice but to use the prison. It was available for immediate use and there was no way we could simply build another prison overnight. Bremer sent the paper to Secretary of Defense Donald Rumsfeld. He approved our re-opening of Abu Ghraib with the caveat that we not use any part of the prison located in proximity to the execution room. We were told that would be part of a museum one day.

The entire detainee mission was becoming more complex and I couldn't wait for Karpinski to take over. But before she took over, and three days before I was tasked to write the decision paper, there was a disturbance at the enemy holding area I had co-located with Camp Cropper. On the night of June 12, I incorporated the problem into my briefing:

> "We had an attempted escape at the Corps Holding area at 0245 hrs this morning. Two detainees got outside the wire while the guards were yelling for them to stop. The closest guard gave chase, and a guard fired at one escapee hitting him in the chest and leg. He later died in the hospital at Dogwood and the other escapee was captured."

On the evening of June 20, I was delighted to report that I had turned over the responsibility for my two internment resettlement battalion headquarters and four MP companies to General Karpinski. The detainee mission, except for the nearly 2000 detainees that I had in my police stations, was now in her hands.

Earlier that month, Major General Wojdakowski asked me to

give him an update on detainee operations. Evans and the staff put together a great brief. I went to Wojdakowski's office and sat down with him one on one. We went through the brief. About two or three weeks later, Karpinski was on her way to Baghdad. Sanchez was in charge of the Army in Iraq. I was focused on the local jails, police training and policing the streets. The solution I thought we'd found to our prisoner and detainee issues actually set the stage for the "torture war." Karpinski and Sanchez would become its biggest players.

When the decision was made to bring Brigadier General Janis Karpinski into Baghdad to assume responsibility for the regional jails, Camp Cropper and Abu Ghraib, General Wojdakowski told me he was going to send her to my office. He wanted me to give her the same "battle plan" briefing I had given to him. Then, he wanted her to repeat the briefing to him, with me in the room, to ensure that she understood her new mission.

This was not an unusual move. Frequently, when one military commander assumes a mission from a fellow commander, the best way to make the transition is through these kinds of battle plan briefings. I didn't realize until after I retired that Karpinski had resisted her new mission so strongly. Apparently, Wojdakowski was concerned about her resistance and wanted to ensure that nothing fell through the cracks as we completed our hand-off.

When word came of her deployment to Baghdad, Karpinski was already fulfilling another mission in the northern part of Iraq to secure capitulators. She was running a large detainee operation in Bucca, and a smaller one at Tallil Air Base. This was at the same location where we had initially established our first enemy prisoner of war holding area after the start of the ground war. During the same time that Karpinski took over, a U. S. Navy ship carrying the equipment of the 72nd MP Company was preparing to embark for the Middle East. The 72nd was initially assigned to me upon their arrival in Kuwait, and while awaiting their journey to Baghdad.

Karpinski and the soldiers of the 72nd didn't know it at the time but they were on a collision course to make history. Less than a year later, photographs would surface showing an army private, Lendie England of the 72nd MP Company, abusing prisoners at Abu Ghraib. Karpinski and Lt. General Sanchez would see their army careers cut short by the tip of the sword that led to far greater allegations of torture inside Iraq, eventually involving high level officials of the U.S. government.

In an ironic twist of fate, about the same time Saddam seized control of Iraq, I'd heard the name Janis Karpinski. I'd never been introduced to her. When I signed into the 503rd MP Battalion at Ft. Bragg, North Carolina, in May of 1979, as a brand new second lieutenant, a first lieutenant named Janis Karpinski had just been removed from the battalion. She was still at Ft. Bragg, but assigned to a unit outside of the 503rd. Later there were various unconfirmed accounts and gossip of Karpinski's history with the U. S.Army. The stories went that Karpinski had attained the rank of Captain, but was turned down for promotion to Major. Karpinski left the regular Army and went into the U.S. Army Reserves in the early 1980s, retaining her rank as a Captain while in the reserves.

Karpinski recalls events differently. In an interview with *Signal Newspapers* of Santa Clarita, California on June 29, 2004, she said she left the Army just short of ten years:

> "I kind of put that mark on the wall, that if I didn't feel like there (were) going to be opportunities, and the outside world was more interesting or presented more opportunities, then I was going to do that." [1]

I can't speak for Karpinski. My military experience was that there was almost always a story behind anyone who left the army after completing half of their career. After the 9/11 terrorist attacks on America and the invasion of Iraq, Karpinski was called up from the reserves. She assumed command of the 800th Military Police Brigade in Kuwait from Brigadier General Paul Hill in early June. When the transfer of command was complete, Brigadier General Karpinski joined Brigadier General Dennis Geoghan of the 220th MP Brigade, another reserve brigade, to become one of the two highest ranking MPs in the war zone.

The tension was thick when Karpinski and I met for the first time in the foyer of my headquarters palace. Karpinski was about two weeks away from pinning on her general officer one star and was still wearing the U. S. Army eagles of a colonel, same as me, when she arrived at my headquarters at Camp Victory. While I had prevailed in implementing my plan to give her responsibility for the prisons, Karpinski's vision had been undercut. She had wanted her unit redeployed to Kuwait and as far away from Iraq as possible. Our different fortunes colored the tone of the meeting.

General Karpinski's security detail delivered her to the front door of my ornate palace, its marble floors and textured walls a perfect backdrop, as some of my staff and I greeted her in front of a massive spiral staircase in the vast open foyer. Bombed out craters that disrupted the floor space and holes in the ceiling tiles were the only indicators the meeting was not being held in the middle of a Beverly Hills mansion. Even though she was technically the same rank as me, I deferred to her soon-to-be rank and addressed her as "ma'am" during our meeting. It was the appropriate army protoColonel I extended my hand to welcome her to my headquarters, but she refused to extend her own, instead glaring into my face.

"You fucked me," she stopped short of saying more, waiting for a reply.

"Ma'am, if asking for you to come up here and do your damn

job, like you've been paid to do, is fucking you then you're exactly right!" She immediately pissed me off. Had she been a male, I probably would have punched her first and talked later. Our meeting would have looked like a World Wrestling Entertainment match. My soldiers and I had already been through too much for me to have any sympathy for a whining, upcoming general. Her attitude and the example she was setting in front of her soldiers and mine made me sick. I just didn't expect that I would end up getting into a fight with a fellow MP commander. She wasn't the enemy I expected to fight during my time in Iraq.

"I was ordered to come here and get a brief from you, so let's get on with it," she glared.

Karpinski made her displeasure known to me during the entire meeting. As we went into my personal office, I sat down beside her to begin the same briefing that I had given to Wodjakowski earlier. She refused to take any notes on the slides and she didn't ask any questions of me.

"General Karpinski, you realize that Wojo wants you to give this briefing, not me. He can be tough and moody. He'll ask questions of you and you'll want to know the answers. That's why I'm trying to give you some of the questions he'll probably ask."

I told her that if he had any sense that she didn't understand her new mission, he would be like a shark in water. She didn't seem to care. I found Karpinski impossible to like, but it was my duty to prepare her for the meeting with Wodjakowski. Karpinski continued to show little interest in the slides or the briefing. I didn't let it deter me.

As I tried to impress upon her our responsibilities and the missions she would be working while in Iraq, she again stopped me short to make sure I knew how she felt.

"Some of the work I've taken over from you, Colonel, is not part of the doctrinal mission of my enemy prisoner of war brigade," she delivered her words with brevity and bluntness, prompting my own flat response.

"General Karpinski, my final bit of advice is this. No matter what comes up in the meeting with General Wodjakowski, don't ever act like you don't want to be in Iraq and don't ever tell him that a particular job is not part of your doctrinal mission. I've seen other people trip Wodjakowski's switch because they didn't know what they were talking about. This is one of his flash points. In the past, I've seen him kill people when they tell him something is not part of their doctrinal mission." My dislike of Karpinski grew as the meeting progressed, but I tried my best to give her one final warning. On the day of the actual briefing of General Wodjakowski, only Karpinski and I were in the room. My worst fears became reality. Karpinski fumbled the briefing. She was unable to answer several of General Wodjakowski's questions.

"That's not a part of my doctrinal mission," she burst out in a moment of frustration.

I wanted to turn away and laugh, but I managed to keep a straight face and watch Wojo's response. It was just as I had warned her.

"Damn it, Janis, Ted hasn't done a fucking doctrinal thing since he's been in the country, but his brigade has accomplished all of their missions." General Wodjakowski was livid. She had succeeded in pushing him over the edge. By this time, she was wearing her star. Unfortunately for her, Wojo was wearing two stars. I wanted to take my eagles and fly under the table. The incident was the first sign of the rocky relationship that would develop between the two and play out over the coming months. Their relationship would become even more tense years after they retired and during the numerous investigations of the abuse at Abu Ghraib Prison.

During my subsequent interactions with Karpinski the remainder of the time we spent in Iraq, she never accepted ownership of anything. I found it very difficult to even be around her. She simply never lived up to the standards of leadership expected of an officer in the United States armed forces. Karpinski was more obsessed with redeployment than doing her job. She was more concerned about letting everyone else know she was a poor female reservist. She was more prone to hand ringing than making things happen. I know my comments sound harsh. If anything, they're not harsh enough. Brigadier General Karpinski was a textbook example of why politics should never interfere with military tactics or become involved in the selection of military leaders. I had to prove myself every day as an officer in the MP Corps in the middle of combat. She gets no sympathy from me.

In her June 29, 2004 interview with *Signal Newspaper*, Karpinski's attitude surfaced as she recounted her career in the United States Army. When asked by the reporter if she felt she was entering "a kind of boy's club," she answered:

> "Oh, absolutely, we were intruders. And my first company commander when I was a lieutenant had just come from jump school and arrived at Ft. Bragg, and my first company commander told me that he didn't agree with women being in the military police. He didn't agree with women being in any of the branches. 'Go back to being WAC's.' And actually he was married to a woman who wanted to be a mother and be a wife, and that's the position he thought all women should be in."

It's little wonder, given her attitude, that Karpinski's relationship with General Wodjakowski was strained. The subsequent lack of any association between Karpinski and I didn't promote our communication with each other. Perhaps if we established a better relationship, I could have assisted her in a better understanding of the way things should work in a war zone. Maybe her problems in Iraq could have been prevented if I had overcome my initial negativity towards her. Her lack of leadership skills and inability to access her superiors contributed significantly to the detainee and prisoner abuse that was in her immediate future. I continued to keep all the detainees in the jail cells of my police stations and never had any issues related to their incarceration. Karpinski went on to run Camp Cropper and Abu Ghraib Prison and made military history, though not in a good way.

There had to be clear cut lines of authority when managing everything in Iraq—from jails to police stations to American military assignments. I never realized just how important this principle was. Ignoring it would bring the wrath of the world down upon the U.S. Army and America itself.

As time wore on, I saw increasingly that the lines were blurred by the competing and often conflicting interests of the Coalition Provisional Authority (CPA). The military commanders in the field, military and civilian intelligence agencies, and a level of mysterious civilian political leadership operating outside of the CPA that owned the nighttime and answered to no one, all had differing agendas.

I felt most passionate about the final point. It tested my definition of leadership and accountability. At the same time, it shaped my disdain for all things political, especially during a war where my soldiers were being shot at all the time. I had already experienced run-ins with people whose names I didn't know and whose U.S. government agency associations I was never sure of, by the time of the transition from the 18th MP Brigade to the 800th.

As Karpinski took over command responsibility for Camp Cropper and Abu Ghraib, orders from invisible politicians in Washington D.C. became the kindling for a firestorm that would burn for years. Those fires are still burning today. I believe they threaten the successful outcome of America's engagement against terror.

In late summer, 2003, a U.S. Army Major General, Geoffrey Miller from Guantanamo Bay visited Iraq. He told General Karpinski he wanted to take charge of Abu Gharib. When she said no, Miller appealed to Lt. General Sanchez. Miller prevailed on Sanchez and was granted the authority to take control of the prison. The change came even as allegations of prisoner abuse and torture swirled around Guantanamo.

Over the next few months, the prison population at Abu Gharib grew from about 1200 convicted criminals to over 6000 suspected terrorists, called "security detainees."

Karpinski ceded control of Abu Ghraib to Miller's designee, Colonel Thomas Pappas. Pappas was a fellow brigade commander of mine. He was the commander of the military intelligence brigade. Karpinski told her MP subordinates that although they were still administratively assigned to the 800th MP Brigade, they would have to take their orders from military intelligence.

In early January, 2004, Karpinski met Colonel Marcelo, a criminal investigation commander, who was looking into allegations of abuse in cell blocks 1A and 1-B at Abu Ghraib. Karpinski allegedly had heard rumors about torture and abuse earlier. However, she took no action herself at the time to confirm whether the allegations were true. Colonel Marcelo showed her photographs that left little doubt in her mind as to the kinds of activities going on at the prison. Karpinski was appalled. It was a little late.

I had also been told of the pictures showing abuse of some detainees around the middle of January. By that time we were scheduled to depart Iraq the first week of February, once we handed our mission over to the incoming 89th Military Police Brigade. I'm ashamed to admit that I hoped the media wouldn't hear about the pictures until after our departure. I was concerned that if they did, we would be extended in Iraq, pending the investigation, since we had opened the prison. Fortunately we were safely back in Germany when the photos were revealed by the media. Some of the photos showed U.S. Army Private Lynndie England holding a dog leash with an Iraqi prisoner attached. In another photo, England was standing in front of a line of naked Iraqi prisoners. In one photograph, England and her fiancé stood behind a pyramid of naked Iraqi prisoners piled on top of each other.

The Article 15-6 investigation interview of Karpinski, conducted by Major General Taguba at Camp Doha, Kuwait on Feburary 15, 2004 is most revealing. She placed the blame for the abuse on everyone except herself, including many of her subordinates. She even managed to drag me into the investigation. As part of the interview, General Taguba asked her if she felt overwhelmed. Her answer was, "No, sir. I didn't feel overwhelmed, but I knew that they (referring to General Wojdakowski) were taking their instructions from Colonel Spain." Anyone that knows Wojdakowski knows he didn't take instructions from anyone with less than three stars on their collar, much less me.

Charges and counter charges still fly today about who was responsible for the abuse of Abu Ghraib detainees. While it appears that some of the highest level officials inthe U. S. government were aware of, and even approved the use of interrogation techniques that were tantamount to inhumane treatment of detainees in American custody, only England, her fiancé and several other soldiers have ended up serving prison sentences.

The subsequent convictions of England, her fiancé and others on charges connected to prisoner abuse based on the events that unfolded at Abu Ghraib have cast a cloud on the military police and the work we did inside Iraq to establish law and order.

A tiny minority of MPs who were out of control threaten the image of everyone. But a close examination of all the facts surrounding the abuse and torture that occurred at the prison clearly illustrate that Lt. General Sanchez, through Major General Geoff Miller, created an organizational structure and chain of command that at the very least was vague and at its worst, intentionally designed to insulate military intelligence from criticism forits harsh interrogation techniques, while assigning the blame to the 800th MP Brigade. Even in his testimony to the United States Senate on May 19, 2004, Lt. General Sanchez painted a confusing picture of the lines of authority he had developed todeal with military interrogations at Abu Ghraib. In response to a question from Senator John Warner of Virginia, Sanchez confirmed that he had placed all of the army elements at Abu Ghraib under the tactical control of Colonel Thomas Pappas, the commander of the 205th Military Intelligence Brigade:

"The order did not intend to eliminate any of the responsibilities of the 800th Military Police Commander. And that was a specific purpose for the tactical control. Tactical control placed the 320th under the 205th M.I. Brigade commander... the M. I. brigade commander authority to conduct local direction and control of movements or maneuvers to accomplish the mission at hand...All of the other responsibilities for continuing to run the prison for logistics training, discipline and the conduct of prison operations remained with the 800th Brigade commander...there was never a time when Brigadier General Karpinski surfaced any objections to that tactical control order." [2]

In fact, when she first heard about the prisons being transferred from the military police to military intelligence, Karpinski has said she tried to protest the move to Lt. General Sanchez. In an interview with reporter and journalist Marjorie Cohn on August3, 2005, Karpinski recalled:

"...When I found out, I went to Sanchez first, and his deputy went in to tell General Sanchez I was there and I needed to see him, and the subject was the transfer of the prison. General Sanchez would not see me, but he told his deputy or his—I think it was his SGS or his executive officer—he was a full colonel—he told me to go see General Fast (General Barbara Fast who was working with General Geoffrey Miller), that she had the details. So I went to see General Fast, and General Fast pointed to the order...it's a done deal." [3]

During the same Senate hearing, Senator John McCain quoted a statement made to army criminal investigators by Colonel Thomas Pappas:

"Policies...at Abu Ghraib relative to detainees operations were enacted as aspecific result of a visit by Major General Geoffrey Miller...key findings were...interrogators and analysts develop a set of rules and limitations to guide interrogation and provide dedicated MPs to support interrogation operations."

Major General Miller responded to a question from Senator McCain that his instructions actually pertained to, "intelligence fusion, the interrogation process and inhumane detention," and not to operational use of MPs by military intelligence interrogators. However, McCain countered with the results of interviews of soldiers during the army investigation that appeared to paint a different picture.

McCain: "Soldier number two, have you ever been told by M.I. personnel to work over a prisoner?"

Soldier number two: "Yes. M. I. told us to rough them up to get answers from the prisoners."

McCain: "Why didn't you report the abuse?"

Soldier number two: "The wing belonged to military intelligence and it appeared military intelligence personnel approved of the abuse."

McCain: "Soldier number four, 'have you ever heard M. I. insinuate to guards to abuse inmates of any type of manner?'"

Soldier number four: "Yes."

McCain: "What was said?"

Soldier number four: "They said, loosen this guy up for us, make sure he has a bad night, make sure he gets the treatment." [4]

Since the war ended for me and I've had the chance to learn so much information to fill in the blanks on my suspicions, I feel almost sick about what was going on that we didn't know about on the front lines. With the passage of years, it's become apparent that pressures, policies and guidelines from top levels of the United States government established an atmosphere that led to the abuse of prisoners and torture at Abu Ghraib. The MPs who were caught up in the ensuing scandals and criminal charges were performing the practices that had been set forth and condoned by former Secretary of Defense Donald Rumsfeld, former Vice-President Dick Cheney and even tacitly accepted by the President of the United States, George Bush. To this day, Bush, Cheney, Rumsfeld, and even Michael Mucasey, the last Attorney General to serve in the Bush Administration, defend the practice of water boarding in public appearances and speeches.

The role of the MPs in the torture and abuse scandal at Abu Ghraib can't be defended. It never should have happened. Its cause wasn't only traceable to defective soldiers who just decided one day that they would start abusing detainees. It was also traceable to poor leadership.

Lt. General Sanchez' fragmentary orders transferring command and control of the prison to military intelligence put the last nail in the coffin of bad practices and poor organizational structure. This contributed to the torture and abuse at Abu

Ghraib. And Lt. General Sanchez was fine with his role because it was exactly what his civilian bosses at the Pentagon and in the White House wanted. Following their orders at the time was the best way for him to get promoted. He always wanted that extra star.

As I will discuss in the next chapter, it wasn't the first time that Lt. General Sanchez made decisions in Iraq that would cause problems for the army. I simply saw far too many examples of a complete lack of leadership from Sanchez. His fellow soldiers saw it too.

It's even easy to find some sympathy for Karpinski, locked in an organizational structure that she says robbed her of the ultimate decision making authority for her own soldiers, and unable to influence Sanchez and his staff enough to change it. I can relate to that because Sanchez had placed me in a similar situation with one of my battalions that was assigned to me, but working for the Polish Division south of Baghdad. One of Karpinski's final warnings about Abu Ghraib is haunting in the context of the overall war on terror.

When news of the detainee abuse at Abu Ghraib became public and Karpinski left the army, she maintained in public appearances that she was not responsible for cellblocks 1A and B, where the abuses occurred after November 19 of 2003. At that point, she was ordered to cede control of Abu Ghraib to military intelligence. She told her MP subordinates that while they were administratively assigned to the 800th MP Brigade, they would have to take their orders from military intelligence, just as my 716th MP Battalion was taking orders from the Polish Division. She continued her role as a member of the security detainee release board. She watched the population of the prison at Abu Ghraib continue to grow because military intelligence wouldn't release anyone. Karpinski protested the growing numbers of detainees to General Wodjakowski "I don't care if we're holding

15,000 innocent people. We're winning the war," Wodjakowski told her.

"Not inside the wire, you're not, sir. Every one of them is our enemy when they get out," was her prescient response. I think that in a sad way for all of us, Karpinski had the final judgment and was one hundred percent correct. Karpinski should have been far more forceful with Lt. General Sanchez when she couldn't get clarity from him on command and control and saw the military intelligence interrogators at her jails. I believe she lacked confidence, experience and leadership skills. She didn't know how to properly challenge the orders of Sanchez, who was also in over his head. Together, the combination proved disastrous for us in Iraq.

CHAPTER FIVE: NOTES

1 Signal Newspaper of Santa Clarita, "SCV Newsmaker of the Week: Brig. General Janis Karpinski; former Commander, 800 Military Police Brigade," June 29, 2004.
2 Testimony of Lt. General Ricardo Sanchez before the United States Senate Armed Services Committee, May 19, 2004.
3 Truthout, "Janis Karpinski, Exclusive Interview," by Marjorie Cohn, August 3, 2005.
4 Ibid, End Note #2.

CHAPTER SIX

THE COMBAT ARMS MENTALITY OF LT. GENERAL RICARDO SANCHEZ

Lt. General Ricardo Sanchez preferred force over policing during his time in Iraq.

We didn't have enough MPs to do the job of putting Iraq back together again when the invasion of Iraq began. Even as we started receiving additional MPs during May and June, it was a never ending battle to ensure they were being properly used, when working with the combat arms units. By mid summer it was evident there would be insufficient MPs for the second year of the occupation, but we had the opportunity to make the right decisions and help correct the problem for the second year. The appointment of Lt. General Ricardo Sanchez as the senior commander in June marked the end of that opportunity, and other opportunities to get Iraq off on the right foot and begin the process of putting humpty dumpty back together again. Lt.General Sanchez believed in the power of combat. Law enforcement, intelligence collection and building trust with the people seemed to be abstract concepts to him and his advisors. He believed in the rule of force, not the rule of law in a war zone.

The U.S army rolled into Iraq under the command of Lt. General William Wallace. Wallace could best be described with three words: a soldier's soldier. From my assumption of command in August, 2002, until his departure from Iraq in June, 2003, Wallace let me know how much he would count on me and his other senior commanders. He emphasized how much he trusted in my judgment and the capabilities of the men and women of the 18th MP Brigade. There's no easy way to begin the invasion of a country. The sure way to get off to a good start is to instill confidence in the soldiers under one's command. Wallace did that as good or better than anyone with whom I have ever served. Wallace had a way of gaining the respect of his subordinates, whether they were privates or colonels. He never had to intimidate or threaten. I just wanted to bust my ass for him. I knew he would have my back if I was doing what was right—accomplishing our mission, and taking care of my soldiers. He was a brilliant strategist and tactician, yet he was able to talk at everyone's level. He never tried to act like he knew more about the capabilities of the military police than I did. He asked for advice, listened to the advice he was given, and then held us responsible for our decisions. He was the kind of commander I tried to be.

During what turned out to be our final briefing in Kuwait he looked at all his Division and brigade commanders.

"Next time I see you, we'll be in Baghdad."

The words of Lt. General Wallace reflected his contagious optimism and reassurance that everything was going to work out fine. Regardless of rank and level of confidence, every soldier wanted to hear that kind of tone from his or her leaders.

I wasn't any different. I was gratified that Wallace understood the enormous challenges we faced. His no nonsense approach encouraged his officers to be truthful about their assessments of difficulties encountered by the various units across the battlefield. He was the kind of leader who could adapt to any situation and expected his leaders to adapt as well.

Wallace was almost unique among the combat arms commanders I had known. He had a keen understanding of the proper role of the military police and recognized early on that our mission had been diluted by the MPs being pushed back in the force flow. But there hadn't been any choice. Everyone knew more soldiers were necessary when the war began, but there simply were not enough soldiers to go around, so Wallace made the invasion of Iraq work with what he had.

Lt. General Wallace and I believed in many of the same sets of leadership principles. They always worked—assume risk, understand your commander's intent, understand how all the parts need to fit together to get the job done, and then do what has to be done. Even though I had briefed Wallace every twelve hours on the radio after our final meeting in Kuwait, I never physically saw him again until a gathering in a huge airplane hanger at the Saddam International Airport, later renamed the Baghdad International Airport, not too long after the fall of Baghdad.

Secretary Rumsfeld was arriving in Iraq for the first time after the ground war and was going to the hanger to address the troops. After waiting in the hanger with hundreds of soldiers from across V Corps, I noticed Secretary Rumsfeld, Wallace and McKiernan enter the hanger. It didn't seem like the best time to address General Wallace, since he was walking with Rumsfeld. Walking by me, in the midst of hundreds of other soldiers, he saw me, left the Secretary and came over and gave me a huge bear hug. I simply don't know of many Army generals who would have done that. He was sincerely appreciative of the contributions our brigade had made thus far, albeit with limited resources.

When we started working together in Baghdad, he was ready to fully implement my vision of using the military police to help establish law and order and he knew the police would be a key part of that. We both knew the ground war was over, and soon realized that now the hard stuff started. General Wallace knew my MPs could play a key role in helping to rebuild Iraq. The plan involved using the MPs for the doctrinal mission of handling enemy prisoners of war, but also a critical mission of standing up a new Iraqi Police force, something we would have to make up as we went along. More importantly, General Wallace knew we couldn't accomplish our unique mission of working with the police, if we were being controlled by, and tasked by the various-divisions. He knew the police mission would be too fragmented if that happened.

The bread and butter of any police effort had to focus on training and conducting operations with the Iraqi police, taking care of the enemy prisoners of war and high value detainees, and building trust among Iraqi citizens by being on the streets and out on patrol. That meant the combat arms would have to permit us to establish a police frame work that I believed had a huge role in the future of Iraq, but more importantly at the time, in helping the Iraqi citizens feel safe, a key component in winning their hearts and minds. General Wallace understood that and counted on me to help implement a plan. He told me late one night in his office that he would put my brigade TACON, meaning tactical control, to the 3rd Infantry Division. TACON would allow Major General Blount, the 3rd Infantry Division Commander to task, but not break up my brigade and put its components into his combat arms brigades. General Wallace made the move based on my recommendation. I clearly understood I could not establish a police force if every combat arms brigade commander did their own thing with the Iraqi police. My new TACON status would prevent that. General Blount probably didn't like it, but he never fought with General Wallace over it to my knowledge. Blount never made me feel bad about the decision.

A couple of his combat arms brigade commanders didn't like the idea. They let me know it. One of them told me after an update with Blount that he didn't want my MPs in his area of operations without his permission. I told him that my MPs and I had to have free access to the Iraqi police stations to do our job and I would send them wherever I needed to. He warned I had better not go into his area without his permission. Even though I had planned to go to another part of Baghdad after that update, as soon as Maj. General Blount released us, I told my security detail that we were going on patrol in that brigade commander's area in Sadr City, recently renamed from Saddam City, and we did.

The few weeks I worked for Blount, before the 3rd was replaced by Sanchez and the 1st Armored Division, I never had any significant disagreement with him. Blount must have known they were soon redeploying, or General Wallace had explained to him how it was going to be. General Blount had been absolutely brilliant in the execution of the ground war and I had the utmost respect for him. We had several conversations about what I thought the Iraqi Police should be doing and what they should look like. General Blount was a good listener and gave me time to explain my plans.

He may not have always agreed with me, but he always listened. Sadly for all of us, in April, 2003, Lt. General Wallace became an early political casualty of the Iraq war. Wallace gave an interview to the *New York Times*. His quote was heard around the world:

"The enemy we're fighting is a bit different from the one we war-gamed against" [1]

This was one of my first, but certainly far from my last, experiences where I learned that the media, just like the enemy, has a vote in combat situations. Throughout the coming months I would learn that the media will get their story. I learned I could cooperate and try to get some of the good news out, or I could fail to cooperate, forfeiting my opportunity to influence what the American people were seeing and hearing.

When the network and print media spread the word that General Wallace was contradicting politicians in the safe confines of Washington, DC, it was the start of his remaining days in Iraq. His departure reduced our chances of success in putting Iraq back together again. Wallace spoke a very clear truth. We had war-gamed against countless scenarios. I had spent dozens of hours with my intelligence advisors trying to understand the capabilities and motivations of the enemy. However, none of us envisioned the commitment of some of Saddam's irregular forces who would ram vehicles into our tanks and fire RPGs at our vehicles. They did this even though they knew it was a suicide mission and they would certainly die as a result.

Secretary of Defense Rumsfeld, General Richard Myers, chairman of the Joint Chiefs of Staff and even General Tommy Franks of the Central Command, came unhinged at the comments Wallace made. Even before the war started, there had been growing tension among some of the top ranking army officers and the civilian leadership in the Pentagon about strategies and numbers of troops required in Iraq.

About a month before the military invasion of Iraq, General Eric Shinseki, the Army's Chief of Staff testified before the Senate Armed Services Committee. Asked by Senator Carl Levin how many soldiers it would take to stabilize the country after the-fighting stopped, General Shinseki responded:

"I would say...something on the order of several hundred thousand soldiers...would be required. We're talking about post-hostilities control over a piece of geography that's fairly significant, with the kinds of ethnic tensions that could lead to other problems. And so it takes a significant ground-force presence." [2]

Shinseki's candid assessment earned him admiration among those of us in the U. S. Army's officer corps. Unfortunately, it led to a bitter public clash with then Secretary of Defense Donald Rumsfeld and his Deputy, Paul Wolfowitz. Two days after Shinseki testified on Capitol Hill, Wolfowitz was telling the House Budget Committee a different story:

"There has been a good deal of comment, some of it quite outlandish, about what our postwar requirements might be in Iraq. Some of the higher end predictions we have been hearing recently, such as the notion that it will take several hundred thousand U. S. troops to provide stability in post-Saddam Iraq, are wildly off the mark. It is hard to conceive that it would take more forces to provide stability in post-Saddam Iraq than it would take to conduct the war itself and to secure the surrender of Saddam's security forces and his army; hard to imagine." [3]

Rumsfeld followed Wolfowitz's comments with a few of his own during a Pentagon press conference, "We have no idea how long the war will last. We don't know to what extent there may or may not be weapons of mass destruction used. We don't have any idea whether or not there would be ethnic strife…the idea that it would take several hundred thousand U.S. forces, I think, is far from the mark." [4]

It was against this backdrop that Wallace provided his candid assessment to the *New York Times*. It was the last straw for the civilian leadership. As a direct consequence of his ill timed interview, Wallace was replaced by Lt. General Ricardo Sanchez in early June. I attended the ceremony where Wallace pinned the third star on Sanchez. Sanchez became the most junior three star general in the Army, with arguably the most important job in the entire military.

I knew that Wallace would be impossible to replace. General Wallace already had us going down the road of winning the hearts and minds. He realized the military forces that were necessary to defeat Saddam's army were not the same type of forces necessary to put Iraq back together again. Even during the ground war, Wallace had to personally approve the destruction of any bridges. His reasons were three-fold. First off, we tried not to destroy any infrastructures that the Army would need after the war started. Second, we knew American taxpayers would probably have to pay for all the destruction we were causing in Iraq. Third, we knew that the Iraqi people would also need these bridges once we started putting the country back together again.

But with Wallace gone, the thinking, style and substance that drove our strategy and thus the war, changed dramatically. I had worked for Sanchez during his final weeks as Commander of the 1st Armored Division and realized that as a combat arms commander his thinking and approach to the role of policing would be considerably different than that of Wallace. I first met Sanchez in my days as the Director of the Force Protection Division, United States Army Europe, from July, 2001 until my assumption of command of the Brigade in August, 2002. At the time, Sanchez was commanding the 1st Armored Division. Our encounters resulted from meetings we both attended after the 9/11 terrorist attacks on America. Part of my job as running the Force Protection Division for General Monty Meigs, another brilliant tactician, was providing him input on how best to spend his limited force protection dollars.

Based on the needs of all the commanders in Europe I had developed a funding requirement of nearly 600 million dollars for General Meigs. When he received only 17 million dollars, General Meigs tasked me to recommend how that paltry 17 million should be spent. I received a lot of help from the commanders across Europe, including General Sanchez. I had talked to then Major General Sanchez several times during my force protection assignment, but never enough or under conditions where any friendship could be built.

Prior to my deployment to Kuwait to prepare for the invasion of Iraq, I was invited to a dinner function given by Lt. General Wallace at a restaurant in Heidelberg, Germany. Major General Sanchez was also at the dinner. He and I recognized each other from our force protection days as we stood together on the balcony of the multi-story restaurant, looking out at the peaceful city.

I wasn't surprised that Sanchez had little to say to me as we stood side by side. At any time there are only about twelve four-star generals in the entire army. Major General Sanchez seemed most interested in talking with the people who could help him become one of those four stars. I certainly wasn't one of those people. Besides, Sanchez had never been a very friendly person. I never saw him smile unless there was a three or four star officer in the room. In his eyes, I was a military police officer. He was a tanker and combat soldier. There was a wide gulf separating the two of us.

The next time General Sanchez and I stood eye to eye, he was in Baghdad as the 1st Armored Division Commander, having just replaced Major General Blount and the 3rd Infantry Division, and my brigade was TACON to his Division, just as we had been with the 3rd. That meant I reported to him.

Shortly after the 1st Armored Division assumed its area of operations from the 3rd Infantry Division, Sanchez visited each of his five combat arms brigades for briefs on how they planned to accomplish their mission. I had already been in Baghdad over two months. I knew there would be changes in the mission, just as happens anytime senior commanders change out, but I wasn't at all prepared for what was about to happen. After getting briefings from all five of his combat arms brigade commanders, Sanchez came to my office to get an update from me. After I provided him my brief, he asked me if I knew about some of the major complaints he was receiving from some of his other brigade commanders. Of course, I had no way of knowing what his other brigade commanders told him. Sanchez said they were complaining that they didn't "own" the MPs in their areas of responsibility. I explained to Sanchez why it was in his best interest for me to maintain control of all the MPs. It was the only way that we could have a clear unity of command over the Iraqi police. I knew it was the best way to establish any type of consistent Iraqi Police training program or conduct consistent police operations with them.

Sanchez and his 1st Armored Division were slated to be part of the initial ground invasion force into Iraq. At the last minute, his division and the 1st Cavalry Division were pulled off the invasion plans. Having missed out on the capture of Baghdad, Sanchez arrived two months later with an attitude. He didn't believe in "winning hearts and minds." I concluded immediately that he wasn't interested in reviewing and assessing with me the program that General Wallace and I were in the process of putting in place.

When General Sanchez traveled to my brigade headquarters to personally make the request that I put an MP company into each of his five combat arms brigades, I was completely honest with him about my feelings on the idea. "General Sanchez, I think that's a bad idea because I need to keep all of the MPs together to accomplish the Iraqi police and detention mission," I attempted to explain.

I provided Sanchez an operational briefing about the overall lack of MP companies in the theater and the MP role in Baghdad. Sanchez made clear to me he was in the decision mode. He wanted me to move my MPs to brigade combat arms support, immediately.

"Colonel Spain, you can put an MP company in each Maneuver Brigade now because I am asking you to, or you can wait a few days until I become the Coalition Joint Task Force 7 Commander, and I will direct you to do it."

Shortly after that meeting in my office I received a call from one of his assistants scheduling me to brief him on why I should, or should not, place an MP company in each of his combat arms brigades. I had been given about a three day notice before the brief, so Evans and the staff starting putting the brief together. I knew it would be a critical brief and we worked it hard. I knew I was fighting an up hill battle, but one that had to be fought and won. It was important for the future of the Iraq police and very important for the future of the Military Police Corps.

I realized that many of the decisions I would be making that first year had the potential to impact the future doctrine and force structure of my beloved MP Corps. The day before I was scheduled to give my brief to Sanchez, his division operations officer released a written order directing me to put an MP company in each of his five combat arms brigades. I was livid. I had the staff change the brief, from a decision brief, to an information brief, explaining exactly how I would accomplish his order, and my first briefing slide consisted of the exact words used in the written order.

I assumed that Sanchez was not aware that the written order had been prematurely issued, but it certainly demonstrated to me that he had made his decision even before he heard my brief. When he saw my first slide he became agitated and admonished me that he had not made the decision yet and reminded me that was the purpose of my brief. I then told him that my first slide was word for word from an order his staff had issued the night before. He looked at me like I didn't know what I was talking about and then looked at his operations officer. The look on his operations officer's face was priceless. I'm not a mind reader, and they certainly didn't discuss it in front of me, but it was apparent that his operations officer had only done what he had been directed. I couldn't tell and never confirmed who had done the directing.

Sanchez was clearly embarrassed, but had me continue with my brief, repeating he had not made his decision yet. After I concluded the brief, Sanchez directed me to put a company in each of his five brigades. I knew this was coming, and had already directed my staff to work with my battalions and come up with a recommendation on which five companies I could ill afford to lose that I would essentially be losing. Even though the five companies would be in direct support of the combat arms brigades, I would be losing my ability to task them, and could not use them to support my overall mission of standing up the Iraqi police, and detention operations in Baghdad. This was a huge blow towards my mission accomplishment and to establishing law and order in Baghdad.

I quietly listened to Major General Sanchez, giving him the respect he had earned by virtue of his position. There was little I could do to change his attitude and thought process if he simply didn't want to hear me out or rejected the premise of my arguments about policing in Iraq and the proper role of the MPs. I finally decided to stay silent and minimize the damage I would do to myself and my brigade by continuing to try and press my position on Sanchez. I assigned the MP companies to the combat brigades as ordered. I personally visited each of the five combat arms brigade commanders to give them an MP capabilities brief. As I had predicted, each of the MP companies was wasted. Some became involved in static security missions. The MP Company that was put in direct support of a Brigade from the 82nd assigned to the First Armored Division was put to work guarding bridges over the Tigris in Baghdad.

Many MPs were used to escort the senior leadership of the brigades as they traveled around Baghdad. Portions of some companies were assigned to running brigade detention facilities. Of course, the brigades shouldn't have been running their own detention centers anyway. They called them "holding areas" to avoid getting into trouble. When I asked the brigade commanders why they were doing this, they said they were trying to get as much intelligence from the detainees as possible before turning them over to the division holding areas. Of course, the division was running a holding area and told me they were running holding areas so they could get as much intelligence as possible before turning the detainees over to the main holding areas that were being run by my brigade at the time, at Abu Ghraib Prison and Camp Cropper.

I was appalled at the decisions combat brigade commanders were making. In one instance, a brigade had been looking for a particular terrorist leader for some time. They had no luck finding him. They decided to hold the terrorist's young son and kept him from his mother for a week. They took care of him and played soccer with him during the day. They told his mother they would release him after his father turned himself in. After about ten days, the father surrendered to the brigade. His son was turned over to his mother. My fellow combat arms brigade commanders were clearly focused on killing the bad guys, they weren't much into the hearts and minds concept.

Maintaining sufficient military police to take on the assignments my brigade had been given while trying to support the division commanders was a continuously difficult job. Whenever I couldn't provide enough MP support to other units, I was always reminded of the consequences. The shortage of MPs significantly effected the overall operation, including the ground war that Sanchez sat at home and watched on TV.

The Military Police Corps is small when compared with the infantry and other elements of the regular army. During the administration of President Bill Clinton the army was cut from sixteen divisions to ten, reducing its overall size from 780,000 to 470,000. The Army never had the time to fully reorganize after the "peace dividend," resulted in such massive reductions. Troop deployments in the name of nation building in Bosnia and Kosovo and the "war on terror," as a result of the attack on the World Trade Center put continuous strain on the availability of military assets. The invasion of Iraq illustrated the negative impact the Clinton era reductions had on the Army's capabilities.

At the time the ground war began, there were only six tactical active duty MP battalions stationed in the United States. I knew that five of the six battalion headquarters were already deployed to Iraq by the time the ground war was over. In August, I convinced Sanchez' Provost Marshal to summon all of the MP battalion commanders and Provost Marshals across Iraq to my headquarters in Baghdad so I could host a conference. During this conference we conducted what the army calls a "troop to task" assessment.

Down to the team level, we identified each instance where MPs were not performing an MP mission, which meant they weren't contributing to accomplishing our overall mission of standing up a functioning Iraqi police that I thought was so critical to putting Iraqi back together again. We identified the equivalent of twelve MP companies performing functions that were not contributing to this critical goal. Meanwhile Major John Perrin was working with headquarters in both Kuwait, and in Washington, D.C. to get a good feel for what was left in the active army and reserve component to come in to replace us, whenever we were to leave. The math simply didn't add up. There just weren't enough MPs left in the force structure to come close to replacing what we currently had in Iraq.

It only made sense to me that we needed to release the twelve active duty MP companies that were being improperly used. They could return six months later to support the forces coming in for the second year of the occupation. I knew we could do this with minimal impact on standing up the Iraqi Police. I also knew that these companies would not want to return home, having to return to Iraq in only six months. We were dealing with complete chaos in Iraq at the time. Drastic times called for drastic measures. It was obvious to me that we would not have all the equipment, training, and personnel that the Iraqi Police needed during our time there, and that this mission would take years to accomplish. The fact that I could not properly use the MP assets we had in Iraq made matters worse.

Our final product illustrated where each MP unit stood in the deployment cycle. My staff concluded that there would not be enough MP companies to replace those deployed during the first full year of the invasion. Many of the incoming MP forces would need to be composed of companies that became to be known as "in lieu of " (ILO). This meant that combat arms soldiers would receive minimal training as MPs atthe MP School at Fort Leonard Wood, Missouri, and then be deployed with incoming MP brigades, "in lieu of" real MP companies. I knew that such a significant mistake would prove costly to the army and the U.S. government's mission in Iraq. "ILO" MPs would never understand the complexities of training Iraqi police and working alongside them to establish law and order. The MP brigade commanders following my time in Iraq were also my good friends. Colonel Dave Quantock and Colonel Dave Phillips made the most of these "ILO" units, but it simply wasn't the same as having real MP companies.

As a brigade commander, I had the authority to release individual soldiers from Iraq, but not entire companies. Major General Wodjakowski, Sanchez' deputy commander did have the authority. I wanted to convince him that my plan was in the best interests of Iraq's future. I asked Evans to prepare a brief for him. When the time came, Evans and I went to his office to present our brief. We showed him how he could release twelve MP companies with little impact on our current. operations. The planwould produce great benefits for the second year of the war in Iraq. We would be able to rotate sufficient numbers of real MP companies into the country to replace the ones returning home. When we briefed our conclusions to Major General Wodjackowski, in the hope that he would implement our plan and release the companies, his response was rapid fire.

"General Sanchez will kick my butt if I release this many

MPs," General Wodjackowski bluntly told us. He agreed with our proposal, but directed that we give the same brief to Sanchez. I begged him not to make us do it, since he had the authority to release the MPs. He wouldn't relent. He didn't want to get on the bad side of General Sanchez by releasing so many MPs. Two hours was reserved on General Sanchez' schedule for our brief.

Wodjokowski told me to contact General Karpinski, commander of the 800th MP Brigade and ask her to attend the briefing. I didn't understand his rationale for having her attend, since she wasn't working with the Iraqi police, but I did as directed. Two days prior to the briefing, Lt. General Sanchez' office called and asked that the slides for the two hour briefing be sent to him ahead of time. The request was not unusual. The following morning, his office called me and told me I was off the schedule, because Sanchez had reviewed the slides and was not going to release any MPs.

The next day, while I was out on patrol, Tom Evans took another telephone call from Sanchez' staff. The meeting was back on, but the time allotted for the brief was reduced from two hours to fifteen minutes.

On the day of the brief, Evans, General Wodjackowski, General Karpinski and I met outside of Lt. General Sanchez' office and were motioned inside by a staff member. Sanchez was seated at his desk, and without looking up, said that he would be with us shortly. There was a small four person conference table in the room. Since Evans was actually conducting the brief, I told him to sit at the table beside Sanchez. Wodjakowski sat at the other end where he always sat. In deference to her rank as a brigadier general, I offered the final chair to Karpinski. I pulled up a chair a little to the rear and sat behind her. Lt. General Sanchez finished perusing his email, grabbed the slides sent to him the night before, and sat down at the table in the empty chair next to Tom Evans.

"Who is doing the briefing?" he barked.

"I am, sir," Evans responded crisply.

"What have you got?" Lt .General Sanchez gave every impression he was in disagreement with the brief before it even began.

I decided to answer the question myself, jumping into the fray, as if instinctively coming to the defense of my deputy before Evans ever opened his mouth to give Sanchez an answer.

"Sir, I don't think you called us up here to give a brief today. Since this went from a two hour brief to a 15 minute one, I think I'm here to be in the receiving mode," Sanchez smiled at me and said I was right, validating my instincts.

"If I were an Army commander I'd agree with you, but I'm not an Army Commander. You are an Army commander," Sanchez paused for my reaction.

Initially I was confused as I looked at the three-star American general wearing an Army uniform just like me. It was hard to believe we worked in the same Army.

"You're an Army commander, I'm a joint commander, my job is to identify my joint requirements. It's up to the Army, Air Force, Navy and Marine Corps to fill those requirements," Lt. General Sanchez repeated as he flipped through the first few slides, asking who assembled the "facts" referenced in them.

I told him I did and that given the current number of MP units in Iraq, it would be impossible to send in sufficient MP follow on forces for the second year. He told me that wasn't his problem, and reminded me again that he identified requirements and it was the Pentagon's job to fill the requirements. He didn't care if they were Army, Air Force, Navy or Marines. I tried to defend and fight for an opening so we could intelligently discuss the ramifications of General Sanchez' decision.

"You're not listening to me Colonel. It's not my problem." Lt. General Sanchez stared at me, waiting for me to argue further.

General Wodjackowski said nothing in defense of the plan he had liked a couple of days before. He left me to fend for myself. As soon as the one way "discussion" between Sanchez and I began, Karpinski pushed her chair away from the table so that Lt. General Sanchez could have a clear shot at me. He took fifteen ensuing minutes to mentor me on joint operations, something he thought I needed since I was just an army commander. He then looked at Evans.

"Maybe in three months you can plan on coming back to me and we'll look at this again." Lt. General Sanchez cast a glance at the officers sitting in front of him, then back at Evans.

"We'll be looking forward to that ass-whipping sir," Evans felt compelled to respond. There was a quickened silence.

General Sanchez then smiled, taking the quip as a symbol of his power and position. He dismissed our group. We left his office and walked into an outer hallway.

"Ma'am, thank you for your support in there—moving your chair out of the line of fire," I started directing my anger from the meeting by addressing Karpinski. General Wojakowski started laughing. I turned to him.

"Sir, thank you for your support, saying nothing in there, you thought this was a good idea a couple of days ago." General Wodjokowski was a great leader whom I greatly respected, but it was evident he didn't want to tangle with Sanchez on this issue.

I had no intention of being disrespectful, but felt that Tom Evans and I were left hanging in the wind as we tried to convince General Sanchez of the problems inherent in rejecting our strategy. In the coming months and years, Iraq plunged into turmoil, in part by lacking a sufficient number of military police and any plan to instill the rule of law on the Iraqi people. The result was a complete breakdown of law and order and years of insurgency and criminality that would extend the war, a contributing factor to increased American casualties in Iraq.

Had Sanchez approved our redeployment proposals, there would have been twelve additional active duty MP companies available for the second year that could have significantly contributed to the standing up of the police, perhaps reducing much of the chaos that got out of control that year. Instead, during that second year there were fewer MP companies across all of Iraq, than we had just in Baghdad in the first year of the war. The briefing Tom Evans and I tried to give to Sanchez was critical to the policing effort in Iraq, but was never requested again. The subsequent lack of MP assets deployed during that second year could be traced directly to the decision made by Lt. General Sanchez. When he ignored our best advice on how to maintain sufficient numbers of MPs in Iraq over the long haul, he created the foundation for a lasting problem.

But the root cause of the smaller Army without sufficient assets to meet all of its commitments could be linked directly to the decisions of President Bill Clinton and theUnited States Congress during the decade of the nineties. Contrary to what Congress believed then, it takes a lot longer to rebuild an Army than it does to tear one down. Given our current situation in 2013, President Obama hasn't learned that lesson and is making the same mistakes President Clinton did nearly two decades ago. The politics of the budget is causing the military to cut personnel they need, and buy some equipment they don't need. This time around, the potential consequences might be far greater to America.

I stood by the side of Sanchez at the 709th MP Battalion headquarters in Baghdad just a few weeks before my brigade left Iraq in 2004. He presented the J.P. Holland Award for the best MP company in the Army, to the 615th. It was an organic company that I had brought to Iraq from Germany. By that time, Sanchez was a media celebrity and the cameras clicked as he gave a speech at the ceremony.

The soldiers were truly appreciative that he personally presented the trophy to their commander, Captain Russell-Tutty. I had already scheduled Maj. General Don Ryder, the Provost Marshal General of the Army to present the award. Sanchez decided at the last minute it would be more appropriate for him to do the honor. Even though Sanchez had previously told me he was not going to make a speech, he decided to get up and deliver one after I made my comments at the ceremony. There is little question that the soldiers were delighted with his decision and attendance at the function.

After the ceremony was over, I walked Sanchez back to his helicopter as he prepared to depart. On the walk back, Sanchez cast a questioning glance at me.

Someone had obviously told him about my recent decision to retire after I left brigade command.

"Why are you really retiring colonel?" he asked

"Family reasons, Sir," I answered, not in much of a mood to discuss anything with him at that point in time.

"I respect that," Lt. General Sanchez climbed aboard his helicopter and although we saw each other after the encounter, Sanchez never again inquired about my reasons for retiring.

Had there been different leadership in the army, perhaps I would have re-thought my retirement plans. I can't say for sure. But there is little doubt in my mind that Lt. General Sanchez pursued the wrong strategy as he replaced General Wallace in Iraq. Had Wallace been in charge, things for America—and me, might have turned out differently.

Sanchez talked a lot about leadership, but from what I observed, he didn't understand and didn't care about the need to win the hearts and minds of the Iraqi people. He was constantly focused on the wrong things—numbers that briefed well in the media like how many police stations had we turned over to the Iraqis or how many police had we trained. He focused on quantity, I focused on quality. Instead of the quality of the police we were training and whether a particular police station was ready to turn over, his staff pressured me to produce numbers. With Sanchez, the time lines became the product. He definitely didn't understand that the military police were the force needed to deal with the Iraqi people because of the outstanding interpersonal communication skills and the understanding of the minimum use of force that military police possessed, because of their law enforcement experience. The combat arms soldiers just didn't possess these skills, critical in the environment we found ourselves in.

Even though the initial units in Iraq rotated out after our first year, Sanchez was there for nearly five more months. Even had we stayed there with him, Lt. General Sanchez and I would never have come to an understanding on the proper use of the MPs. I had a keen awareness that came from experience as a real policeman in a democratic society, both as a civilian police officer before joining the army, and as a military policeman for 26 years. I knew the population had to be engaged with the police if crimes, regardless of type, were to be prevented or solved. To be engaged, they had to trust and have confidence in their police departments. If they did, they would provide intelligence and help solve crimes and they would do it without fear.

In the late summer of 2003, Lt. General Sanchez was asked whether more American troops were needed in Iraq to combat growing crimes of violence and terrorist activities. His response set the tone for the next few years of war and rising American casualties:

"Putting more soldiers on the ground is not going to solve the problem if I don't have the intelligence to act on." [5]

He went on to emphasize that the Iraqi police had to "establish linkages to the Iraqi people."

Using MPs in the mission they were designed to perform instead of "ILO" MPs would have resulted in the right kind of soldiers on the ground. They would have properly trained Iraqi police in how to develop relationships with the Iraqi people so that those people would step forward and provide intelligence. They would have understood law enforcement as well as being combat cops. But after early 2004 there were insufficient numbers of MPs assigned to Iraq—a direct consequence of the decision made by Lt. General Sanchez not to approve the MP rotation plan submitted to him by my Deputy Commander Tom Evans and I.

Ironically, after Sanchez redeployed to Germany in June, 2004, he started to prepare my brigade to redeploy to Iraq in November, for their second tour, about three months after my departure. This meant they would have only been out of Iraq for nine months. They were the first brigade to do a second tour in Iraq. After my departure, and as the brigade prepared to return to Iraq under the command of my replacement, Colonel Jim Brown, Sanchez had a different perspective on the units that would be joining the18th MP Brigade for their second tour. In *Wiser in Battle, A Soldier's Story*, a book he wrote after he retired, Lt.General Sanchez blamed the Army for the fateful MP decision that he and he alone made in the summer of 2003:

"When we learned that our MP brigade was going to be filled with reserve 'in lieu of' units from the United States, we began to ask questions about the certification of those units. To my surprise, I learned that not only were they placed on an accelerated two-week training schedule for quick deployment, but many of the soldiers were being thrown together at the last minute to fill the units. Even more disturbing was that in some cases, people were put into the units, underwent training, and departed the unit. The permanently assigned personnel arrived later and received no unit-level training at all. From our perspective in V. Corps, it appeared that many of the 'in-lieu of' units were not receiving sufficient training for their mission and were being filled in a haphazard manner, without any regard for long-term effectiveness."[6]

These comments by Lt. General Sanchez are nothing short of remarkable. He learned about the future shortage of MPs during our briefing and rejected our plan to overcome this problem. At the time he said it wasn't his problem. I suppose there is some poetic justice that it somehow became his problem. I guess back in his role as an "Army commander," he saw things different than he did as a "joint commander." The plan we had presented to him would have prevented the very outcome that his decisions brought about. He had the rank and information to make the right decision. He made the wrong one in spite of our pleas. He and his staff never asked for a second briefing from us after August of 2003.

When I think of the lost opportunities in Iraq during 2003, Lt. General Sanchez comes vividly to mind.

During the several weeks I served under him when Sanchez was the division commander, he was more interested in killing bad guys and not interested at all about standing up the Iraqi police or winning the hearts and minds of the Iraqi people. Ordering me to put an MP company in each of his five combat arms brigades over my strong objections resulted in them being seriously misused.

Maj. General Martin Dempsey, Sanchez' replacement as 1st Armored Division Commander (and the current Chairman of the Joint Chiefs of Staff) and General William Wallace had a much greater understanding of the importance of training the Iraqi police and the unique skills that the MPs brought to the battle-field. While Wallace had to exit Iraq prematurely and couldn't help right the bad choices that Sanchez made, GeneralDempsey eventually overturned Sanchez' MP rotation decision.

However, Dempsey's orders didn't become effective until September 1, and even then he made me leave a platoon, which is about a fourth of a company, in each brigade. I assume this was a compromise to appease my fellow brigade commanders. Of course,they wasted the platoon, just as they had the company. By that time, significant damage had already been done. It wasn't the only decision made by Sanchez that caused problems for the Army, the soldiers in the thick of the battle for Iraq and the U. S. government. His failure to insure that his officers adhered to a strict accountability standard through a clear cut chain of command, contributed to the torture and abuse scandal at Abu Ghraib that gave America, and the Military Police Corps, a terrible blackeye on the world stage. The ensuing scandal kept him from getting the fourth star he so coveted in the army and led to his retirement.

Sanchez' leadership style, combined with the cumulative decisions of civilian leaders in the states, created an environment which allowed for interrogators from military and civilian agencies to subvert the army's command structure when dealing with Iraqi prisoners of war and high value detainees. Torture and prisoner abuse were the direct result. This development did substantial damage to America's reputation in the region and around the world and hurt the prosecution of the war. Lt. General Sanchez bears some serious responsibility for that toxic situation.

CHAPTER SIX: NOTES

1 The New York Times, March 28, 2003, "A Nation At War: In the Field-V Corps Commander: A Gulf Commander See A Long Road," by Jim Dyer.
2 February 25, 2003 Testimony of Eric Shinseki Before the United States Senate Armed Services Committee.
3 February 27, 2003 Testimony of Paul Wolfowitz Before the United States House of Representatives Budget Committee.
4 February 27, 2003 Pentagon Press Conference of Donald Rumsfeld, from CNN Transcript.
5 Baltimore Sun, August 29, 2003, "U.S. General in Iraq Says Facts Needed, Not Force."
6 "Wiser In Battle, A Soldier's Story," by Lt. General Ricardo Sanchez, published May 6, 2008, by Harper, pages 414-415.

Practicing defense against
anticipated chemical attacks

Coming up on a typical explosion,
with crowd gathering.

Road sign on the way to Baghdad
(about 167 miles away).

Road sign upon entering Baghdad.

The two seat toilet that SFC Brown built from scratch.

Bombed civilian commercial airplanes (Iraqi Airways) at the airport.

The main foyer of palace with the crystal tree.

Back of palace formerly "pleasure palace" of Saddam's sons.

Small child kissing CSM.

Ambassador Bremer, Claire Shiffert, and Colonel Spain after the 20/20 briefing, leaving Colonel Spain's headquarters—Tom Evans, Gill Boice, and a Blackwater guard are in the back ground.

The "fake" jail commander cuting the ribbon to open the jail. Command Sergeant Major Guyette behind him.

Confiscated enemy weapons.

Ambassador Bremer and Jim Steele arriving at Colonel Spain's headquarters for the 20/20 briefing.

Sanchez, Bush, Bremer—Thanksgiving Day before President Bush worked his way through the crowd and started serving chow.

Left to right—Colonel Dave Quantock—coming in as the 16th MP Brigade Commander out of Ft. Bragg, NC—currently Major General and Provost Marshal General of the Army; Brigadier General Geoghan, the 220th MP Brigade Commander; Colonel Spain, Brigadier General Karpinski, the 800th Enemy Prisoner of War Brigade Commander, and blamed for the Abu Ghraib Prison scandal and later demoted to Colonel by President Bush; Colonel Dave Phillips arriving as the 89th MP Brigade Commander out of Ft. Hood, Texas, who retired as Brigadier General and Commandant, US Army Military Police School.

Small section of Abu Ghraib Prison.

Detainees captured during looting of the police academy.

Captain Steve Caruso and Colonel Ahmed shortly after the fall of Baghdad.

Room of a weapons cache found in a school, during the ground war.

Meeting with the Sheik. Kuwaiti translator sitting between both cautioned Colonel Spain not to threaten to shoot the Sheik.

A sign a soldier made and put up at one of the entrances to Tallil Air Base, the first major re-supply point—also the site of the first major battle for the Army.

Colonel Spain and his Command Sergeant Major standing with the family of the detainee he ordered released for insufficient evidence.

One of the first meetings with some of the previous Iraqi police—the gentleman in this picture was the Baghdad Police Chief before the invasion.

Iraqi policemen receiving final instruction from General Ahmed before running checkpoints with Colonel Spain's miltary police.

Ambassador Bremer, Bernie Kerik and Colonel Spain during briefing for the 20/20 session.

A typical search, /frisking of someone before entering the perimeter
of security around each of our
police stations.

Colonel Spain and senior Iraqi generals at transfer of power.

Arriving at the bombed UN building.

General Sanchez with the soldiers of the
615th MP Company, after he presented
them the JP Holland Award for the best
MP Company in the Army Author
standing behind him and to his right.

Huge poster Kuwaiti people made
after the capture of Saddam.

From left to right—Corporal Mathew Dillon, Colonel Spain, Major Rob Dillon, Mathew's older brother—Major Dillon asked to have a picture made with Colonel Spain and his brother, who was visiting him in Baghdad, from a different unit stationed in Northern Iraq. Corporal Dillon finished his tour, went back to college, joined the Marine Corps, returned to Iraq, and was killed by an IED.

DEPARTMENT OF THE ARMY
Headquarters, 18th Military Police Brigade
APO AE 09302-1322

April 30, 2003

Mrs. Robin Legair
595 Lee Avenue
North Brunswick, NJ 08902

Dear Mrs. Legair,

   The soldiers of the 18th Military Police Brigade join me in extending our deepest sympathy on the death of your son, Specialist Narson B. Sullivan.

   We know the great loss you have suffered and realize there is little we can say to help you in this moment of sorrow. We offer our continued support and understanding and hope that time will make some sense out of this tragedy.

   Our heartfelt condolences are extended to you and the members of your family in your bereavement.

Sincerely,

Teddy R. Spain
Colonel, United States Army
Commanding

The first of the 13 letters Colonel Spain had to write to the families of the soldiers who were killed under his command—this was to the mother of Specialist Narson Sullivan, killed on April 25, 2003, before making it into Baghdad. His memorial was held in the desert.

CHAPTER SEVEN

L. PAUL BREMER'S CPA,
CAN'T PRODUCE ANYTHING

**Disbanding the Iraqi army and Ba'ath Party complicated
establishing law and order.**

On May 21, during my nightly radio update with Lt. General
Wallace, I reported the following:

> "We conducted a ribbon cutting ceremony at our first jail
> this morning with Ambassador Bremer. The senior Iraqi
> police officer in Baghdad actually cut the ribbon, and then
> Ambassador Bremer made comments and answered media
> questions. He then toured the jail and went to a police sta-
> tion where he witnessed an MP/Iraqi Police joint patrol.
> Lots of media were on hand.

A minute or two later I ended my update by saying:
"Mr. Bernie Kerik, New York City PD is here tomorrow, he
is Ambassador Bremer's Police Advisor."

Little did I know just how much my initial meeting with
Ambassador Bremer and Commissioner Kerik would change the
course of my time in Iraq. It all started with a call from Bremer's
staff about four days earlier. The staff member told me that
Bremer wanted to highlight some of the progress being made in
Iraq and wanted to know if I had any suggestions. I told him that
I was opening my first regional jail in a few days, and if they were
looking for a media event, I could create a ribbon cutting cere-

mony. He later got back to me and told me that Bremer loved the idea, so we starting planning a sham ribbon cutting to play to the media. We had renovated the jail in order to prepare to house the initial detainees that would be some of the first to be tried in the new court system. We selected the facility based on its proximity to the court rooms that were being renovated to begin trials, but they were not based on security for visiting dignitaries, such as Bremer. I told Bremer's staff member I had security concerns for the safety of the ambassador, given the numerous high rise buildings in the vicinity of the soon to be jail. I received a call-saying that Bremer's security detail, contractors from the newly arrived Blackwater Corporation, would be doing a reconnaissance in a couple of days and would determine if it would be safe enough for his visit.

Subsequently my security detail, Bremer's security detail from Blackwater, and I met at the facility. I was sure they would cancel the visit once they heard my security concerns, but they didn't. They explained how they would secure the area, even though there were numerous potential sniper positions around the building. I explained to them how my security detail normally set up security for me, albeit much less than what Bremer required. They were all in civilian clothes, with hair longer than military regulation and some had facial hair, another "double no" for the military. My security detail was in military uniforms, with trimmed hair. I expressed a concern that some of the Blackwater detail blended too much with the locals and was worried that if shooting started, my security detail might possibly mistake them for "bad guys" and shoot some of them. After a lengthy discussion, we agreed that they would take the counter sniper positions and everything beyond ten yards away from Bremer. My security would take the close in security where the Iraqi police would be and should there be a threat from the Iraqi police, my security would do the shooting, and they would do the shooting for all external threats. At the time, I didn't know Bernie Kerik was in Iraq, nor did I know anything about him.

Later that week, about an hour before the ribbon cutting, I arrived at the jail with my security detail. We went over last minute discussions with Bremer's advance team as the media started to arrive. It was evident this would be a big media event and that Bremer's staff knew how to play to the media. Earlier that week his staff said Bremer wanted several Iraqi police officers to be present to conduct the ribbon cutting with him. We hadn't been working long with the police, and certainly didn't know who we could trust, an issue that lasted our entire time in Iraq. I told my battalion commander responsible for the area of the ribbon cutting that I wanted about ten Iraqi police in uniform. Preferably, they would be sharp looking and we could designate one as the jail commander. Yes, as sad as it is to admit it, I was already playing the media game myself.

When Bremer arrived, I met him as he exited his vehicle and introduced myself. I quickly told him how we would conduct the ceremony. He had someone with him who looked very familiar and was very sharply dressed, but I couldn't identify the person. I found out later that day it was the former New York City Police Commissioner during the9/11 attacks on New York City, Bernie Kerik.

We conducted the ribbon cutting, and carried the media through the newly renovated facility. As we exited the facility, Bremer stood on the small porch and answered additional media questions. He then told me that he had been made aware that I had a police station nearby and wanted to visit it. I told him I had one several hundred yards away. He said he would hand pick some media representatives to take with him, and that he wanted me to stay behind and conduct media interviews with the remaining media, emphasizing our progress since our capture of Baghdad. As he turned to depart, one of the staged Iraqi policemen walked through the crowd towards Bremer at such a fast pace that I was concerned he intended to do him harm. I quickly looked at my closest security member and placed my hand on my pistol. In the split second I was deciding whether to pull my weapon and shoot the person, he stopped, clicked his heels, stood at attention and said in nearly perfect English how much he appreciated the United States, and President George Bush for freeing his country from Saddam.

We immediately went from a potential media fiasco, to a media grand slam home run. Bremer was delighted and accepted the gratitude of the policeman. I likewise was extremely delighted I hadn't shot the man dead on national TV. Bremer had a staff member find out who the policeman was as he departed. It was then and there that Bremer and Kerik started their relationship with Ibrahim Ahmed, who would later become a three star police general and the acting Minister of Interior for Iraq. It was also the hour that I started my relationship with Bremer, Kerik, and Ahmed. The course of history for the Iraqi police was established with that single momentous event.

Even though I did not accompany Bremer and Kerik to the police station, I suspect Ahmed did. While some of my officers were conducting the second, even though unplanned, media event at the police station, another unscheduled event took place. I had been convinced by one of my battalion commanders that Iraqi Police General Rizak should be the first post war police chief of Baghdad and I was working to make that happen. As luck would have it, Rizak was at the police station Bremer and Kerik visited with the hand picked media members. Someone created a scene, saying that Rizak had committed crimes against the Iraqi people prior to the toppling of Saddam's government. After the media wrote stories about Rizak, I was told by Bremer's people that he could never be the police chief and I was directed to send him into retirement. Ironically, he was brought back to a very prominent position within the Iraqi police, after my own retirement from the U.S. Army.

So what started out as a ribbon cutting stunt for the media turned out to be the beginning of a lasting relationship between Ahmed and Bernie Kerik. Kerik and Bremer used Ahmed for whatever purpose they had in mind and Ahmed used them. He played well to the media. It was a match made in heaven, a win/win situation for Ahmed and the CPA. I would soon find out there were complications to the Ahmed/Kerik relationship, and once again I was going to have to play the hand I was dealt. The Coalition Provisional Authority (CPA) was the successor to a short lived political office established to help distribute humanitarian assistance to Iraq in the aftermath of the invasion. The civilian administrators assigned to the CPA made some key decisions in 2003 that contributed to Iraq's drift towards civil war a year later. My soldiers and I watched helplessly as the CPA and its stalwarts paid little attention to our advice and the opinions of other military and police experts, placing the U. S. Army on a collision course with disaster. The CPA's decisions to disband the Iraqi army and the highest levels of the Ba'ath Party, had a huge impact on our mission to stand up the Iraqi police. The decision to disband the Iraqi army alone resulted in tens of thousands of unemployed people turned lose in the streets with guns. They blamed us for the loss of their jobs and often turned those guns on soldiers of the U.S. Army.

Much argument exists to this day on who made the decision to disband the army and take out certain levels of the Ba'ath Party. Bremer said it was Rumsfeld, Rumsfeld said it was Bremer. But in Colin Powell's book, *It Worked for Me*, he provides quite a revelation,that I haven't seen any where else:

"When we went in, we had a plan, which the President approved. We would not break up and disband the Iraqi army. We would use the reconstituted army with purged leadership to help us secure and maintain order throughout the country. We would dissolve the Ba'ath Party, the ruling political party, but we would not throw every party member out on the street. In Hussein's day, if you wanted to be a government official, a teacher, a cop, or postal worker, you had to belong to the party."

"...The plan the President had approved was not implemented. Instead Secretary Rumsfeld and Ambassador L. Paul Bremer, our man in charge in Iraq as head of the Coalition Provisional Authority, disbanded the Iraqi army and fired Ba'ath party members, right down to teachers."

"...These actions surprised the President, National Security Advisor Condi Rice, and me, but once they had been set in motion, the President felt he had to support Secretary Rumsfeld and Ambassador Bremer."

Are you kidding me? You can ignore the President's plan? I've been faced with numerous leadership dilemmas throughout my career where I was torn between supporting a subordinate's bad decision or doing what was right for the mission. The mission has to trump the bad decision. If only President Bush would have forced Rumsfeld and Bremer to reverse their decision, we would have been much better off on the streets of Baghdad.

The removal of senior levels of the Ba'ath party resulted in a loss of many of the high level leaders within the Iraqi police. Although they had served under Saddam, most did so out of necessity to avoid losing their heads. They would have been loyal to a more independent Iraqi state when Saddam was overthrown and extremely helpful in rebuilding the police force. In fact, they were desperately needed if the job was to ever get done. In the early stages of post-invasion Iraq, I was constantly asked by the media how I could be certain that some of the senior police I was working with weren't part of Saddam's former regime. My response to the media was that I didn't know and didn't care. We had to play the hand we were dealt until we could get the right leadership in all of the Iraqi police stations. My strategy was to get the Iraqi police under control. Whether I liked it or not, some of the former Ba'ath party members could help us do just that. It was my belief that over time we could weed out the ones who were going to be part of the problem, rather than part of the solution.

We came to view many of the people staffing the CPA as political hacks with terrible judgment. Some of the time, they simply caused more harm than good in Iraq. Often, it seemed like they spent more time fighting with us than helping in the fight with the trouble-making elements left over from Saddam's regime. We started referring to the CPA as, "can't produce anything," thinking the phrase was a far more appropriate description of the results we saw from the agency's efforts. Most of the CPA staff came and went on a frequent basis. There was little consistency in opinions or finishing tasks.

Most of the CPA appointees came and left so often that no one was ever in a job long enough to stake out a reasonable position to address a problem and then embark on truly fixing it. Hardly anyone stayed around long enough to be held accountable and responsible for the consequences of the decisions they made. Some of the CPA members I worked with were dedicated great Americans who tried to make a difference, got extremely frustrated and went home. Some were there for the money, realized it wasn't worth the danger, and went home.

The old saying, "if you can't stand the heat, get out of the kitchen," certainly applied to some of them. Baghdad was a dangerous place. I didn't have any sympathy for them because they were relatively safe in the Green Zone. I felt if they really wanted to see danger, they should experience what my soldiers experienced every day. My soldiers fought the enemy, in the worst of conditions, with a lot less pay, and they didn't have the option of going home.

But as dangerous as Iraq was for American soldiers in the spring of 2003, it was even more threatening to civilians. Arriving from coalition countries and the United Nations to help rebuild Iraq after the ouster of Saddam Hussein, civilian authorities weren't immune to increasing violence. The story of how the foundation for that violence was built started early on—even before we invaded Iraq.

Two months before the invasion of Iraq, a retired U.S. Army Lt. General, Jay Garner was named Director of the Office for Reconstructions and Humanitarian Assistance (ORHA). The ORHA was created to act as a temporary government for Iraq until a civilian election could be held.

Garner had served in Operation Desert Storm during the first Gulf War in 1991 and had ties to Defense Secretary Donald Rumsfeld. In his book, *Known and Unknown*, Mr. Rumsfeld confirmed that he had recruited Garner for the job:

"I had met him when we served together on the Space Commission in 2000. General Garner knew Secretary Powell and had fought in Iraq during the 1991 Gulf War, when Powell was chairman of the Joint Chiefs of Staff. In what was called Operation Provide Comfort, Garner had led twenty thousand troops to assist Iraqi Kurds battered by Saddam's regime... Thousands of Kurds delayed his departure by lifting him on their shoulders in celebration of his work.

"I saw Garner's military background as a valuable asset. I knew the civilian reconstruction effort in Iraq would have to be done in close cooperation with

CENTCOM's military personnel... I believed a retired general, one who knew many CENTCOM officers and understood military culture, would have the best chance of avoiding friction with the military personnel. I also thought that Garner's prior association with Colin Powell would foster good relations between the reconstruction office and the State Department...

"Garner believed, as I did, in empowering local populations to do things for themselves... Once the military had toppled Saddam's regime, I thought it was strategically important to put the United States in a supporting role to the Iraqis as soon as possible. This was the Pentagon's and—at least as I understood it—the President's vision." [2]

Garner was actually a good fit to help in Iraq's government transition. However, he ran into trouble almost immediately. He fought the decision favoring the wholesale dismissal of Ba'ath Party members, which included some of my high level Iraqi police officers. Garner refused to give in to pressure from within U. S. government circles to remove former members of Saddam's Ba'ath Party from their police, military, and government jobs. He believed their educations and backgrounds would benefit the rebuilding of Iraqi society. I definitely agreed with his assessment. We were working aggressively with Garner to put the police back together in Baghdad when his continuous resistance to dismissing them led to his own sudden dismissal in May, 2003, after less than a month on the job.

Bob Gifford and Phil Hall, two of Garner's senior police representatives, and I met on several occasions. We were on the same sheet of music as to where we should begoing with the Iraqi police. This was also my first experience dealing with the politics of working with members of our most supportive coalition, the United Kingdom. Bob Gifford was from the United States. Phil

Hall was from the UK. They didn't alway sagree with one another on the issues. However, they were always respectful of each other and I could never figure out which one of them was actually in charge. Even when I asked them, they told me they were "equals." Theirs was a strange arrangement in my mind, because I had been taught from day one in the army that someone is always in charge. I never saw that command and control philosophy altered during my military service. Even if there were two privates together, one of them is senior to the other, based on their date of rank. I was extremely naive about the organization, or lack thereof, of the civilian leadership that was entering Baghdad. It became as foreign to me as the land we invaded. It was a philosophy that caused one problem after another for all of us—civilians and soldiers.

President George W. Bush appointed L. Paul Bremer as the Administrator of the Coalition Provisional Authority (CPA) on May 11, 2003. The CPA functioned as Iraq's interim government until it was dissolved on June 28, 2004. During this time, I witnessed some of the worst decision making I had ever seen in government.

In his book, *Decision Points*, President Bush talks about the clear mandate he gave to Bremer upon his appointment:

"Bremer arrived in Iraq on May 12, 2003. One of his first tasks was to assemble an Iraqi Governing Council that would take responsibility for key ministries and prepare for a formal return of sovereignty. Navigating Iraq's tribal, religious, and ethnic politics was highly complicated. But Jerry and his team did a superb job. The Governing Council took office in July, just four months after liberation. It included twenty-five Iraqis from all backgrounds. Iraqis still had a long way to go, but they had taken their first step toward a representative government.

"Forming the Governing Council was an important way to demonstrate that Saddam's tyranny was gone forever. With that in mind, Jerry issued two orders shortly after his arrival in Baghdad. One declared that certain members of Saddam's Ba'ath Party would not be eligible to serve in the new government of Iraq. The other formally disbanded the Iraqi army, which had largely disappeared on its own...

"In retrospect, I should have insisted on more debate on Jerry's orders, especially on what message disbanding the army would send and how many Sunnis the de-Baathification would affect."[3]

My soldiers were among the first to see and feel the negative effects of the de-Baathification decision on the effort to rebuild Iraq's police and government institutions. Major Boice had this incisive assessment of the situation:

"The decision to restrict Firqah level Ba'athists from serving in the new Iraqi governmental institutions was a major mistake. To get any semblance of a higher education in Iraq, a person, out of necessity, would have to be a high enough level Ba'ath party member. The Firqah level was a pretty moderate level if an Iraqi wanted to gain a college or specialty education. Those with the education, leadership, and managerial skills needed to rebuild Iraq were thrown out of the solution set. These people needed to be deeply vetted, but retaining them was the key to gaining early success in Iraq.

"Because these educated Iraqis were excluded, progress was hindered. One man, Jamal Abdullah, was a true hero in the early days of the post-invasion time frame. He was by far the man of the hour in getting Iraqi police back to work. He was respected by the new Iraqi police and his education and former work in the Iraqi patrol police made him a superb and hands down choice for Chief of Police during our tenure in Baghdad. But due to Ambassador Bremer's policies and the lack of listening to senior MP advisors like Colonel Spain, Jamal was not selected. A far inferior choice was made to the real detriment of law and order in Baghdad. The right leader for the position was not chosen and progress in securing order suffered dearly."

From May, 2003 until the 18th MP Brigade was re-deployed in February, 2004, Major Roger Hedgepeth served with me in Iraq. He returned again to Iraq in November, 2005 with the 709th MP Battalion. When Hedgepeth first joined me in May, he took over from Major Boice the responsibility for hiring, training, and equipping the Iraqi Police Services in Baghdad. He strongly believed that the decisions of the CPA worsened security in post-invasion Iraq. He never hid how he felt:

"The CPA was not properly staffed to execute the mission they were assigned. They lacked the right people, size, or expertise to plan and execute such an enormous and complicated mission, particularly in the Provisional Ministry of Interior (MOI). This resulted in military units having to frequently step into the process. Without a staff to plan and coordinate, or assets to accomplish tasks, the MOI would frequently rely on the 18th MP Brigade and other military units to execute detailed planning, coordination, and task accomplishment.

"Both the CPA and the military units in Baghdad had a much too tactical focus on the mission, instead of a strategic or operational focus to rebuild the police/security infrastructure. The CPA had frequent turnover of personnel in both staff and leadership positions. It took a long time to earn the trust of the Iraqi people, and to understand the complexity of the operational environment. The MOI became a revolving door of MOI personnel in a hurry to make their mark and depart 60-90 days later.

"The CPA failed to understand several important cultural factors, including the Sunni-Shia divide, resistance to democratic ideals, lack of rule of law within the Iraqi criminal justice system, and the ill-advised de-baathification process. The influence of these three factors prolonged the process of reconstituting the Iraqi police and resulted in a deterioration of the security situation."

Another much discussed controversy that lingers to this day is Bremer's alleged order to shoot the looters. The news media back in the U. S. was showing looters roaming the streets of Baghdad, giving the impression to the American people of chaos in Iraq. That was probably because there was chaos in Iraq at the time. Bremer later said he only asked his staff what they thought about the idea. All I know is that my staff told me that an order came down from our higher headquarters to shoot the looters. I told my staff to put out to all my units that they were to not shoot any looters. I told the staff that until I heard this personally from one of the generals I was answering to, we would not shoot people that were stealing from store windows.

One of my fellow Brigade commanders referred to this as wealth redistribution. I didn't think this was a laughing matter, but I also didn't see how shooting the looters would help us win the hearts and minds campaign. A good leader will always seek clarification on an order that either appears to be a misunderstanding at best, or illegal at worst. Bremer's alleged order turned out to be a huge misunderstanding and I am thankful to this day that we didn't follow it.

By any measure, Iraqi citizens were feeling far less safe as they approached their first post-invasion summer. Dominant leadership figures in the Shia and Sunni populations allowed their own egos and centuries of distrust to spur acts of violence against each other, coalition soldiers, and Iraqi police recruits. Violent criminals released by Saddam from Iraqi prisons savaged neighborhoods and returned to committing the crimes that landed them in prison to begin with—burglaries, armed robberies, murders, extortions, and kidnappings. Terrorists, sometimes supported by other nations such as Syria and Iran, and other times by the growing influence of al-Qaeda in Iraq attacked civilian and military targets with impunity.

A variety of terrorists, in groups and alone, went after military convoys and the civilian administrators trying to rebuild Iraq. Iraqi citizens who got in the way of any of these people or groups often ended up dead. Even as President Bush declared an end to combat operations in Iraq on May 1, the war that was supposed to be over was just getting started. Attacks on Iraqi prisons, assassination operations directed at coalition leaders, the use of rocket-propelled grenades, checkpoint ambushes, and IED assaults on military convoys were just the warmup for what would be the next few years of war and thousands of American soldiers killed or wounded. For example, on August 7, seventeen people were murdered when a car bomb exploded outside of the Jordanian Embassy in Baghdad. On August 15, Iraq's oil exports were stopped when a major pipeline was destroyed in an act of sabotage.

The decisions made by the CPA were completely failing to contribute to the stabilization of Iraq. President Bush, Vice-President Cheney, Secretary of Defense Rumsfeld and his Deputy, Paul Wolfowitz had all been wrong—Iraq was not shaping up to be a short war. It was turning into a disastrous lesson of how not to plan, organize, and anticipate.

I read an article in the September 1, 2003 issue of *Newsweek* where I believe that journalist Fareed Zakaria captured the problem facing us at the time:

> "...Security is the first task of government; everything else rests on it. And important parts of Iraq—including its central city, home to 20% of its people—are insecure...It is time to recognize that the occupation of Iraq needs fixing. This has been a massive enterprise undertaken with little planning and extreme arrogance...
>
> "The Coalition Provisional Authority must assert its authority and ensure rapid progress on governance and reforms—even when Iraqis are slow or unable to act...If things fall apart, Iraqis will...blame America. After order, the first priority must be to create a system of justice: courts, police and a legal system." [4]

Confirmation that major combat operations were not over in Iraq came on August 19. The ensuing scenes were eerily familiar to the first international terrorist attack on the World Trade Center in June, 1993, the home grown terrorist attack on the Alfred Murrah Federal Building in Oklahoma City in April, 1995, and the al-Qaeda attacks on theUnited States on September 11, 2001.

Late in the afternoon, a lone Iraqi guided a Russian-made military vehicle towards Baghdad's Canal Hotel which was serving as the headquarters for a United Nations contingent dedicated to the rebuilding of Iraq. The truck's flatbed was packed with a variety of munitions as the driver made his way to an unguarded paved road that ran by the building. Likely in possession of insider information provided by another Iraqi working security in the building, the truck pulled to a stop below the office of the U.N.'s top diplomat in Iraq, Special Envoy Sergio Vieira de Mello. At 4:30 p.m. the 1500 pounds of explosives carried in the truck detonated with devastating results, leaving 24 people dead and more than 100 injured in a field of burning rubble. Among the dead, crushed by the weight of the building, was Sergio de Mello.

The commander of the 519th MP BN, Lt. Colonel Dave Glaser immediately sent MPs to help with the tragedy. Dave recalls the terrible tragedy that happened on that day:

"We helped dig most of their bodies out of the rubble after the truck bombing on the compound. The 812th Military Police Company was the first major element on the scene and they literally sawed several guys' legs off to free them before they burned to death and the rest of the building collapsed."

The brutal and cowardly murder of Sergio de Mello and his colleagues sent a clear message. There would be no quick ending to war inside Iraq. A combination of indecision, poor decisions, and no decisions by the CPA would change the face of America. In the eyes of many Iraqi citizens, we were no longer viewed as a welcomed liberator, but as the evil invaders of their country. I personally saw it on the face of the average Iraqi citizens that I interacted with daily. It was difficult to surmount the propaganda spreading this myth, when it was our army tanks occupying the main streets of their towns and cities.

It didn't matter that the majority of Iraqis supported the ouster of Saddam. What did matter were the legions of criminals he released from prison prior to the invasion; the divide between three ethnic groups; terrorists supported by international sponsors of terror and terrorist organizations; and dominant personalities inside Iraq who wanted to impose their own local and regional agendas on the national stage. Violence and destruction of Iraq's institutions, cities and neighborhoods by Iraqis became the post invasion face of America's attempts to bring democracy to the Middle East.

The American Army was caught in the middle. As a transparent symbol of the transition from tyranny to democracy, my U. S. Army MPs were particularly vulnerable as we patrolled Baghdad and other Iraqi cities and towns. The MPs followed a chain of command, clear set of established guidelines, and a code of conduct and discipline honed by generations. The collision of politics with the Army's transparency set the stage for ugly disputes and distrust among the very Americans that had to change the same attitudes of Iraqis.

Sometimes I witnessed the politicians and the media interacting first hand, creating a double whammy. High level U.S. government officials who traveled to Iraq were sensitive about the presence of the media and what they were saying about the war. None was more obsessive and detail oriented than Secretary of Defense Donald Rumsfeld. During a visit from Rumsfeld to Bremer, he stopped by the 1st Armored Division Headquarters to get an update.

On September 6, I participated in a briefing given by General Dempsey to Rumsfeld. The day before the briefing, Dempsey had reviewed the slides with all the Brigade Commanders to ensure they were all accurate and to ensure we knew what he would say, since we would be in the room with him during the briefing. He had a slide that addressed the Iraqi police. After he stumbled on a couple of facts, I suggested to him that perhaps I should brief the Iraqi Police part, because he certainly had a lot more important stuff to focus on. He said no, he would conduct the entire brief.

The next day Rumsfeld, his entourage from Washington

D.C., and all of the brigade commanders sat around a conference table as Dempsey briefed the Secretary. When the slide related to the Iraqi police showed up, Rumsfeld had a question of General Dempsey.

"I have the commander of the 18th MP Brigade right here, Mr. Secretary. He can answer your question," Dempsey passed the hot potato to me.

"Colonel Spain, are you aware of a newspaper article going around the United States that says there was a journalist in Baghdad who had gone around to the morgues and counted the dead bodies and wrote about the high homicide rate in Baghdad?" Rumsfeld glared.

Realizing that the media was in an adjoining room watching the briefing on a live feed, I was careful and deliberate in my answer to the secretary's question. "I haven't heard of the article you're talking about, but we average 45 dead bodies a month, either discovered by my MPs or the Iraqi police."

"Colonel, that's less than the journalist is reporting," Rumsfeld stopped me in the middle of my response.

"Sir, I don't have any control over the journalist you're referring to and I don't have any idea where he's getting his information. The information I am giving to you is all that I have." I decided the best tack was to respectfully hold my ground.

"Forty-five dead a month from homicides, that's less than some major cities inthe U. S., isn't it?"

Rumsfeld paused to wait for his observation to be confirmed. As the discussion continued, turning into a side bar in front of the other conference participants, Rumsfeld wanted me to clarify an issue that had arisen as to the number of cars in Baghdad after the invasion as compared to before the war started.

"The Iraqi police have told me that there has been an increase in the number of cars in Baghdad as compared to before the war. "They've also told me many of the cars have counterfeit titles from Jordan," I told the Secretary. The smile left Rumsfeld's face and he leaned a little forward towards me. I realized something was wrong, I just didn't know what.

"Colonel Spain, remember that the media is watching us. You're not suggesting that the country of Jordan is counterfeiting titles to vehicles and sending them into Baghdad are you?" Rumsfeld cautioned.

"No, sir, the counterfeit titles are being made here in Baghdad without the knowledge of the country of Jordan, my MPs busted the counterfeit ring," the Secretary smiled as I clarified my response.

I figured that Secretary Rumsfeld wanted the news media to hear me give the answer to the counterfeit issue, as if it was something that needed clarification in the states. After several more minutes of direct questioning of me, where I provided information that I thought he needed to hear, not necessarily what he wanted to hear, he went on to the next subject.

When the briefing ended, Rumsfeld walked around the room shaking hands. When he came up to me he said, "We need more people like you," he told me as he shook my hand. I assumed he meant he needed more MPs in Iraq, unless he was referring to more people that stood up to him.

As the delegation was leaving the conference room, one of the Pentagon generals traveling with the secretary came up to me and shook my hand. "Few people handle the secretary that way," he told me.

"Sir, Did you think I was being disrespectful?" I was getting concerned. "No, you weren't disrespectful. It was just the way that you stood up to him." The general seemed to be sincere, so I said to him, "Sir, he's like the bully on the playground, you just have to stand up to him."

As the general turned to catch up with the Secretary, he turned to me, smiled, and said, "You're damn right."

I saw myself as answering Secretary Rumsfeld's questions as honestly as I could. I wanted Rumsfeld to know that my soldiers had been accomplishing miracles since entering Iraq. I didn't care whether the media was present or not. Shortly before Thanksgiving, 2003, I was tasked to assign a platoon of MPs to a "special event" on Thanksgiving Day. I tasked the 709th MP Battalion with the mission The day before, Lt. Colonel John Garrity told me that the platoon would be working with the United States Secret Service. Rumors spread throughout Camp Victory that Hillary Clinton was going to have Thanksgiving dinner with the troops. The rumor quickly escalated to include the possibility that Vice-President Dick Cheney would be our surprise visitor.

As I woke up on Thanksgiving Day, I caught a glimpse of *FOX News* on the television in my office. It showed President Bush at his ranch at Crawford, Texas. The story even included the menu for the First Family's Thanksgiving dinner. Thinking to myself that it would be cool if Vice-President Cheney showed up at the mess hall, I got dressed for the feast.

My soldiers and I stood in shock as we gathered for our Thanksgiving break and found that the special guest who joined us for dinner was President Bush himself. Soldiers always conduct themselves with a reserved professionalism, but it was easy to feel a certain "rock star" sensation among us as the President greeted one, then another, as he slowly made his way around the dining area and ended up with the servers behind the chow line.

President Bush picked up a tray of turkey as photos flashed around the room. When he placed the serving tray back down on the table, Buchmeier joked, "Let's take that tray and sell it on eBay."

The president then gently moved aside one of the soldiers serving chow, asking "What's your job?"

"Well, it's to ask them if they want peas or corn and then to give them the one they ask for," the soldier answered the Commander-in-chief.

President Bush, handling a serving spoon and wearing an easy smile, seemed to get it and turned to the first soldier lined up in front of him.

"Do you want peas or corn?" the president asked.

As the speechless soldier momentarily froze at the sight of the President of theUnited States about to put vegetables on his plate, the President made the decision forhim.

"I'll give you both, what are they going to do to me?" We broke out in a respectful and grateful laughter.

For the next 30 minutes, in the middle of the war zone, President Bush fed the soldiers he had sent to liberate Iraq from tyranny and terrorists. If any of us had any questions about the sincerity of the man who was responsible for our being there, the questions disappeared on Thanksgiving as he stood among us, having little regard for his own safety. Finally, the head of his Secret Service contingent turned to me and said it was time to get the president out of the chow hall. I ordered my security detail to set up a path so that the president could make an exit.

But as he finished serving President Bush walked off in the opposite direction, visiting with all of us standing on the other side of the chow hall from where he had been serving. As he passed by me, he paused, shook my hand and said, "thank youfor your service."

When President Bush finally left, everyone was told to stay in the building until Air Force One had cleared Iraqi air space. Without any discussion of politics and a warmth that made the occasion seem so kind and real, I captured a permanent mental image of the day as an awe inspiring display of leadership and courage by President Bush. The president's visit left a feeling from home that gave me and the others the boost we needed to continue forward with a job that seemed to have no end.

The visit by President Bush stood in stark contrast to a more politically motivated trip by a congressional delegation. I was asked to set up a dinner with the troops. Politicians always love it when the voters back home see them in the war zone mingling with America's fighting men and women. Over half of the 18th MP Brigade was made up of National Guard and Reserve MP Units, representing a vast pool of voters during the next election cycle.

"Sir, do you want us to set up anything special?" John Garrity asked me as he was planning for the visit of nine Congressmen and women from several states.

"No, in fact, before the delegation has their meeting with Ambassador Bremer, arrange for them to be linked up with their constituents so they can eat what the soldiers eat." I knew that would mean standing in the same lines and eating out of the same Mobile Kitchen Trailers, or "MKT(s)" as the war fighters. I also knew that during the meetings before dinner it was always the same tone—Democrats tried to encourage the soldiers to say that things weren't going well. Republicans tried to justify that everything happening was perfectly according to plan. My reaction was always the same—Politicians made me sick.

After this particular delegation finished their meeting with the soldiers, I was waiting in the chow line when I saw Congresswoman Sheila Jackson Lee of Texas. She was taking pictures of the MKT. I walked up to her with an outstretched hand. "Ma'am, give me the camera and jump up there. I'll take a picture of you getting your food."

She was happy to oblige and eagerly jumped up to the MKT while I snapped several photographs of her with the troops from back home. When it was her turn to retrieve the camera, she had questions of her own for me.

"Colonel Spain, do you agree with the President's decision to invade Iraq?"

I knew the wrong answer would immediately land me on headline news. I pulled a cell phone from my pocket and looked at her.

"Whenever any senior person in Iraq wants to talk to me they can call me on this phone. If the President wants my opinion, he'll know exactly how to get in touch with me. I won't give you my opinion but I'd love to tell you about the brave men and women in my brigade."

"Colonel Spain, is there something you want to tell the American people?" she then asked.

"Yes, ma'am, there is. Tell the American people you spent a few hours with heroes. You're in the middle of America's real heroes here. Some are just out of high school, and all of them have seen stuff that people shouldn't have to see their whole lives." I had her complete attention, so I continued.

"I've seen horrible things too, but I'm an old man and I've lived a good life so it's okay for me. But it's not okay for them. There are a lot of these soldiers who aren't even old enough to buy a beer back in the states, but some will be emotionally changed the rest of their lives because of their duty over here in Iraq," I knew that I was probably close to saying too much, but couldn't shut up.

"Congresswoman, I've seen you several times criticizing our President on *Meet the Press* and I know that's your job. The only reason you have the freedom to do what you did is because of my brave men and women and what we did here." I cast a glance at the faces of the soldiers around me.

"Colonel Spain," Congresswoman Jackson defended, "you understand that is politics."

I stopped her abruptly.

"Ma'am, you can explain that to the families and other loved ones of the soldiers I've lost. You've spent a couple of days in the Green Zone and you're going back to the states and you'll be on

TV next week telling the American people about your experiences in Iraq. You'll tell the story as if you've gone across the desert like we did, waited to get hit with chemical weapons as we did, ate MRE (s) all day as we did, had nowhere to take showers, as we did, and never knew from day to day whether we would live to see the next.

Congresswoman Jackson remained hushed as I brushed a portrait of our feelings of war.

"You've not seen the real Iraq—the good, the bad, and the ugly. But if you want to spend a week with me and go where I go and see what I see, then you can return to the American people and tell them the real truth about what their young men and women are enduring to defend freedom. You can stand with me at a memorial and say good-bye to a soldier that has given his life for his country. A soldier who was under my command and was my responsibility; you can watch me stand there as a commander and say good-bye and pray that I had done everything I could to keep this from happening. Then you'll understand this isn't politics to me. Politicians told us when to enter Iraq and they'll tell us when to leave. When the President ordered us to enter Iraq, we didn't have enough equipment and we didn't have enough soldiers, but we pushed ahead with the mission we were given and I'm so damned proud of the soldiers for what they accomplished with what they had. There's nothing like the American soldier!"

"Can I have my picture made with you?" was the Congresswoman's response.

"I don't normally have my picture made with Democrats, but I'll make an exception this time," trying to break the tension, the mood lightened as Congresswoman Jackson started looking around for a suitable backdrop for the picture.

She chose a place in front of a picture of me presenting a purple heart to another young soldier. I told her the story of the ambush at Abu Ghraib police station that killed Rachel Bosveld and earned the young soldier in the picture the purple heart. "He was just 18 or 19 years old and his foot was blown up during a mortar attack. I lost a female soldier in the same attack and another young soldier lost his leg. This picture was taken when I went to the hospital room to present him his purple heart. He recognized me and pulled the covers back and started getting out of bed. He was wearing his uniform. When I asked him why he had his uniform on in bed, he told me he put it on because he knew his brigade commander was coming by and he didn't want me to see him in his pajamas. That, ma'am, is the American soldier."

I worried constantly about some of the personalities inside the CPA who seemed to add to our problems instead of helping find resolutions to them. One such personality was Jim Steele. Steele is self-described as an "expert in the areas of security and counterterrorism," and has used this marketing pitch to render his services since leaving Iraq. His resume says:

> "From May 2003 until assuming the position of senior counselor to Ambassador Bremer for Iraqi security forces in November 2003, Jim Steele was the senior police advisor with the Iraqi police SWAT unit in Baghdad. He headed the advisory team that organized, trained and operated with this special unit. He personally led the unit on a series of highly successful operations that netted former high-ranking members of the Saddam regime as well as numerous other criminal and terrorist elements..."[5]

I was in Baghdad in November, 2003 and if Steele 'was the senior police advisor with the Iraqi police SWAT unit in Baghdad,' it was such a secret that even I didn't know. He definitely was involved in some night time operations. I'm just not sure they were helping us accomplish our overall mission. In fact, I think Steele and others like him hindered our mission in Iraq.

During my first meeting with Steele he asked me if I had a pistol I could give him. I certainly wasn't going to give him one of our military pistols, but I did give him one of the countless pistols we had confiscated at various check point operations or during numerous raids. One of the liaison missions assigned to Major Roger Hedgepeth was the responsibility to interact, and keep a close eye on Jim Steel. Hedgepeth has a different recollection of Steele from our time in Iraq with him:

"I'm not sure what his official role was, but he would often commandeer large groups of Iraqi police and conduct operations to 'hunt down bad guys.' These operations were disruptive and tactically-focused, rarely resulting in any operational advantage. Steele worked closely with Bernie Kerick. The lack of coordination of his operations in the Division battle space resulted in much strain between the Minister of the Interior and Coalition forces. Steele would leave Iraq frequently, often returning with some new supposed mandate from 'Wolfowitz.' Since he was a retired army officer, I tried to appeal to him about what I saw as a lack of detailed operational and strategic planning ordirection at the MOI—but he mostly wanted to focus on targeting and tactical operations."

I took Major Hedgepeth's observations to heart. His opinion of Steele confirmed my own instincts. They told me to keep a watchful eye on Steele from the beginning. It would be the only way to keep my soldiers out of trouble. During one of my first meetings with Steele, he said that when he was in the army he had been on the promotion list for brigadier general. He said he decided to retire instead of accepting the promotion. His story raised an immediate red flag. He also made it clear to me that when he was a brigade commander, one of his battalion commanders at the time, was Lt. Colonel Wallace, the same Lieutenant General Wallace who was my boss. I suppose he thought he could intimidate me if I thought he and Wallace were friends. Knowing Wallace as I did, I knew that he would not approve of Steele's method of operations. Wallace had principle and integrity—both qualities sorely lacking in Steele.

I never did know what Steele's official position was at the CPA. When he first arrived in Iraq I was told his job was to help set up the electric grids, which made sense if I believed the story that he ran an electric company back in Texas. To my knowledge, he never had any involvement in setting up any electrical power capability in Iraq. Steele was a wild card who was well connected to the top. He could walk into Paul Bremer's office any time of the day or night without an appointment. Even though I frequently saw Bremer, and occasionally briefed him on police matters, there's no way I could have just walked in to talk to him without him asking for me, or me having an appointment.

Steele did his own thing and conducted many operations out on the streets. As a consequence, he really pissed off General Dempsey. On one memorable occasion, Dempsey asked me to bring Steele to see him. I did as directed by General Dempsey. Dempsey voiced our concerns to Steele about his activities, behavior and failure to keep us apprised of whatever it was he was doing in Iraq. General Dempsey's talk went nowhere. Steele gave every indication that he didn't much care whether Dempsey or I liked what he was doing. One thing is certain—our talk never changed his behavior, not even for an hour.

I recall a fire fight one afternoon involving Steele and "his boys" which was endemic of the types of problems Steele could cause with his brand of adventurism and lack of accountability.

Steele was involved in a shootout one day in downtown Baghdad. He and his cronies were pinned down by the enemy. He called me on my cell phone and asked for immediate help. As he was trying to give me his exact location in a city of six million people I could hear gunfire in the background. Regardless of my issues with Steele or however I felt about him, once someone comes under fire, the only thought you have is to come to his assistance. Personal feelings never get in the way when the shooting starts. I sent an MP response force to save his butt, however, Steele and his guys got out of the situation before my MPs ever arrived.

It was this kind of judgment that caused me to worry about the safety of the MP units that worked with Steele. At one point, elements of the 812th MP Company supported Steele's excursions into Baghdad. In early July, I pulled them back, because Steele put the unit into unnecessary danger. Bernie Kerick, the former New York City Police Commissioner, and another character who believed he could do whatever he wanted to in Iraq without any accountability, appealed to me to return the unit to supporting Steele and his independent patrols. I steadfastly refused. They went over my head, but when my superiors questioned my decision, they supported it after I explained what was going on.

I never did understand how Jim Steele's actions fit into the overall CPA plan. I think Jim Steele just did whatever he wanted to do and never answered to anyone. Somehow, Steele was closely tied to Bremer, with perhaps even a greater godfather somewhere up the line in the U. S. government. I never fully understood how and why he came to be assigned to Iraq.

Regardless, Steele often came between me and the Iraqi police. When I wanted General Jamal to become the chief of the Iraqi police, Jamal told me that Steele had been spreading derogatory information about him. Bernie Kerick and Jim Steele supported General Ahmed for the Iraqi police chief position. Subsequently, when Ahmed didn't get the job, they appointed him to be the first acting Iraqi Interior Minister, giving him authority over the individual we had chosen to be the chief. The result was constant bickering and infighting.

Major Roger Hedgepeth worked with Ahmed and saw the trouble that Steele and Kerick created with Ahmed's appointment to the Ministry of the Interior:

> "Ahmed was completely unqualified for the critical position. It was like placing a platoon leader in charge of a division. Ahmed was a disgraced junior officer in the Iraqi police. Allegedly he had been a horse trainer at one of Saddam's many palaces. Bernie Kerick appointed Ahmed to the ministry position because of his vocal distaste for the Ba'ath Party and Saddam. Ahmed horded police assets at the Baghdad Police Academy and conducted operations sometimes involving 200 police cars to take down targets that were often unvetted. We later discovered unofficial police jails hidden throughout Baghdad that housed prisoners who were not afforded due process. Ahmed was the target of many assassination attempts. He lived in his office at the Baghdad Police Academy. He worked closely with Jim Steele. Ahmed eventually moved to New York, presumably arranged by Kerick."

Although I was never able to determine exactly what was going on with Steele in Iraq, I think my instincts were on target. With a little personal research I found out that Steele was no stranger to assignments where there was no accountability or transparent chain of command. Steele was no stranger to violence and allegations of wrongdoing in his wake. Jim Steele came to Iraq with a past record of bad behavior that should have been the best indicator of his performance with us and the most accurate indicator of how he would perform in the future. During the mid-1980's, seven American citizens in Lebanon were kidnapped and held hostage by Hezbollah. Iran was in the middle of its war with Iraq. The Iranians worked out a secret deal with members of the administration of President Ronald Reagan. They would use their influence with Hezbollah to secure the release of the hostages if the United States would supply Iran with TOW anti-tank missiles. Although this sort of arrangement was a violation of American law, the plan was implemented. Israel received the weapons and sent them to Iran. Although the hostages were never released, the Iranians paid millions of dollars for the weapons systems. Since the money couldn't be returned to the U.S. government because it should never have been accepted in the first place, Marine Lt. Colonel Oliver North, working in the White House, devised a plan to filter the money to Central America. At that point in time, the U.S. was also covertly working with the "contras" in Nicaragua to overthrow its leftist Sandanista government. Funding the contras was also against U. S. law, in the form of the Boland Amendment, and thus the entire operation needed to be accomplished with complete secrecy.

No one knew of the "Iran-Contra" affair until the Nicaraguans shot down a CIA airplane carrying supplies and determined America was funding the contras. The ensuing scandal resulted in indictments and convictions of North and a number of Reagan cabinet members, advisers and CIA officials. Several of the convictions, including that of Lt. Colonel North, were subsequently overturned.

In 1986, Steele testified before the Senate Intelligence Committee to answer questions about his role in Iran Contra. He was asked whether he had helped Lt. Colonel North provide assistance to the contras, contrary to U.S. law.

"I certainly didn't do that," was Steele's response to the United States Senators.

Steele did admit to meetings with North during the time frame that Iran-Contra was occurring and while Steele was leading a military mission in neighboring El Salvador. Steele told Congress the meetings:

"'Weren't focused on the contras,' and he, 'never saw' any weapons being shipped through the pilots` main staging area in El Salvador." [6]

However, two years later, members of the Senate Armed Services Committee didn't believe Steele had been truthful in his earlier testimony and blocked his army promotion to brigadier general. In a July, 1991 article in the *Chicago Tribune*, I believe I found the "rest of the story" that explained to me why Steele operated so independently in Baghdad:

"But as Congress 'Iran-contra committees expanded the investigation in 1987, they found that Steele was one of the six principal members of North`s supply network. Steele kept in touch with North through the use of a coded transmitter and helped him coordinate numerous deliveries of arms to the contras, the committee said.

"At various times, Steele provided North's pilots with weather data, intelligence on Nicaraguan government forces and advice on how to avoid radar detection, the committees found.

"The committees even located a crew member of one of the supply planes who described how Steele had walked through the cargo bay and asked if a load of assault rifles was properly padded. The leaders of the Senate Armed Services Committee, questioning the truthfulness of his testimony, refused to act on the Army`s request to promote Steele to brigadier general in 1988.

"Defense Secretary Dick Cheney's office then delayed a second attempt to promote Steele for more than a year and a half while Iran-contra special prosecutor Lawrence Walsh also scrutinized Steele's actions, several sources said.

"But a prosecutor working for Walsh recently told

Pentagon officials that he had decided not to seek criminal charges against Steele, the sources said. Supporters contend that Steele deserves the promotion because he had an exemplary record as a troop commander in Vietnam and Germany and as a military adviser in Panama, where he helped quash an armed revolt by the Panamanian security forces last December without anyone being killed." [7]

Everything started to make perfect sense to me. I understood why Steele probably never pinned on his general officer star. He couldn't get congressional confirmation. Why would American politicians want people like Steele inside Iraq in such a sensitive-position after the mess from the 1980's on how not to do business? It was like the saying in psychology circles. The best indicator of future behavior is past behavior. In fact, it shined a light on many of the problems we experienced with the CPA, the people who staffed it, and the decisions they made. It turns out that much of the time the CPA was staffed by political operatives who had made terrible judgments in the past. Why should we have expected a different outcome from their help in Iraq?

The conduct of men like Kerick and Steele, under the apparent operating authority of L. Paul Bremer and the CPA, undercut trusting relationships with the U.S. Army. My MP brigade knew its mission in Iraq was to help secure the Iraqi people through their building of the Iraqi police, but all too often we ran up against interference from the CPA rather than help. I tried to develop and implement the strategies and tactics that offered the best potential at accomplishing the mission, but found many of my proposals and advice going unheeded. Even some of the soldiers under my command quickly grew to doubt the initial premise of the war itself and viewed all politicians, including those who led the CPA, as people who couldn't be trusted and who were more interested in oil resources and other agendas than the welfare of soldiers fighting the war.

Sgt. Buchmeier echoed what many of us felt as he observed our mission in Iraq from his vantage point as a soldier and MP close to the action on a daily basis:

> "As the days and weeks went on, we all kept asking where all the terrorist training camps and chemical weapons plants were that President Bush was always telling Congress about. What was really upsetting was that all of my soldiers wore Vietnam era flak jackets instead of body armor. But every time I saw an employee of Halliburton, they had body armor. It didn't make us feel very trusting!"

Increasingly frustrated, Major Hedgepeth concluded that, "the whole push for democratic policing and rule of law was pretty much a waste of time. Rebuilding the police stations, training the police, and hiring new cops, which was the focus of the 18th MP Brigade was the only effort that really impacted the security situation."

Against the backdrop of violence, military and political leaders in Washington,D.C. seemed detached and disconnected from the reality of post-invasion Iraq.

General Richard B. Myers, in his book, *Eyes On The Horizon, Serving on the Front Lines of National Security*, offered these rather naïve comments about what he thought was happening in Iraq at the time we were in the middle of "phase IV post-hostility operations when the ORHA and CPA were in charge:

> "Small-scale looting by 'couch pushers' stealing furniture from government buildings quickly gave way to organized bands of vandals stripping anything of value they could lay their hands on in ministries and hospitals,even museums. Coalition forces should have done more to stop this."[8]

There weren't enough coalition forces to manage these problems, and those that were in Iraq were not the proper mix of forces in the first place. Myers' elementary assessment of the situation was even more remarkable given the conclusions of the Defense Policy Board in a February 28, 2003 briefing, titled, *Establishing Post-Conflict Security in Iraq.* Ironically, February 28 was the exact day I moved from my temporary housing at Camp Doha, Kuwait to my intermediate staging base in the desert near the Iraqi border at Camp Virginia. I wish I would have known about this assessment at the time. Although I didn't learn of this briefing until after my retirement, I'm surprised that Myers didn't seem to be aware of its key assessments:

1.) The U.S. military administration will be responsible for security, public order, and law enforcement.

2.) There is also a distinct difference between military and police forces. Military forces are trained to concentrate mass and firepower to destroy the enemy.

3.) Police are trained to deal with civilians, to preserve and protect and to use only the amount of force required to control the situation.

4.) Establishing the rule of law at the outset will free the military to perform its duties and speed its withdrawal.[9]

If I would have known about this assessment at the time, and been given an opportunity to comment on it, I would have added a fifth comment:

5.) U.S. Army Military Police are the only part of the Army that is suited to, using the words above, "be responsible for security, public order, and law enforcement," but more importantly, "deal with civilians, to preserve and protect and to use only the amount of force required to control the situation."

Former Secretary of Defense Rumsfeld concluded as much in

his book, *Known and Unknown*. Disputing Bremer's recollections that he had recommended to the secretary that more troops were needed in Iraq in 2003, Rumsfeld confirmed the post-CPA American plan to save Iraq:

> "Since the end of the Coalition Provisional Authority in 2004, our recalibrated strategy had centered on moving responsibility to the Iraqi security forces as quickly as possible. I believed it was the right approach and would work given time and sufficient patience by the American people." [10]

This was the approach I had recommended to Lt. General Wallace early on in Baghdad and the one that the soldier police of the 18th MP Brigade tried to implement from the minute we set foot in Baghdad in May, 2003. It was clearly not the approach-being pursued by the CPA after America broke Iraq in 2003.

America's political leaders simply had no post-war plan to build a foundation for freedom and the rule of law in Iraq after the successful invasion. They failed to understand and address the challenges of standing up the Iraqi Police and the Iraqi Prison system after the ground war was over.

The Coalition Provisional Authority should have defined the desired end state of the Iraqi police, courts and prison system, but never did. This required a level of liaison and discussion on the part of the senior military and civilian leaders that never occurred. If you don't know where you are going, all roads will lead you there.

Without a desired end state and consistency of leadership, building a system to administer justice as the first step towards implanting the rule of law in Iraq never happened. During just a year of deployment in Iraq, I answered to five military and eight civilian leaders. I had multiple military and civilian bosses at any one time. All of them had great ideas but none of them ever defined a focused end state for the administration of justice in post-war Iraq.

Several decisions made by America's civilian leadership before the war and the Coalition Provisional Authority after the invasion complicated our mission. There were simply not enough military police in the theater to do the job. Senior officers within the military police provided countless risk assessments to our civilian and military leadership outlining the danger of too few military police on the ground, but our advice went unheeded. This proved costly during the invasion and slowed progress afterward in establishing law and order in Iraq's cities and towns.

Concerned that America would be viewed as an invader, civilian leaders on the ground in Iraq, led by Ambassador Paul Bremer, decided against declaring martial law and imposing a nighttime curfew. American combat forces and the military police, as well as Iraqi citizens, paid the price for his decision. My staff and I crafted a policing strategy for Baghdad, realizing we could never surrender the night to the enemy. Citizens would be terrorized by criminals and terrorists would be free to plot, plan, roam and prepare for attacks against the Americans and the Iraqi police, free from disruption. These kinds of political decisions made the nights less safe for Americans and Iraqi police.

One of Ambassador L. Paul Bremer's first decisions was to disband the Iraqi army. He followed that with the de-baathification process, where we lost some of the most senior levels of the Iraqi police. I continue to believe these officers would have been a significant help to us and wish they had remained long enough for me to sort the good from the bad. He had no one on his staff with oversight of all three of the components of a functioning criminal justice system—police, courts and prisons.

Lt. General Sanchez and Ambassador Bremer should each have had a person reporting directly to them who was responsible for the entire system of justice in Iraq. The two individuals would have been the focal point of communication between the army and the civilians. They would have been responsible for establishing the rule of law by building a system for the administration of justice. But during my entire year in Iraq, I never heard anyone recommend or propose a desired end state and articulate what was wanted in the way of police, courts and prisons.

In the very early stages of the post-invasion process, terrorists confined their attacks to coalition forces, thus not impacting the average Iraqi. It was the perfect time to select a "criminal justice guru" who could tie in the police, courts, and prison system, ensuring the overall desired end state. Identifying the "right" MP general or colonel to fulfill this role on the staff of Lt. General Sanchez, while also having access and a direct connection to Ambassador Bremer, would have made a big difference in the immediate establishment of a civilian criminal justice system, but neither the military or the CPA took the lead. To his credit, Sanchez sent a request for an MP General to become a member of his staff, but there were only two on active duty at the time, and neither one was dispatched. We desperately needed some senior MP leadership advising Sanchez, but I was in no position to push the issue, or I would have been forced to move up there—myself.

Had Ambassador Bremer clearly identified a vision of what the end state of the criminal justice system looked like, and appointed competent people to implement that vision, precious time would not have been wasted. The insurgents in Iraq would arguably never have formed the foothold that subsequently prolonged the war, increased American casualties and turned Iraqis against each other.

In a strange twist of fate, two years to the day after the attacks of 9/11, I met with one of the most interesting, and insightful Iraqis ever, Nori Badran. Even though he initially was answering to the CPA, he, "Could Produce Something." Ambassador Bremer had just named Badran to be the first post-war Iraqi Minister of Interior, the role that Bernie Kerik originally attempted to fill, when he requested to meet with me in Ahmed's office at the Police Academy.

Badran had been the Iraqi Ambassador to Afghanistan, until the Soviets invaded in 1979. Later he fled Iraq, went into exile and worked hard to overthrow Saddam. He spoke perfect English and had an excellent vision for the future of the Iraqi police. I can only imagine what could have been if we would have had his leadership once we began our occupation about four months earlier. That leadership, in conjunction with stable CPA leadership, that we never had, and the proper emphasis by Sanchez, that we never had, could have gotten the Iraqi police on the right footing from the beginning.

When I arrived for the meeting on September 11, Minister Badran was waiting for me. He was very impressive looking and sharply dressed. It was evident immediately that I was in the presence of a politician. When I entered the room with my interpreter and one member of my security team he asked me in perfect English if that was my interpreter. When I told him it was, he asked me to have him leave the room. He wanted to meet with me one on one. I told my interpreter to wait outside with my security team. I told my security member to let the team know I was okay in the room by myself, but to have one of them stand just outside the door in case I needed them.

I started the meeting by telling Badran where we currently stood with the police. I explained our mission, our task organization, our support to the police stations, and needed to know which ones he wanted us to continue to support. I briefed him on the status of the police equipment and let him know that I knew he now controlled the Iraqi police budget and that I now had to come to him to get money. I explained where we were in the training and recruiting of new police officers and the work we had done standing up the police academy. I told him about the joint operations we had been conducting with his police. I briefed him on the current police structure, and let him know there was much work still to been done and that we had a long way to go. I explained the support we were getting from the 1st Armored Division and how my military police lashed up with them. I closed out my brief with the details of the Major Crime Unit we had established and their current and future operations.

Minister Badran quickly absorbed my comments. He then spoke for the next two hours, during which time I received a professional development session equal to anythat I had received at the Army's War College. His comments were prophetic. He started out by saying we were not in normal times and starting from scratch. He said his first priority was to understand the current situation and then prioritize his resources. He needed lots of cars, and the Iraqi citizens had to cooperate with his plan, or otherwise nothing would work. We had to work as a team. He believed most of my comments fit inwell with his vision, but emphasized we needed to put his plan on paper, so it would be memorialized for the ages.

Badran went into excruciating detail on his vision. He would decree all kinds of crime in order to mobilize forces to defeat the terrorists in Iraq. First, however, we had toget crime under control. The Iraqi police stations had to be effective to do this. Terrorism was the most dangerous threat because the terrorists could bring additional assets into Iraq since the country was their main target.

Badran believed that the main effort had to focus on Baghdad and it would take a lot of resources. He said police patrol was the main tool to show Iraqis there is real authority in Baghdad and that he was big into the visibility of the police. He said that the traffic police had to be a patrol force by themselves. They were the first thing the Iraqi citizen would see in the morning on the way to work, and the last thing they would see on their way home.

Like I had said so many times, Badran said the police had to have the trust of Iraqi citizen to achieve security and support against terrorism. He wanted to control the border of Iraq. He said if we calmed Baghdad, the other provinces of Iraq would be calmed as well. He wanted local police to handle local problems. He felt the local people would come forward, if they saw the local police solving their problems, not outsiders. He wanted to bring back the local mayor concept. He said the only job Saddam failed to impose on the Iraqi people was the local mayor. Saddam never screwed with the local mayor. He said his vision was simple and clear, and we were already way behind. He was exactly right!

Badran felt it would take time to change the way detention operations were conducted before the war, such as family members bringing food to the jails. He was getting lots of citizen complaints because bad guys were being released, which was a function of an inadequate court and prison system. He wanted detainees kept at the police stations until investigations were complete. He wanted records of detainees kept to a minimum because Saddam kept too many records.

He wanted to coordinate my military police role with him. He asked me to pull my MPs out of the police stations because it looked like we were propping up the police, which we were. He said that didn't help the confidence of the Iraqi people. I told him his police were not ready for my MPs to be removed from the police stations, but he said he wanted to do it anyway. I told him I would think about it, but I thought it was a mistake. At the time I intended to ignore that part of his vision, because I knew it would be a mistake.

Ambassador Bremer eventually revisited the issue with me and directed that I pull my MPs from the police stations. I explained to him why such a move would be a big mistake.

Bremer said he needed to support Minister Badran. In Bremer's subsequent book, he talks about pulling the MPs out of the police stations over my strong objections.

Badran expressed his views on police training. He said he would put together a training plan, and we must be able to evaluate its effectiveness. He said he would determine police training needs, and decide if he wanted to send them somewhere else to train. Not long after this, some of the police went to Jordan to train. He wanted to train current Iraqi police before hiring new officers. He then asked for my help in assessing what was currently going wrong. He said we couldn't give any one person too much authority because that caused corruption, and that we had agree on the right level of authority, so that the police couldn't get away with anything.

From our initial meeting until my departure I periodically met with Minister Badran. We attended several joint meetings together. I was always impressed with his understanding of the Iraqi people and police. I learned a tremendous amount from him. Unfortunately, I wasn't smart enough to use him to get some of my agenda items approved. I simply didn't want to do an end run on my military bosses.

My involvement with him nearly backfired. When he learned of my redeployment, he asked to see me. When I met with him, he wanted me to know that he was going to ask Ambassador Bremer to talk to General Sanchez to request that I stay in Iraq and work with him. I was stunned! I asked him why he would do that. He told me that I understood the Iraqi people and the Iraqi police and the senior Iraqi police leadership didn't want me to leave.

I quickly had to figure out how I was going to get out of this mess. I explained to him that my brigade was redeploying to Germany and I needed to return with them, because as soon as I returned, we were going to start training additional units to deploy to Iraq. That was true, even though I knew I would have more than adequate leadership in Germany that could train the follow-on forces. I held my breath as he thought about what I was saying. I knew that if he requested of Bremer that I stay in Iraq, I would endup being a brigade commander without a brigade. I was relieved when he said he understood and would not make his request to Ambassador Bremer.

In peacetime, the MPs are the experts on policing and prisons. Combat arms leaders usually listen to their advice and consul. But in Iraq, the MPs were not represented at a high level on the staff of Lt. General Sanchez. Sanchez never gave credence to the advice I gave him that might have assisted in turning from combat arms to a civilian policing mode. I believe had he done so we would have improved our chances for the host nation to embrace a "buy-in" of an approach designed to secure citizen cooperation and understanding of our mission. The lack of support from Lt.General Sanchez and Bremer's CPA for our approach contributed to a missed opportunity, longer war, and ancillary crises like the torture scandal. We have only people like Bremer, Lt. General Sanchez, Kerik and Steele to thank for that.

CHAPTER SEVEN: NOTES
1 "It Worked For Me," by Colin Powell, published by Harper, May 22, 2012.
2 "Known and Unknown, A Memoir," by Donald Rumsfeld, published by Sentinel, February 8, 2011.
3 "Decision Points," by George W. Bush, published by Crown, November 9, 2010.
4 Newsweek, Fareed Zakaria, September 1, 2003.
5 Premiere, Motivational Speaker/Jim Steele/Jim Steele Biography, May, 2003.
6 Chicago Tribune, July 7, 1991, "Testimony on Contras Still Haunts Colonel," by Christopher Drew.
7 Ibid, End Note # 5.
8 "Eyes On The Horizon: Serving On the Front Line of National Security," Threshold Editions, March 17, 2009, by Richard Myers and Malcolm McConnell.
9 Defense Policy Board, February 28, 2003, "Establishing Post-Conflict Security in Iraq,"
10 Ibid, End Note #1.

CHAPTER EIGHT

BERNIE KERIK, "THE COMMISSIONER"

Former NYPD Commissioner Bernie Kerik rolled into and out of Iraq with his agenda.

I'd never met Bernie Kerik, but like most people, had heard his name and could spot his serious scowl from a mile away. As I watched him on television before I ever ran into him in Iraq, I always thought he'd be a great guy to have a beer with. Once Bernie and I got to know one another, I still would have a beer with him. But before leaving the bar, I'd just look back one more time to make sure he didn't pick up the tip I left for the bartender.

In Iraq, whenever I wanted to find Bernie Kerik, all I had to do was look for the lights, cameras, action, reporters and Associated Press. For the national and international news media, keeping up with the former New York City Police Commissioner was like the pot of gold at the end of the rainbow and could reap big rewards. Kerik loved commenting for the evening news and made himself available and accessible for any cameras that needed his picture.

When President George W. Bush tapped him to oversee the rebuilding of the Iraqi Police in May, 2003, Kerik wasted little time getting to the press, telling the *New York Daily News* he'd be in Iraq, "in excess of six months, but no one really knows…as long as it takes to get the job done."[1]

Kerick left Iraq years ago and there is still wide ranging debate among those of us who knew and worked with him on exactly what his job was and what he did during his short tenure in Baghdad.

Kerik was a policeman, politician, and magic act. When it served his purpose, Kerik was easy to find. When it didn't, he was all but invisible. The media was mesmerized by the Kerick show and naïve in its addiction to his illusions. No one really knew the real Bernie Kerik, nor fully understood the difference between what he said and what he did.

In a twist of irony, Bernie and I found that we shared some common background.

He had joined the U.S. Army in 1974 and subsequently became a Military Police Officer. He was initially stationed in South Korea, but in early 1976 was reassigned to the 21st Military Police Company, part of the 503rd Military Police Battalion, at Ft. Bragg, North Carolina. I was the Commander of the 21st MP Company in 1982-1983, and the 503rd was one of my Battalions in Iraq for a short period of time.

After the 9/11 terrorist attacks on the World Trade Center, Mayor Rudy Guiliani instantly became "America's Mayor" and a personification of leadership. He was everywhere after the tragedy, consoling victims and their families at Ground Zero, comforting New York City citizens, standing alongside a reassuring President Bush vowing to seek justice. Always somewhere close to the mayor was Bernie Kerik, wearing the serious face that seemed to combine the best theatrical portrayal of the perfect cop from *Criminal Minds*, *Law and Order* and *NYPD Blue*.

Mayor Guiliani and Bernie Kerik were seemingly inseparable. When the mayor appealed for the public's help a day after 9/11, Kerik stood behind him. A month later Kerik took the podium with Mayor Guiliani to answer questions about the anthrax attacks along America's eastern seaboard. In January, 2002, Kerik joined and became a co-founder of Guiliani Partners. The firm describes itself as, "dedicated to helping leaders solve critical strategic issues, accelerate growth, and enhance the reputation and brand of their organizations in the context of strongly held values."[2]

The media gushingly followed Kerik into his new position in Iraq. His title was almost as big as his ego, "Senior Policy Advisor to the United States Presidential Envoy of Iraq, Coalition Provisional Authority, Ministry of Interior, Republican Guard Presidential Palace, Baghdad, Iraq."

To actually do the job, Kerik had to have at least some knowledge of the facts on the ground. On May 22, the day after I met him at the ribbon cutting ceremony at my first regional jail, he tracked me down in my office to get some of those facts. My first impression of Kerik when he came to me to discuss training and rebuilding the Iraqi police was that he was one of the most charismatic people I've ever been around. He gave me a hat and T-shirt from the New York City Police Department, and a signed copy of his book, *The Lost Son, A Life in Pursuit of Justice*, an ironic title given his current location.

"Ted, all the best and thanks for everything, Bernie," he wrote inside the front cover.

Two hours after I provided him with the facts, Kerik appeared on NBC's *Today Show*, where he was interviewed by Matt Lauer.

"We—we've heard…from a military point of view, that Iraq and Baghdad are still very dangerous places…You've been there just over a week now. What are your impressions?" Lauer treated Kerik as if his responses should be considered gospel.

"…There is a lot of resistance out there yet…those that were in power in the past, those that are losing their power… they come out and resist," Kerik answered solemnly.

"You're talking members of the Baath Party…How do you go about getting at those people?" Lauer asked.

"Weapons all over the country will be confiscated…This morning I met with Major Boice and Colonel Spain in charge of the 18th Military Police Brigade here in Baghdad with the ambassador. We're enhancing patrols and mixing the MPs with the Iraqi Police that are coming back to work…Things should be getting better in the very near future." Kerik thought his own credibility would be enhanced if he invoked my name. Kerik went on to say other things about Iraq, some of which I was hearing for thevery first time.[3]

Later, Kerik visited my office again.

I stayed behind my desk and looked up from him, trying to maintain a professional demeanor but frowning nonetheless.

"Bernie, I saw you on the *Today Show*. You lied to the American people. I know you lied, but you were very convincing."

I paused and watched for any reaction from the former top cop.

"Guliani did that to me." Kerik's smile grew larger before his split second response, taking great pleasure in my assessment of his television interview.

"Well, you are not Guliani, and I am not you," I reprimanded Kerik,who wasn't used to being exposed to non-worshippers.

Kerik had keen instincts, sharpened from his political knife fights. He immediately picked up on my contempt for his manipulative behavior. As we continued our shortened meeting, Kerik quietly studied me as he sat across from my desk. He reacted to my comments and feelings by turning up his charisma, flashing his magic smile, and mentally backslapping my shoulder. It was clear he was momentarily puzzled by why an army colonel from the deep south would get so upset at such a small display of no integrity.

After all, it was Kerik's job to get the media's attention and make sure that it reported only the good things to the people back home. In Kerik's eyes, there was no downside to his little lies or whatever I chose to call them, because America was at war and the kind of lies Kerik told were for the good of the war effort. Kerik cast a look at me that conveyed a clear message—he would keep a careful eye on me and what I was doing in my job. I returned the glance so that he would get an equally clear message from me—I would maintain Bernie Kerik at a safe distance from my soldiers and make sure that he didn't get in our way. Kerik would let me know from time to time that he wasn't very happy with me for it!

Iraq became a whistle stop for Kerik on the way to bigger and better things, at least that is what I believe he was thinking. Touching down on the tarmac in late May, by early September, Bernie Kerik departed Iraq as quickly as he had entered the country. There are many people still asking what Kerik was sent to Iraq to do in the first place. Far fewer care to debate the proposition that he did nothing, except create the potential for problems for someone else. As I look back on Kerik's focus while he was in Iraq, it seems pretty apparent that Kerik did little to nothing to help rebuild the Iraqi police, which was his ostensible mission when he arrived. At least that is what the administration and Kerik always said he was there to accomplish. But there is no question in my mind that Kerik had a specific agenda, and he worked hard to implement his agenda during the ninety or so days he was inside Iraq. It's just that Kerik's agenda had little to do with the mission his country allegedly sent him to Iraq to get done. Events on the ground led me to conclude that Kerik had six goals while he was in Iraq.

(1.) Kerik spent his days in Iraq as a cheerleader and spokesperson for the Bush administration. He was a master at charming the news media and directing them at whatever message(s) the administration wanted delivered to the people back home. Kerik didn't mind being deceitful to get the job done. Since he had the knack to sell beachfront property to a Missouri pig farmer, he always got rewarded for his deceptions.

Take the example of one of our earlier press conferences. In late May, I was summoned to Ambassador Paul Bremer's office and told to prepare a briefing on developments in standing up the

Iraqi Police. The television news show, *20/20* planned to spend May 27 with the ambassador and Kerik. Bremer wanted to share success stories with the American people, stressing that the security situation in Iraq was getting under control. He decided having me give him and Kerik an update on National TV would help him get his message out.

I called my staff together to prepare for the event.

"Bremer and Kerik will be with the *20/20* crew. We'll want to brief police patrols, weapons, Task Force Vigilant Justice, uniform and joint patrols. I want to emphasize the MP capability to shoot, move, and communicate."

My staff knew exactly what I wanted. On the combat side of the MP house, the descriptive language referred to the adaptability and versatility of the MP force to possess large quantities of quality weapons systems and superior mobility to move around a battlefield or through a city of civilians. Complemented by a highly functioning radio network, my MPs could respond quickly to any type of hot spot and bring whatever type of force necessary to answer a variety of crises. Unlike the rest of the army, their training and prior experience helped them think like street cops and bring cop like solutions to citizen problems. The difference was crucial if Iraqi citizens were to ever grasp the concept that the rule of law trumped the corruption and brute force of any government. I didn't want anything, including our discipline and even the way our office space looked, to stand in the way of that message. Most important, I believed in sticking with the facts, giving the right answers to media questions and telling the truth about the situation we faced in Iraq. Our pre-meeting was vital if my MPs and I were to be speaking from the same sheet of music.

I knew that Bremer and Kerik would ask me to quantify the amount of crime occurring in Baghdad prior to the invasion and afterwards. I had no intention of appearing on national television to tout crime statistics. This was just the first of many occasions where officials of the United States government encouraged such comparisons to let American citizens know the situation in Iraq was improving.

The news media, the Coalition Provisional Authority, Secretary of Defense Donald Rumsfeld, Bremer, Kerik, and Sanchez all desired to use any statistical reduction in crime as proof that security in Baghdad was better after the occupation and that Iraq was getting safer every day. I have always been a firm believer in the old saying that statistics lie and liars use statistics. I didn't plan on becoming a liar so I decided to talk about conditions in Baghdad when we arrived versus how they were each time we gave a press conference.

Each month we were in Iraq, things seemed to be getting a little better so that's the message I liked to give to people whenever they asked questions that begged me to argue with statistics.

Ironically, during a visit by President Bush visit on Thanksgiving Day, Ambassador Bremer walked up to me and said, "We've come a long way since we first met."

I agreed with him and said that I measured success by conditions on the ground, as opposed to statistics. He said he did the same thing, but I think it was the politician in him that made the comment.

Everyone was under tremendous pressure whenever we held media conferences in Iraq, but I had studied math and psychology statistics in earning my undergraduate and master's degrees and decided to stick to my guns. I adamantly refused to become a mouth piece for the statistics crowd. There were enough positive things to talk about inIraq without having to embellish the facts. It would become the mantra for me and my soldiers during our stay in Iraq.

At the time of the *20/20* broadcast, the Bush Administration needed repairs to its public image. The debate over the merits and wisdom of the military invasion of Iraq was just starting. The underpinning of the justification for war, Saddam's possession of weapons of mass destruction and the desire to use them, was weakening as each day passed. We weren't finding any such weapons on the ground, nor any indicators that Iraq ever did possess them.

Even though I was absolutely convinced they existed when we invaded, even I started to question the likelihood as each day passed. I turned to Tom Evans not too long after our move to Baghdad and said, "Wouldn't that be something if we don't find any type of weapon of mass destruction?"

Even then I thought it would be just a matter of time before we did, then the invasion would be justified to the American people. Sadly, that day never came.

If there was any doubt as to why Kerik was selected to come to Iraq as the Bush Administration point man on the rebuilding of the Iraqi police, the reason was obvious after the *20/20* briefing. Kerik lied to people in the way he manipulated crime statisticsthat I had provided to him. I had to focus so much on what Kerik said to avoid being taken in by his mis-statements that I decided never again to do a news related briefing with him. Kerik was constantly upset with me over the differences in our views of the crime stats. But at the *20/20* briefing, Ambassador Bremer and Bernie Kerik came through for the president. My wife spoke with many of my relatives and friends in the states following the airing of the *20/20* show and all of them told her the show seemed to go very well.

Reluctantly, I would have to admit that the *20/20* briefing appeared to be one of the best success stories of the time. But the attention from the media kept coming. During my nightly update to General Wallace on May 27, after I briefed the daily events, including the *20/20* interview I told the boss, "David Martin from *CBS News* will be with metomorrow."

Even though these were high risks meetings, the potential pay off of getting the positive story of what my brave men and women were doing, was worth the risk. Another day of high adventure.

(2.) Kerik didn't come to Iraq to help rebuild the Iraqi police with their buy in. He tried to control the police through his involvement in the selection process for the chief. Kerik placed himself in the middle of our carefully crafted effort to identify a new chief for the Iraqi police. He so subverted the selection process that our ultimate choice was severely hampered in his attempts to do the job.

Unfortunately, behind the scenes the decisions Kerik was making on his own or as a front man for the administration, Bremer or the CIA were negatively impacting our MP efforts to rebuild, re-staff and reorganize the police. There was no area where this became more obvious than in our selection of a new police chief for Baghdad. Kerik destroyed the integrity of our selection process through his unwarranted intervention.

After the infamous ribbon cutting media event, Kerik became tight with Ahmed, to the dismay of other Iraqi police officers. There were many of them who didn't like or trust Ahmed, referring to him as "little Saddam," because of his striking resemblance to Iraq's former ruler.

Nonetheless, through Kerik's influence, Ahmed became a very powerful force in Iraq. Ahmed often accompanied Kerik and James Steele on all night operations that were never cleared with or coordinated with the United States Army or the military police. Suffice it to say that Steele was more of a political operative and holdover from previous scandals that scalded the U.S. government and some of its highest officials during Iran Contra.

Most of the time we didn't know what Kerik, Steele and Ahmed were doing, but I soon figured it out. Occasionally, Kerik had no choice but to request our assistance. On August 30, just four days before leaving Iraq, during my nightly update to General Dempsey, I briefed:

"Bernie Kerik called the TOC this afternoon to request support—a raid was conducted this morning by Jim Steele and Iraqi police and they picked up four detainees during questioning one of the detainees allegedly admitted to carrying out an attack on a U. S. soldier here in Baghdad about three weeks ago—based on this info we picked up all four detainees and are currently moving them to the DIF."

Since Kerik missed so many scheduled meetings during the day, I could only reach one conclusion. He was up all night running operations and inserting himself into the business of the U. S. Army and Iraqi police who worked with us. Kerik slept all day to get ready for his activities on the next night. But he never told us what those activities were or what he was doing. Ahmed obviously knew the answers to our concerns, but never cooperated with us long enough to tell us what he and Kerik were up to most of the time. Kerik's relationship with Ahmed, so distrusted by mainstream Iraqi police who were working with us to rebuild the police force, became a constant source of tension and conflict.

I concluded that Steele, Kerik, and Ahmed were out conducting operations with the CIA. In fact, Ahmed was slightly wounded during one of these late night adventures. I was forced to maneuver through countless decisions made by Kerik that led to frequent collisions with the interests of the army, including delays in appointing a new police chief for Baghdad.

Kerik followed up on his developing relationship with Ahmed by promoting him to Brigadier General of the Iraqi Police Academy on June 12. An opening developed at the academy when the Iraqi Police General running the academy before the war was arrested for being an active Baath Party member. I was certain that the information creating the opening had been given by the CIA to Kerik and Steele. Shortly afterward, the Iraqi police chief for East Baghdad was retired through pressures from the CPA because he also had previous involvement with the Ba'ath Party. Subsequently, Kerik told me to develop a retirement program for all of the Iraqi police officials with the rank of colonel or above before the war. The program was intended to complement the initiative undertaken by Bremer to strip all of the top three levels of Baath Party officials from positions in the government and police.

All of these moves made it more difficult for us to stand up the Iraqi Police. Iraqi police generals consistently told me that they had no choice but to belong to the Ba'ath Party under Saddam or they would be killed. Many of these senior people were respected by the police rank and file and having to re-establish the police without them delayed progress. So I was pleased when Kerik approached me one day in early July to tell me that General Jamal would be announced by Ambassador Bremer as the next Chief of Police of Baghdad.

I had always liked Jamal and had a great deal of trust in him from our first meeting. I also knew that Jamal was well regarded by others in the police force. I was especially pleased that with Jamal's appointment as chief there would be a single point of contact within the Baghdad police department, simplifying my efforts to coordinate a variety of operational and administrative needs between the army and the police. I briefed Major General Dempsey that Jamal would be our choice to be police chief of Baghdad.

Jamal never got the job during my time in Iraq. Just hours before the announcement was to be made, someone showed Kerik a video of Jamal encouraging Iraqi police to resist the American invasion force. Jamal later explained to me that he had to tell the police to resist or be killed by Saddam. I believe that Ahmed was the individual who showed Kerik the video. Ahmed let it be known that Jamal punished many Iraqi police officers before the war began. Ahmed's motives were pretty easy to figure out. He wanted to be the police chief of Baghdad and would do anything to eliminate the competition.

The 709th's Battalion Commander, Lt. Colonel Garrity kept Jamal as his advisor after Kerik forced his retirement from the Iraqi Police. I had to return to Major General Dempsey to tell him that Jamal would not become the Baghdad police chief. I also had to tell Jamal. I recall his concerns after we discussed the issue.

"Colonel Spain, if not the chief position, what is my future?"

Jamal knew that Ambassador Paul Bremer had set up a "city council," and that everyone who came before the council alleged that when Jamal ran the intelligence section of the police department and was Chief of Patrol, he supervised executions. To be in such an influential position, they concluded he had to be a member of the Baath Party. I didn't have any encouraging response to Jamal's worries.

Although my time in Iraq convinced me that Jamal would have been the best police chief and accepted by the new police force and local citizens, there was no future for Jamal as long as Kerik was in town. Ironically Jamal later became a senior leader of the police, after my departure.

A few months after I left Iraq I was sitting in my office in Mannheim, Germany and received a call from Major General Ryder. When I answered the phone he said someone wanted to talk to me. It turned out General Ryder was at a police conference in England and met General Jamal. When Jamal found out Ryder was an American MP General he asked him if he knew me. Not only did Ryder know me, he got me on the phone with Jamal. It was so wonderful to talk to an old friend. The last time I had spoken to Jamal was the day before I departed Iraq. As we said our goodbyes he told me his dream was to pick me and my wife up at the Baghdad airport one day. I told him that was my dream also. He is currently in exile in Dubai, but I hope he still has his dream. I do.

Kerik told me that Jamal could never compete for chief of the Baghdad police and established a four person panel to interview other candidates for the position. Kerik wanted Ahmed to be the Baghdad police chief, but he wanted it to appear to be fair. To Kerik the ends always justified the means, so he had us conduct what he thought was going to be a sham selection board, but it back fired on him. But as always, he got the last laugh.

Gerald Burke, David Barlow, Douglas Brand and I were selected to conduct the interviews of three finalists. In addition to Ahmed, whom Kerik wanted as a candidate for chief, Iraqi Police Brigadier Generals Salah, and Hassan were the finalists in the selection process. The interviews gave all of us great insight into Iraqi society and the pressures on everyone during Saddam's reign.

During his interview Ahmed stressed that he was never a Ba'ath Party member.

"Most of the high level leadership is Ba'athist. The gossip will come against me, but what prove me are my deeds and not the words of others."

Ahmed told us he had worked as a police officer in Iraq as a young man until 1979 when he was alleged by the regime to have made a statement that Saddam was a bad leader. When the Iraqi intelligence service caught wind of his comment, he was arrested and placed into a small jail that more closely resembled a cage. After being confined for a year and subjected to various forms of torture. Ahmed was released and ordered to work in a civilian job until he was placed back in the military and sent to Kuwait in 1991 during the first Gulf war. Afterwards he was sent to northern Iraq to fight against the Iranians. Ten years later he was allowed to resume a career as an Iraqi police official.

Ahmed told the panel of his intense hatred for the Ba'ath Party, which stemmed from his witnessing of the hangings of nine people who were executed as Israeli spies inthe 1970s and left hanging in a square where their bodies were guarded for two days.

"It was a horrifying sight," he said, describing the moment as the time he started hating the Ba'ath Party and all it stood for.

Ahmed appealed to our panel that he wanted to lead the police in a way that would encourage citizen trust and pleaded,

"Please don't believe the gossip. Ask me directly. I will know the truth."

Unlike Ahmed, the second candidate, Brigadier General Hassan had been an active member of the Ba'ath Party. "I am a government employee, I had to," he explained to us.

Hassan came from a police family. His father had been appointed a policeman by the British when they first came to Iraq. Hassan graduated from the Iraqi Police Academy in 1972, working in several Iraqi cities afterwards. He felt a close connection to the Iraqi police at every level.

"I was a very good officer and there was never any negative connotations and have always been a police officer only. As an officer, commander, and director of an administrative unit, I have been able to get the trust of all people. Even those sentenced considered me to be a colleague."

Hassan acknowledged that Saddam and the Ba'ath Party brought bad times to Iraq and its citizens. The police were often caught in the middle of things and always under the vigilance of Saddam's intelligence services.

"In the beginning of the 70's there was a security service so my friends and Iwould talk that this man's hands were tainted with blood and we expected things to happen from wars to executions so we were very careful to try and help people not make mistakes to cause them to get into trouble."

Hassan explained to our interview panel that his goals were to modernize the Iraqi police, get police patrols out with the citizens and to improve pay, clothing and equipment. Most important in his view was to "organize the police life and choosing the good police and giving security and safety to the society because we can't provide this if the police are not of good ethics and work."

Like Hassan, the third candidate, Brigadier General Salah had been a member of the Ba'ath Party because, "they would never allow me to have a position without it."

Salah became a policeman in 1978 and was sent off to an intelligence post within the police department. He didn't want to work in the intelligence area and after a year was brought back to the regular police. In the intelligence department he strongly disliked the "monitoring, follow-up and playing with people."

Salah told our panel there was nothing about the Saddam regime that was good and that everything was centered on fear and terror.

"I saw torture and there were things outside the law that were being done. The police right now are under the rule of law, they weren't then."

Salah expressed pride in the reputation he had established with his fellow Iraqi policemen.

"They like me because I have never harmed anybody all my life and have never harmed anyone and have only done the truth."

Our panel's choice was unanimous after the interviews. Brigadier General Hassan was recommended to Kerik and the CPA as our choice to be the new Baghdad Police Chief. I gave the news of the panel's choice to Major General Dempsey, only to learn that the entire process had been a sham. Although Kerik approved the selection of Hassan, he designated him a two star general while promoting Ahmed to a three star position working directly for Kerik as an advisor.

Hassan then became a direct report to Ahmed, completely compromising the work of the panel and our final choice as chief. Kerik's decision set the stage for continuing conflict with me and the senior leaders of my brigade, as we were trying to bring cohesion and clarity to the rebuilding of the Iraqi police. Kerik just couldn't be trusted to pursue any of the issues plaguing the Iraqi police with integrity, but could be counted onto aggressively pursue his own agenda.

(3.) Kerik skillfully cultivated Ahmed as his "source" of information from inside the Iraqi police. He used that information to organize his personal police "operations" without any coordination or communication with me, putting American troops at risk.

For example, Kerik asked me to provide him with an MP "liaison officer" who could serve as a planner, but I knew any of my soldiers assigned to Kerik would be used as "flunkies" and I refused to come through. My notes from June 12 mentioned that I really needed a liaison officer/planner at CPA but there was nowhere for them to operate that would get them far enough away from the influence of Kerik. Unfortunately, I concluded that the lesser of the two evils was to just not have anyone permanently sitting in CPA, even though I needed someone.

My defiance angered Kerik, who brought the issue up repeatedly while we were in Iraq, but I was never ordered by my military chain of command to provide one.

Captain Ann Dunscombe was one of my MP officers who worked most frequently with Kerik, even though I never allowed her to have any office space at CPA. Her experience working with Kerik sheds light on his character and style. She later said:

> "Kerik was in charge of the Ministry of the Interior. He operated out of the Coalition Provisional Authority with the guys from the Department of Justice. Kerik used the South African mercenary guards and spent a lot of time with Ahmed and working with Bremer. He neglected a lot of other portions of the ministry and that caused problems. He never delegated authority to anyone and he never

showed up at meetings to make decisions. From a military standpoint it wasn't very productive. I had to go to him to get money for contracts and was always amazed that he kept stacks of money in a water box under his desk."

It was difficult to find Iraqis appreciative of their new found freedom because it came with such a high price tag. Many believed they traded their fear of Saddam for fear of violent criminals and a variety of terrorists, supporting one cause or another.

I circulated constantly among Iraqi citizens and always heard the same concerns, they frequently told me about something good they had under Saddam that they didn't have after we invaded. They never identified things they had after the invasion that were good that they didn't already have under Saddam. It was enough to really frustrate me and my MPs.

Kerik's solution to dealing with some of the more violent criminals and terrorist issues was to identify Iraqi police to put on his "special team." He wanted to staff his own Major Crimes Unit, independent of the Iraqi Police and asked me to provide names of Iraqi police fit for such an assignment.

I refused to cooperate with Kerik's request. I think Jim Steele was behind Kerik's build-up of a special police squad and simply wanted to conduct his own operations based on information he was getting from intelligence agencies. Kerik and Steele were loose cannons. Their conduct constantly placed my soldiers at risk. The same was true with Kerik's desire to establish an amnesty program. There was much discussion about giving the bad guys amnesty for some of the things they had done in Iraq. Kerik thought he would buy loyalty with the amnesty idea, as well as information.

I completely disagreed with Kerik on this issue as well, telling him the military and I were adamant that no Iraqis would ever get amnesty for killing or trying to kill American soldiers.

(4.) One of the issues Kerik worked harder than many others from the day he arrived in Iraq, was implementing a contract with Motorola to supply the Iraqi police with radios. I had deep concerns about Kerik's aggressive efforts. I believe the entire Motorola contract was shaky and if we could have run the rabbit far enough down the hole we would have found plenty of things wrong with his involvement in it. Within days of his arrival in Iraq, Kerik participated in a Department of Defense Central Command briefing with Lieutenant General McKiernan, the Commander of the CFLCC. Before he answered any press questions, Kerik provided some introductory comments intended to provide an overview of his major objectives in rebuilding the Iraqi police:

> "I had the opportunity this afternoon to meet with several of the commanders of the Iraqi Police Service...I informed them...they will be receiving a new radio system; that we now have people in Baghdad from Motorola that will be implementing the system, putting in the technology they need to communicate with each other."[4]

Kerik was referring to a specific $15.8 million contract between the Pentagon and Motorola to furnish the Iraqi Police Force with a radio system in Baghdad. Kerik was no stranger to Motorola Corporation.

In 1997 when Rudy Giuliani was mayor, he made the decision to place the New York City Office of Emergency Management on the 23rd floor of 7 World Trade Center. Diesel fuel tanks were placed inside 7 World Trade to power the office in the event of an outage. One of the functions of the office was to coordinate police and fire services throughout New York City during any type of emergency. Early in 2001 New York City entered into a no-bid contract with Motorola, to replace the fire department's old analog radio system, which had failed to operate properly during the first terrorist bombing attack on the World Trade Center in 1993.

The Motorola system was never field tested before its installation and it too failed to work properly. The system was recalled and the old analog radios, which had failed during the first World Trade Center attack in 1993 were reinstalled. Thus, it was the same old radio system that failed during the 1993 terrorist attack that was in use during the 9/11 attacks.

When chiefs from the New York City Fire Department ordered firefighters to evacuate the towers on 9/11, the orders were never heard. During the collapse of the towers, 343 firefighters died. Subsequently, memos surfaced that had been written by the first Director of New York City's Office of Emergency Management and the New York City Police Department showing they had recommended against the location of the office in the World Trade Center because it had been a target of terrorists, preferring a location in Brooklyn instead. Giuliani overrode their recommendations.

Only eight months after the 9/11 attacks, and a year before Kerik went to Iraq, Nextel and Giuliani Partners entered into a strategic alliance. All of Nextel's phones were made by Motorola. According to a press release issued by Nextel on May 2, 2002:

"The public safety community is facing two critical communications challenges—the need to resolve interference to their communications systems and to allow for instant, rapid, secure communications capabilities between public safety authorities across multiple jurisdictions... The effort will be supported by the extensive public safety background and experience of senior executives from Giuliani Partners including New York City's former Police Commissioner Bernard Kerik... former Fire Commissioner Thomas Von Essen."[5]

(5.) Another issue I had real concerns about was Kerik's efforts to enter into a contract to acquire thousands of glock pistols for the Iraqi police. It appeared to me he was far too wedded to this ill conceived plan.

Kerik's insistence about entering into a contract to procure the glocks never let up while he was in Iraq. First and foremost, the glock was not the right pistol for the poorly trained Iraqi police. The glock had no external safety. Employing the safety involved the trigger. Once the shooter placed their finger on the trigger, the safety was already disengaged. The glock was simply an unsafe weapon at that point for untrained or poorly trained people, like the Iraqi police. Even my highly trained soldiers used the safer to operate 9MM pistol.

Nonetheless, on September 17, exactly two weeks after Kerik departed Iraq, I briefed General Dempsey that CPA had received 10,000 glocks for the police across Iraq and that half of those were going to stay in Baghdad. We immediately went to work to attempt to mitigate the safety concerns. We started glock weapons training to teach some Iraqi police the basic skills needed to operate and maintain their new pistols. By September 27, with the help of glock representatives, we completed training of 400 Iraqi police officers and some of my military police so that they could handle and teach further glock training to the Iraqi police.

Amazingly, we ran into numerous snags in getting CPA to issue the glocks, reinforcing the synonym we used to describe the CPA— "can't produce anything." September and October went by without the pistols being issued. We were setting up ranges and preparing to qualify the police once we were given the go ahead. Even the police generals were constantly asking me when they would get the pistols. Two months after Kerik departed Iraq I finally briefed General Dempsey on November 11 that we had 5640 glocks and as the Iraqi police qualified with them, we issued them.

(6.) Yet another issue that concerned me was the procurement of 1000 M16s for the Iraqi Police. To this day, I am unable to understand the reasoning behind this decision. I found out about the M16s just as Bernie was leaving Iraq. I'm not sure about his involvement. I suspect that his running buddy, Jim Steele, was involved with procuring the weapons. I expressed my disagreement up the CPA chain and my own military chain. I knew the enemy could easily get their hands on some of these M16s, commit murders, and blame it on the American soldiers. My disagreement is very apparent in my briefing to General Dempsey on September 6:

"As directed, we picked up 1000 M16s and dropped 600 of them off at the police academy—the rest are going up North—I called the Minister of Interior's office and requested input on the distribution of these M16s. I will get back to the 1AD when they approve the distribution plan."

I had been ordered to pick up the M16s, so I thought the least I could do was try to influence who would use them. I recommended they only be used by the special police, not the normal police. During my last few visits to the police academy before I departed Iraq I saw the guards around the academy carrying some of these M16s. To my knowledge they had never even fired them. In my meeting with Minister Badran, he asked me to get him ammunition for them. I'm not sure of any role he played in obtaining the weapons either. In my final attempt to establish some type of accountability I briefed General Dempsey on September 12:

"We inventoried the 600 M16s the Iraqi police have at the Police Academy and have recorded all serial numbers. I sent an email to the CJTF7 PM to ensure he knew the weapons were there and recommended they use them for their special units, across Iraq."

I can't even imagine how these weapons have been used over the years. In hindsight, the judgment of all three men looks terribly flawed. Kerik brought the same poor judgment with him to Baghdad, with a priority to secure Motorola's interests there. He left the country quite abruptly, as suddenly as he came.

In a final flurry directed at me, Kerik was angry that I had challenged him on the location of priceless Iraqi artifacts recovered in a raid which were supposed to have been placed in appropriate secure storage facilities but wound up instead, in Kerik's office.

In a September 2, 2003 e-mail addressed to "Colonel Spain," Kerik spent four paragraphs chastising me for the alleged failure of Baghdad Police Chief Hassan to follow Ahmed's orders, stating in his e-mail, "Make no mistake that there is an Iraqi chain of command and in so, General al-Obeidi (Hassan) reports to and must obey the commands of the Interior Minister and Deputies. Failure to do so cannot be tolerated."

Sandwiched within the chain of command warnings, Kerik gave this explanationof the artifacts:

"...based on our conversation of late yesterday, there are several priceless items that were recovered during the arrests of a violent kidnapping group...Because Ibrahim (Ahmed) didn't feel comfortable securing them in the property room, safe. Or whatever location is maintained at the academy, he had them delivered to me in my office and I in turn personally turned them over to Ambassador Bremer."

The next day, Kerik departed Iraq and never came back. The total time he spent with us was less than three months. Ahmed eventually left Iraq and ended up in New York City, where he still resides today on the Upper East Side. Ahmed was a well intended person that I personally like, but had simply been promoted beyond his abilities, not unlike a few Army generals I've seen in my career, a couple of which are mentioned in this book.

Even though I personally liked Bernie, I professionally disagreed with much of what he did. I strongly disagree with the old saying, "the end justifies the means," if the means are illegal, immoral, unethical, or reflect poor leadership. Not everything or every idea Bernie Kerik had was a bad one. Kerik traveled back to New York City while he was working in Iraq to attend an International Donor Conference pledging to get us police cars, motorcycles, boats and police gear donated to the Iraqi Police. He went to the networks emphasizing the mission. But we received absolutely nothing from his travel or attendance at the conference. I have to give him credit for trying.

After the Baghdad Chief of Police was finally selected, Kerik turned his attention to some of the real issues confronting the Iraqi Police as we worked to rebuild the force. Following our invasion, many of the cops had disappeared, so a major push was mounted to identify and encourage them to return to the force. At least 200 more police cars were necessary if Iraqis were to hit the streets with patrols—a function they had to be taught. Before the war, Iraqi police simply sat inside the police stations waiting for citizens to come and report crimes. Patrol was a uniquely American policing concept that they needed to learn and integrate into their policing strategy.

Kerik supported a reward program to buy criminal intelligence. It was vital that Iraqi citizens report criminal behavior and the locations of terrorists to their newly rebuilt police departments. A variety of "thugs" had taken advantage of the invasion to prey on their fellow citizens, stealing from businesses and attacking the innocent and helpless.

One of Bernie's final actions in Iraq was a noble one. The night of August 29, Bernie made a presentation to many of my soldiers. When I briefed General Dempsey the next night this is what I said:

> "Last night we filled the auditorium at the 709th Headquarters for a presentation by Mr. Kerik about the 9/11 attacks in New York City. I requested this to help focus our soldiers on why we are here and to re-enforce that what we are doing really matters. It was an incredible presentation and I received extremely positive feedback all day."

Today, Kerik resides in a Federal prison where he is serving a four year sentence for pleading guilty to charges that he lied on his application to be the Director of Homeland Security, lying to FBI agents, tax fraud, and using a company with mob ties to do $250,000 worth of renovations to his home. Of course, the work was free and he didn't have to pay a dime.

The Federal Judge who sentenced Kerik was moved by his own perceptions of the magnitude of the former commissioner's crimes in the aftermath of 9/11:

"The fact that Mr. Kerik would use that event (9/11) for personal gain and aggrandizement is a dark place in the soul for me." [6]

General Sanchez, in a May 5, 2008 interview with the *Daily News*, had little good to say about Kerik:

> "...He was very superficial in his understanding of the requirements of his job. His whole contribution was a waste of time and effort." [7]

Sanchez used some of his harshest language to describe the activities Kerik engaged in, while assigned to Iraq that put American troops in danger:

> "I went to see Kerik and asked him to knock it off...You're going to wind up in a firefight with our soldiers. We've got troops patrolling the neighborhoods and if they see a group of unknown armed Iraqis show up, they're going to engage." [8]

Sanchez knew that "territorial issues" were at the heart of Kerik's resistance to communicate with Army commanders, proclaiming that Kerik spent more time "conducting raids and liberating prostitutes" than helping the 18th MP Brigade train the Iraqi police. [9]

Sanchez was not alone in his criticism of Kerik. Former State Department senior adviser to the Iraq Interior Ministry Robert Gifford described Kerik with these words:

> "He didn't listen to anything. He hadn't read anything except his emails. I don't think he read a single one of our proposals." [10]

I'm not surprised. I think back to the first time I confronted Kerik about lying to the American people. Kerik thought he was Giuliani and I was him. Thankfully, it never turned out that way.

CHAPTER EIGHT: NOTES

1 New York Daily News, May, 2003, Interview of Bernie Kerik.
2 www.gp.com, Home Page For Giuliani Partners.
3 NBC Today Show, May 27, 2003, Bernie Kerik interview with Matt Lauer.
4 Bernie Kerik briefing with Central Command in Iraq.
5 Nextel Press Release, May 2, 2002, "Nextel and Giuliani Partners Announce Strategic Alliance to Improve Public Safety Communications," Reston, Virginia and New York, New York.
6 "Kerik Is Sentenced In Corruption Case," by Sam Dolnick, February 18, 2010.

7 New York Daily News, May 5, 2008, "Former Iraq Commander: Bernard Kerik Was A 'Waste of Time in Iraq.'"
8 Ibid. End Note #7.
9 Ibid. End Note # 7.
10 History Commons, "May, 2003-July, 2003-9/11 Police Adviser Ignores Rebuilding Process For Iraqi Police in Favor of Media Coverage, Night Raids."

CHAPTER NINE

CAN WE COUNT ON THE IRAQI POLICE?

**Absent: a pre-war security plan for the Iraqi police.
We had to make one up on the run.**

Establishing law and order was critical to the future of Iraq, but we knew we couldn't stay there forever. I realized the Iraqi police would be the key in helping to prevent future chaos, once the decision was made to pull out American troops. President George W. Bush, his advisors and fellow politicians who rushed America into the invasion of Iraq, misjudged how the country would look and behave afterwards. America's professional military made the same mistakes. Senior military leaders were focused on how to take Iraq in the shortest time, with the minimum number of casualties and damage to the country's infrastructure.

We knew that the American taxpayer would have to foot the cost of repairing and replacing all the things we destroyed during the ground war. As a result, from a policing perspective, we focused on the security of "things" and not the security of the people of Iraq, after the ground war ceased.

One of our most significant faults was the failure to give sufficient attention to the rapid rebuilding of the Iraqi police. As I reflect on what was happening in Iraq at the time, I can't help but to conclude that from the perspective of the V Corps, I may be the most to blame for this situation. Despite the misgivings I had and the thoughts I expressed to my commanding officers, I fell in line with the senior combat arms leaders. I focused on ensuring that the 18th MP Brigade supported the ground war. As the invasion grew closer, I realized the resources available to me would be extremely limited. For those reasons, I concentrated almost exclusively on controlling the enemy prisoners of war and moving critical convoys through Indian country. Of course, these are the things that Lt. General Wallace wanted me to do.

The U. S. war plan called for the encirclement of Baghdad, Iraq's capitol. I believed such a siege would last at least three or four months. One of the results would be door to door fighting in the city of six million. I always felt that during that period of time I would be able to assess the effectiveness and level of cooperation of the Iraqi police. I was dead wrong in my own assumptions.

After my fellow brigade commanders from the Third Infantry Division fought their way into the airport and Saddam's Headquarters, they didn't want to fight their way back out. Their plan called for "thunder runs," which involved directing formations of tanks and Bradley Fighting Vehicles at the enemy. They were designed to draw out the Iraqi army, then destroy them from the ground and air. Resistance by Saddam's forces was unexpectedly stiff. After a couple of the combat arms brigades were successful in fighting their way in, they requested to hunker down and fight off counter-attacks, rather than fight their way back out. I was surprised as I heard all of this play out on the radio. Unfortunately, I was completely consumed with ensuring the prisoners of war didn't have a negative impact on our overall operations. I was also involved in tracking the arrival and use of my incoming MP forces.

MP brigade commanders that came before me had learned from our involvement in places like Panama, Haiti, Bosnia, and Kosovo that we would need to count on the help and trust of the local population to move the country forward. We'd also found that the faster we restructured policing systems to deal with the aftermath of an invasion, the quicker the country would recover. Sadly, just like America at large, the military doesn't always learn from its previous lessons and often repeats the same mistakes. This was the case in Iraq.

Before we ever entered Iraq, there should have been just as much planning on rebuilding the police as there was on planning the invasion. I should have been smart enough to see this issue building and pushed it even harder than I did before the war started. Instead, as the previous chapters in this book have illustrated, the invasion plans actually called for the misuse of the military police, assigning them to combat units, delaying their transport to Iraq so that combat units had priority, and otherwise treating the MPs as an after thought. Politicians like Vice-President Dick Cheney, civilian leaderslike Secretary of Defense Donald Rumsfeld and political advisors and supposed intellects like Paul Wolfowitz simply rejected the significance of putting a country back on its feetby quickly rebuilding its police force.

This should have been easy to figure out. After decades of being run by a ruthless dictator, Iraqis would need to be convinced that their safety and security were paramount concerns to the very force that invaded their country. While they waited for reassurance, one decision after another made by American leaders sent them a different message. Ironically, assorted terrorists and criminals saw the weakness in America's strategy and targeted the Iraqi police and their U. S. Army mentors every step of the way. Seeing the people responsible for protecting them become the targets of brutal and repeated attacks, common Iraqi citizens were reluctant and afraid to help their own police force.

The impact of little to no pre-war planning on how to rebuild the Iraqi police led to a variety of decisions and policies that prolonged the war and interfered with the rapid re-establishment of law and order. Somehow, we had to figure out the best way to overcome this weakness while we were literally on the run in Iraq, one minute acting as an army, and the next acting as the country's police force.

Lt. General Wallace established the tone of how we might

accomplish such a mission with these words to his subordinate commanders. "Let your training and your leadership take over," he told us.

It was my responsibility to translate Wallace's words into action. I called my own command staff together and reminded them of the lessons of leadership.

"We're going to have to assume risk. We're it. We have to make all of this work. The only way we are going to bring law and order to Baghdad is to blaze new trails, to set priorities, to serve as an example, and to focus on what is really important. Flexibility and creativity are going to be as important as numbers of soldiers and types of weapons. I'm counting on all of you to get this done and to remember the enemy has a vote. It doesn't matter how great our strategy is—we're going to need to be ready to change and adapt to counter the enemy's plans."

I tasked Major Gillian Boice to develop strategies that would assist us in accomplishing the 18th's mission. I met her shortly after assuming command of the brigade. At the time, Boice was serving in Kosovo with Rich Vanderlinden and the 709th. She had become a specialist on detainee operations. Boice was "all army." She was married to a Lt. Colonel. Her father-in-law was a retired Major General. I had met him in a meeting just months before I assumed command of the brigade.

"You're going to be the brigade commander for my daughter-in-law," he told me.

When the 18th went to Iraq, I thought of Boice. She had experience with detainee operations in Kosovo. She had worked extensively with the Kosovo police. Her prior experience would be a perfect fit. Although Vanderlinden was disappointed in losing Boice to the Brigade Headquarters, he was fully supportive of the decision. Boicere called the day he broke the news to her.

"You're being pulled up to Brigade Headquarters to be the lead agent for setting up the Iraqi Police and liaison with the

ORHA. The experiences you've had in Kosovo make you a natural choice for the position."

In a meeting we had later that same day, Boice learned some of the details of her new assignment from me.

"I want to get the Iraqi Police back to work immediately. There's going to be an announcement that some former Iraqi police are being recalled to help rebuild an Iraqi police force,"

I told Boice all that I knew. There wasn't any formal plan to accomplish the task. The plan would be made up as the day wore on—hour by hour and event by event.

Boice came to terms with the fact that there was no plan. She learned quickly that political leaders and military planners of the war at the strategic level developed a plan to invade Iraq and take down Baghdad, but there was no well conceived plan to rebuild the country afterwards. It would be up to the 18th and her MP friends and colleagues to do the crisis planning that would establish law and order.

Jay Garner from the ORHA arranged a meeting between the senior Iraqi police leadership, ORHA representatives Gilford and Hall, myself and anyone I wanted to bring along. I decided to take Boice, a few other senior officers, and my security detail with me.

"Colonel, what can we expect at the meeting? Do we have any intelligence or information on who will be there and where they stood in the regime? Can we even count on good security?" Boice asked me before we left for the meeting.

I could only grin while she rattled off the questions:

"This is high adventure. We don't have any information. We don't have any intelligence. We don't even know how these guys will react to us. This could be like the OK Corral if these guys are packing guns."

Boice felt the tension as laughter erupted between the two of us.

When we arrived at the meeting at one of Saddam's former convention centers, only a handful of Iraqi police generals showed up. I later found out they were concerned it was a sting operation on our part and they would perhaps be taken as prisoners. I never had such a thought. I was extremely disappointed at the attendance, told them what my vision for them was, and that we would reschedule the meeting for the next day. When we departed I didn't have a clue as to whether I would see them again or not.

Attendance the next day was astounding, and I was overwhelmed with their questions and concerns. After several hours of meeting, I realized that this was truly high adventure. Even though we had won the war, winning the peace was going to be much harder. My military police were going to have to play a bigger role than I had anticipated. Unfortunately, I didn't realize that it would take senior military and civilian leaders so long to get the concept. In fact, many of them didn't get it until a couple of years after my retirement. By that time, extensive damage had been done to America's reputation, inside and outside of Iraq.

Still, with just three days warning and no script to follow, my staff and I transformed the crisis planning session into a major victory. A huge percentage of Iraqi police were recalled to work. They were asked to report to a familiar location at the Iraq Police Academy in Baghdad, which became the Joint Operation Center for the military and Iraqi police to connect, train, and rebuild. The guiding principle developed at the meeting was that former Iraqi and military police would work together in joint patrols to help secure Baghdad in the short term. Police stations and precincts would be set up that mirrored the districts within Baghdad to support local patrolling from the local stations. As part of a longer term plan, the police academy would be revived to retrain former police and train new recruits in proper policing.

I didn't realize that although I had only met General Ahmed

the day of the ribbon cutting event with Bremer, others in my brigade had already been working with him. No doubt, that is how he was selected to be one of the ten Iraqi policemen that were there that day. I didn't know very much of this until after my retirement. Ahmed later relayed his thoughts on his dealings with me, and other members of my brigade. A couple of weeks before his initial interaction with Bremer, Kerik, and I, Ahmed stood in front of Iraq's Police Academy surveying the scenes of war and about to experience his first encounter with an officer from the 18th MP Brigade. He related to me what he had been thinking at the time.

"Everything was out of order. It was hard to tell where to start rebuilding. The situation was bad, with fire and smoke raging through buildings and dead bodies on the streets. The smell of death was the only thing one could be certain of.

Suddenly, three American military vehicles loaded with soldiers pulled in front of the academy. Several other Iraqi police officials and I didn't know what to do or how to behave.

"Should we talk to them or should we wait for them to talk to us. They are well-equipped, fully uniformed and packing weapons. We don't even have guns to protect ourselves," Ahmed was silently thinking to himself.

The highest ranking American soldier approached Ahmed and his colleagues, extended his hand and greeted them with a smile. "I'm Captain Steve Caruso with the 18th Military Police Brigade.

You will be working with us and we are here to help you rebuild and reorganize the Iraqi police. You need to know we support your work."

This was not what Ahmed and the other Iraqi officers expected. The Americans were victorious in war. There was no need to be friendly or even humble, yet Captain Caruso conveyed to every Iraqi police officer that his words were from the heart. The

Iraqis believed his promise that the Americans were there to work with them and came to view Captain Caruso as one of them, a fellow policeman, a friend and a person who would stand behind them. Caruso and his soldiers helped them collect pieces of furniture and made sure they had office space to work and meet. Caruso prepared the Iraqis for their first introduction to me.

In a meeting room at the police academy, Capt. Caruso later brought Major Boice, Lt. Colonel Keith Warman, the Commander of the 519th MP Battalion before Dave Glaser, and I face to face with Colonel Ahmed and several high-ranking officials of the Iraqi police. Even though I didn't remember Ahmed from our initial meeting, it would become the first step in building a partnership to restore order and bring justice to post-war Bagh-dad. The impressions we left with each other would determine whether trust had any chance of prevailing over the clouded decades of tyranny.

Ahmed later told me he had his answer as soon as I started speaking to the group.

"We want your suggestions. We want to know what your needs are. The military police are part of the United States Army, but we are policemen. Many of us come from law enforcement backgrounds in America. We know that fighting a war and invading acountry is not the same as helping citizens feel safe from crime and from violence. We're here to help you rebuild what the war destroyed."

As I finished, the Iraqi police officials grew more comfortable. They told me I sounded helpful. My staff and I tried even harder to convey our professionalism. But to Colonel Ahmed, something far more dramatic occurred in the room. As he came to know us better, he spoke of our first meeting.

"We were encouraged to cooperate with the Americans. They wanted to help us bring security to our people. They wanted us to be equals in being police officers to them. We spoke our minds and the soldiers with higher ranks were fair and let us exchange ideas and even present arguments to them if we disagreed with an idea. After awhile we were not afraid of presenting our ideas and of listening to the ideas of others. At the end of the discussions, we agreed to do what the majority decided to do. It was our first lesson in democracy. Cooperating, listening to others, and exchanging ideas, we learned, was what democracy and leadership were all about."

The pace of change and relationship building grew more intense as the next few days passed. Capt. Caruso set up an office in the police academy to follow the progress of rebuilding the Iraqi police. His sense of humor and the respect they developed for him translated into a deeper trust among two differing types of police agencies, with one trying to rebuild the other in its image. Through the force of personalities, not regulations and bureaucratic guidelines, the Iraqi police caught on quickly. As one of them put it:

> "Capt. Caruso picked up some Iraqi words and used them with our police, he ate with us, he worked with and talked to us, and most of all, he gained our respect when we learned that he was a father and that he left his family behind to support our country and to help us."

The Iraqi police coined Lt. Colonel Keith Warman with an Iraqi name that translated, "the man who does not smile." Colonel Ahmed remembers Warman as a "man who taught us respect, professionalism, justice and the necessity of obeying the law."

Lt. Colonel Warman met Colonel Ahmed shortly after the collapse of Baghdad. As the commander of the 519th Military Police Battalion, he positioned his Tactical Operations Center across the street from the police academy when Baghdad fell.

Ahmed introduced himself and offered his services to the Americans. The Iraqi commander of the police academy had been arrested by the coalition forces during the invasion and a replacement was sorely needed. Warman trusted Colonel Ahmed and his Operations Officer. He decided to place Ahmed in charge of the Iraqi Police Academy.

Shortly afterwards, in a sign of the continuing danger posed to anyone who worked withthe Americans, Ahmed's Operations Officer was killed. But Ahmed continued providing his valuable support to the military police.

Lt. Colonel Warman knew that Ahmed arrived early at the police academy almost every day. Warman recalled the pride he felt when Ahmed spoke at the formal inauguration of the academy as the official representative of the Iraqi Police Services.

"Ahmed praised President Bush for freeing the Iraqi people, shook Paul Bremer's hand, and presented him with a gift at the event. We went on to become very close in a relatively short amount of time."

The bonding described by Lt. Colonel Warman occurred at every level of interaction between the Iraqi police and the American MP forces in Baghdad. However, it was during joint police patrols that Iraqi police officers cemented their relationships with us and saw where examples spoke even louder than words. General Ahmed described the first time he witnessed my men and I in action:

"Colonel Spain gave the order to Iraqi police to accompany an 18th MP Brigadepatrol on a joint mission in a lawless area of Baghdad. Forty-three checkpoints were established. Numerous weapons were taken out of cars and collected from people who weren't supposed to be carrying them. The Iraqi national media and the international media showed stories of the Americans and Iraqis working side by side to protect people and restore order. The mission was a great success.

"We watched Colonel Spain stand up in the middle of the street. He was not afraid to be a target. We learned from him that defeating the enemy required courage. Courage means to be in the middle of the street telling your enemy you are not afraid of them and telling the citizens you will protect them from the enemy. Colonel Spain set a good example to everyone."

The night that I joined them on the simultaneous checkpoints was also a night that my interpreter Bennie will never forget. He was new with us, so it was his first experience at having shots fired at us. He later recalled the scene:

"As our convoy approached a small traffic circle, we heard some shots being fired. The colonel said, 'let's go see what's going on,' and we climbed out of our vehicles and started running toward the shooting. As we got closer to the circle, there were more shots being fired at us from an alley a few meters away. Everybody took positions and we started clearing the alley. It was long, narrow and smelly. The alley curved between two story buildings. Some of the doors we passed were not metal or wood, they were just doors made up of bed sheets or window blinds so it was easy for someone to take a shot at us from behind. At one corner when Sgt. Buchmeier, Staff Sgt. Jordan and I went to pass a wall and turn into the alley in front of us, a shot popped off the corner wall, just missing one of their helmets. We eventually came to a place where we found spent brass but no shooters. Clearing alley ways in Iraq wasn't a fun thing to do but we ended up doing so many it became a walk in the park."

If the Iraqi police academy became a lynchpin to introduce the rule of law into Iraq, the daily examples we tried to set on how to bring law and order to lawless streets galvanized ordinary Iraqi citizens and caught the attention of the bad guys. The lessons learned during extensive police training at the academy were put into action through daily joint Iraqi/American police patrols in the most dangerous areas of Baghdad.

Gunners riding atop our hundreds of military vehicles across the brigade were constantly on edge as we made our way from one police station to another and one combat patrol to another. We were aware that we were not just checking on the Iraqi police. We were also sending a clear message to Iraqi citizens that things had changed and that the American military would not desert them. We would help protect them from the variety of criminals, terrorists and foreign fighters who were trying to blend into their midst.

The message became very clear. We would mentor the Iraqi police in the ways of American policing. Since American policing absolutely depended upon citizen involvement, our patrols took us everywhere in Iraq we could travel on any given day. Even the Iraqi Police Academy wasn't spared from our patrols or criminal activity in its midst.

The police academy was actually many buildings assembled and situated in a huge open area that resembled an American high school complex of buildings, open space, athletic fields and parking lots. The Iraqi Olympic Team trained in a stadium near the academy, so it was clear that no expense had been spared by Saddam's regime to make it appear a model of government efficiency and progress.

One day my convoy pulled in front of one of the main academy buildings while out on patrol, early in the occupation, agitated people were emerging from inside. An Iraqi policeman excitedly indicated to my translator that there were a number of armed people looting the buildings in the back of the academy compound.

I told the police officer to grab his buddies and take us to the looters. As they jumped into a couple of their police cars, my security detail followed them less than a half mile before we saw several looters leaving a building in an effort to escape the scene.

I jumped from my military vehicle, followed by Buchmeier, Staff Sgt. Jordan, my interpreter and other members of my security detail. Prokop, my communications specialist was left behind to guard our vehicles and monitor the radios.

Suddenly, Prokop found himself alone, standing in front of a line of vacant U. S.Army vehicles, watching as his colleagues disappeared around corners of buildings and into the complex. Prokop's conflicted thoughts raced as time stood still. He wasn't even a military policeman; he was a communications specialist who happened to carry aweapon. But he was trained to fight in combat if he had to. What would he do if his colleagues didn't return? What if he was attacked by bad guys? Here he was in themiddle of a combat zone as a communications specialist who now found himself without anyone to communicate with. It just didn't seem right.

Quickly, it would all change. As Prokop brought his army issued rifle to the ready, first a woman, then two adult men came out of the building they were looting in front of him. He ordered them to take their hands out of their pockets, as they raced in hisdirection. Either they didn't understand him or they weren't paying any attention to what he had to say.

"Get down, Get down!" Prokop yelled.

They continued charging, ignoring his commands in a language they didn't understand. Prokop learned a valuable lesson that day. He learned and then applied the same lesson numerous times during his year in Iraq. A loaded weapon in the face of apotential enemy transcended any language barrier. He would use the technique many more times to compensate for his inability to speak Arabic.

Prokop was sweating profusely and almost breathless as he kept trying to stop their advance in his direction. Finally, as he trained the barrel of his rifle on them, they dropped to the ground just short of where he was standing. Feverishly pointing at their pockets as he finally got them to place their hands where he could see them, he realized they were trying to reach for cigarettes before they hit the ground.

For the longest ten minutes in his lifetime, he pointed his M-16 at the three Iraqis, lying face down on the ground and smoking their cigarettes. Had he not shown the discipline of holding his fire while he judged the situation, these cigarettes would have gotten them killed long before smoking would have.

Finally, Prokop saw me walking around a corner of the nearest building and towards the parked convoy. I had an Iraqi in custody. Prokop might have been sweating profusely from fear. I was sweating profusely because of the foot pursuit. The temperature was well over 100 degrees. I was wearing full combat gear at nearly fifty years old. What in the hell was I thinking? During the short foot pursuit, I briefly thought about shooting the guy. I feel very lucky he fell to the ground before I had to make that decision. When I pounced on him, I realized he was so out of shape he couldn't run any more either. Over the next few minutes, more of my military police from the convoy emerged from within the compound. They had arrested other Iraqi looters and criminals and had them in tow. Iraqi police watched with amazement as the bad guys were caught by America's ranking military police. They said later they had never seen their senior Iraqi police leaders react in such a way. They realized we meant business, and if we had to, would show them how it's done.

For Prokop, it was a memorable moment:

"I felt like I became a military police officer on that day. The appreciation I got from that feeling was huge. It was the toughest job in Iraq—to operate in a war zone and not to shoot first. I learned how to take care of a situation like a cop back home, but it was inherently harder in war. I joined the military out of necessity, but become humbled at the thought I had become a part of history. I have never been able to recreate the feeling. I have never been able to feel that way again."

The event at the police academy repeated itself throughout Baghdad. Daily patrols, nighttime missions and dealing with the unexpected became the "stuff" comprising the 18th MP Brigade's plan to restore law and order in Iraq. But, as each day progressed in Iraq it became less clear exactly who we could trust and that included the Iraqi police. We knew they were critical to the future of Iraq, but in some cases the same police we worked with during the day, were providing intelligence to bad guys in Iraq on how to kill us. I believed I could trust over 99% of them, but unfortunately I didn't have a list of names of the 1% I couldn't trust.

My first personal experience in trust and danger was shortly after our work began with them. About two weeks after I announced to the Iraqi police generals that we would meet every Monday to discuss our accomplishments of the past week and future plans, the plotting against us started. I had conducted about two or three of the weekly meetings in a room at the Police Academy that we were renovating. In fact, Tom Ricks from the *Washington Post* had attended one of the meetings with me in that very room. We had used the same room for other meetings, but I failed to realize I was already establishing a pattern, something I learned quickly I shouldn't do.

Even though my security detail was always near the entrances and windows of any room, they could only do so much. I was coming in from patrol in late May on a Friday night and my chief intelligence officer, Captain Jim Reed was waiting for me. He certainly got my attention when he said, "Sir, you are going to be assassinated on Monday at your weekly meeting."

He went on to say that there would be a final coordination meeting on how to conduct the attack the next morning at 1000 hrs at the Police Academy. We hastily planned a raid that would occur about twelve hours later. During the raid seventeen Iraqi police officers were arrested. After that, I immediately looked for a new location for my weekly meetings. I can only imagine the impact in the media if the attack would have occurred during the visit by Mr. Ricks the week before.

Across the street from the police academy, the 519th MP Battalion had a police station they were jointly manning with the Iraqi police. There were a couple of other buildings located inside the perimeter. Beside the station, was an Iraqi police motor pool where we had several police cars. The battalion commander suggested we start using a room in one of the buildings for our weekly meetings. He thought it would be more secure. I had seen the building before. I had visited the police station previously, so I agreed and we started conducting our weekly meetings there. After we selected General Hassan to be the first postwar Baghdad Police Chief we even set up his temporary office in the building until we could renovate a more suitable location.

After a few weeks we discovered it wasn't as secure as we thought. While we were conducting a meeting in a different part of Baghdad, a car bomb exploded, taking out half of the building, including the temporary office of General Hassan, an Internal Affairs office we just established and the room where we were holding our weekly meetings with all of the police generals.

Fortunately, General Hassan was with me and my battalion commanders when the blast occurred. Lt Colonel Dave Glasser, who received the initial call about the bombing from his Tactical

Operations Center, told me about the blast. At least one Iraqi policeman was killed. Dave needed to go to the site, so I told him to take off. I finished what we were doing at the convention center, since there were so many people in attendance from across Iraq and then left to meet him at the site of the explosion. It was obviously an inside job. The car bomb had been parked beside a four foot wall that separated the vehicle motor pool from the building where we met weekly, and where the Iraqi police chief operated daily. The blast was so massive that remains of the car were on top of the wall. While Dave was showing me around, he said he had been told that the Arabic TV station, Al Jazeera had filmed the attack, which to us meant they had advance knowledgeof it.

The attack was on September 2, and that night at my update to Major General Dempsey I briefed the following:

> "At 1115 hours an explosion occurred next to the Rusafa Police HQs. Eleven Iraqi police received minor injuries and one died. *FOX News* is reporting that the police chief who is operating temporarily close by was the target. I was with the police chief at the convention center when the explosion occurred. We will not be able to prove it, but we think the target was Internal Affairs that is located right where the bomb exploded. The FBI is conducting the investigation. We cannot confirm, but we are being told Al Jazeera was there when the explosion occurred."

The possible advance notice to the Arabic media bothered all of us. During a briefing of General Abizaid, the head of Central Command on September 14, he directed a question at me. General Dempsey had obviously told him about the attack twelve days earlier and what my suspicions were. General Abizaid asked me if I thought that Al Jazeera had advance notice of the attack.

I told him the same thing I had briefed toDempsey earlier. In my opinion they did have advance notice, but I couldn't prove it. Dempsey sought to ban Al Jazeera's access to us, but wasn't successful.

It was nearly impossible to know the intended target on some of the unsuccessful attacks. Even though suicide bombers started attacking military units, including my MPs, on a regular basis, I experienced a third brush with them up close and personal while going to a meeting with my Special Crimes Unit. As part of the reorganization of the Iraqi Police, we had built a Special Crimes Unit that operated out of its own headquarters in Baghdad. Iraqi Police were trained in the detection, development of witness information and criminal forensics and put to work trying to halt the rising crime rate that was primarily the result of Saddam's decision to release violent criminals from jail prior to the invasion.

One day I was visiting the unit to get an update, and see some of their special capabilities. Lt. Colonel Todd Harrison and his 168th MP Battalion had one of their MP platoons supporting this unit. Fortunately, we were running close to thirty minutes late that morning. About fifteen minutes before our arrival, Prokop, sitting in the back of my vehicle, received a call from my Tactical Operations Center telling me to stay away from the Special Crimes Units. A suicide bomber in a vehicle had just blown up trying to penetrate the location and created a hole in the wall of its perimeter. A second suicide bomber had entered that hole, and attempted to set off his vehicle, but it had malfunctioned. They didn't know if there were follow on attacks, so I was told that I should return to my headquarters. As soon as Prokop told me all of this, my driver, Sgt. Buchmeier, who knew me like a book, looked my way.

"We're still going, aren't we?" he said in a sick sort of way.

"Haul ass there as fast as you can," I confirmed the answer he already knew.

Upon our arrival, I confirmed that a suicide bomber driving a vehicle carrying an improvised explosive device (IED) had pulled up near the building perimeter and detonated his vehicle borne IED. A second suicide bomber driving another vehicle entered the opening created by the first explosion and drove directly into a meeting area congregated by a platoon of MPs and numerous Iraqi police. He desperately attempted to activate his bomb and when it failed to work, jumped off the truck and started firing on the police.

I arrived with my security convoy as police vehicles were burning, fire trucks were entering the site and the MPs and Iraqi police were engaged in a foot search for the second bomber, following a trail of blood across the crime scene. I jumped out of my hummer and instinctively stopped the fire trucks, motioning for my MPs to search them prior to allowing them entry onto the site. We needed to make sure they were not additional vehicle borne explosive devices.

A combat arms lieutenant colonel was coordinating the search as we joined in, back tracking the blood stains to an area that came out at the rear of the building. A massive military police search party fanned out over the area and combed through the neighborhood trying to locate the bomber, but despite the trail of blood, he was never found.

When I was confident there was no remaining threat from a third vehicle borne explosive device, my MPs and I examined the inside of the remnants of the second vehicle, an SUV, that had failed to detonate. We found it packed with so many explosives it could have leveled the building killing my entire MP platoon, nearly 100 Iraqi police, me and my security detail. The scene was one of the worst memories I have of the war in Iraq. It's still vivid in my mind today. The body parts of the first suicide bomber were lying all around me. I couldn't help but think how fanatical someone would have to be to do such a thing. Since then I've concluded that he gave his life for what he believed in. My soldiers and I were prepared to do the same. Thirteen of my soldiers never returned from Iraq for exactly the same reason. I surveyed the tremendous carnage around us.

My soldiers were working steadfastly across the crime scene. I couldn't help but think, that had the attack been only a few minutes later, the Iraqi police, my MPs and I, would have been standing exactly where the first bomb went off. It had to be an inside-job! To my knowledge, this was the first of many attacks in Iraq that came to be known as the "breech and blow" attack technique. The enemy continued to develop this technique during our time in Iraq.

In subsequent years it was responsible for numerous casualties to American soldiers. Even as the dangers increased, I knew there were no options other than to show Iraqis that the Americans were unafraid to patrol their streets and provide for their safety across the war zone. The example we tried to set, and the training we were giving to the Iraqi police started to pay off. We knew because we saw the results firsthand.

On one visit to an Iraqi police station, an Iraqi police officer was walking rapidly towards me, with a small explosive device in hand. My security detail moved to protect me, as the Iraqi neared. Then, with a proud smile on his face, the officer reported to me, through my interpreter, that he had found the bomb on a road side and wanted to let me know of his good work. The explosive device was taken from the officer's hand before it had the chance to detonate. Clearly, the officer showed great passion but needed a little extra training in the care and handling of explosive devices. The police were constantly looking for positive reinforcement. Each of our police stations had unexploded ordnance pits where we would place the countless explosive devices that were brought to our police stations, until our Army's explosive experts could gather them up and detonate them safely.

Tom Evans was constantly unhappy that I chose to hit the dangerous streets every day. We had breakfast together nearly every morning. I usually laid down before Evans and always got up before he did. I usually hit the sack around 2300 hours and had my first cup of morning coffee between 0300 and 0400 hours, and received my unofficial morning update from the night time battle captain. Evans always joined me at our official morning battle update briefing with the entire staff. After the briefing I would leave on patrol.

He usually walked outside with me to my waiting security detail. Nearly every morning, Evans told me the same thing.

"Some day you know I want to be the brigade commander, but not today."

Throughout our deployment, Tom and the MPs who traveled with me could see that I was trying to practice what I preached. We had to be seen. I had to let Iraqi citizens and the Iraqi police know we weren't afraid to move out into their communities. I had to let my MPs know that I wasn't afraid to do what I was asking them to do, I expected all my leaders to do that, and nearly all of them did. We had to tell the Iraqis the story by example—the rule of law had replaced the rule of fear. I realized I had to be seen living that example—by Iraqis and my own soldiers.

I didn't want to waste any time letting the Iraqi police see the changes we were bringing to the country. I also wanted them to be free of their fear of Saddam. As soon as we moved into the palace, I capitalized on relationships I had been developing with Iraqi police generals during our patrols to Baghdad, inviting a group of them to take a tour of the cleaned up palace that had once belonged to the Iraqi dictator. It was a bold move that would remind them who was in charge, while ridding them of any lingering fear that Saddam might return to order their beheading for treason.

As I personally led them on a walk-through, ending the tour

out in back of the palace where there was an expansive view of the man-made lake that meandered amidst the several palaces that composed Camp Victory. Non-verbal expressions said everything. They were shocked at how Saddam's inner circle had been living.

"I can't believe this son of a bitch was living like this," Iraqi Police General Jamal said in English.

From the looks on all their faces, the anger ran deep ran deep in all of them.

"If any of us had even been caught on one of the roads leading in this direction when Saddam was around, he would have killed us on the spot," said another. The roads leading to the palaces had always been off limits to the Iraqi police during the dictator's brutal reign. The gestures worked almost instantly in establishing trust and rapport with the most senior of the Iraqi police, whose loyalty would be needed if our policing plans were to succeed.

Unfortunately, on a couple of occasions, I had to worry about my own soldiers and how their actions negatively affected accomplishing our mission. Sometimes it would involve innocent civilians getting killed in the chaos of combat. But on one occasion it was one of my staff sergeants who had enough of Iraq and was ready to go home.

In an article published on July 1, 2003 by the *Washington Post Foreign Service*, written by Anthony Shadid, Staff Sergeant Charles Pollard, from my 307th MP Company, a reserve unit out of Pittsburgh, felt the need to share with the reporter exactly what he thought about our involvement in Iraq.[1]

"U. S. officials need to get our asses out of here," Pollard shared with the Post reporter.

He then proceeded to escort the reporter around the police station and point out who he said were crooked cops and lazy cops. While he was at it, he thought it was a good idea to give advice to President Bush. When the article hit the Pentagon the next day, the senior leadership called us in Iraq to express their "appreciation." It was the first I had heard about the incident. I called the battalion commander and told him I wanted to see him and the company commander. When we met, they asked me to sign paperwork sending the staff sergeant back to the United States.

There was no way in hell I was going to allow that so called squad leader to leave Iraq until the rest of his fellow soldiers left. I told the battalion commander to get him out of the police station and I didn't care what he did with him, but I didn't want him to see another Iraqi the rest of the time he was in Iraq. He worked at his company's headquarters his remaining time, which was about another six months. I never saw him until his company was departing Iraq and he came up to me to apologize. I was long over the incident, but I told him what I had essentially told his leadership six months earlier. When the media gets involved in stunts like he pulled, the results are the undermining of what thousands of other soldiers were doing to accomplish their mission. I told him he didn't hurt me, he hurt his fellow soldiers.

Nonetheless, on both sides of the aisle we always worked hard to build trust. For every Iraqi police officer we weren't sure we could trust, there were countless more we could. We simply had to trust them all, until proven otherwise, or we could have never accomplished our mission.

One of the Iraqi police I trusted the most was Basim. He was an Iraqi police captain who spoke perfect English. I met him during my first and only meeting with the general who had been the Baghdad Police Chief before the war and right after the fall of Baghdad. Basim interpreted my conversation because the police chief wanted one of his people doing the job, not one of mine. He distrusted the Americans at the time. Ironically, the chief was not allowed to return to his previous position by ORHA and I never saw him again. During my remaining time in Iraq, I continued working with Basim.

Basim is currently in exile in England. Shortly after we met, I asked him when he knew the Americans were going to take Iraq.

"Colonel Spain, I was hearing news reports where Baghdad Bob was telling Iraqis that the army was pushing back the American invaders. I had no television. I called my sister who lived along the Jordanian border. She had a satellite dish in violation of Saddam's rules and was watching the British Broadcasting station. While she saw Baghdad Bob telling everyone that the Iraqis were defeating the Americans, she watched American tanks rolling into Baghdad. We both realized then it was over. Baghdad Bob was lying."

Basim will always bring to mind moments of comic relief that eased the tension with the police. Sometimes the soldiers created their own humor. Sometimes events simply lifted the sounds of laughter past the sounds of war. Sometimes I created the laughter. There were countless cultural differences between us and the police. They would frequently kiss and hold each other's hand while talking. Sometimes there was weird food they would eat, and their hygiene habits could be a little different. I had to quickly decide which cultural differences I would bridge and which I wouldn't. I frequently tried to get myself out of awkward situations through humor. When I simply couldn't accept some of their customs I would tell them I didn't have to because we won the war. I told them had they won the war I would be in one of their prisoner of war camps doing what they said.

I decided to use the kissing and holding hand issue as part of my comic relief. I told the most senior Iraqi police generals that I met with regularly that I would shake their hand, but not hold it, and that I would not kiss them. I created a three second rule, which meant that when they shook my hand they had to let it go within three seconds, or I would shoot them. I also told them that if they kissed me, I would shoot them. There were a few police generals who couldn't speak any English, but they spent so much time around me that if I told my interpreter to ask them what I would do if they either kissed me or held my hand they would say in broken English, "you shoot me."

Basim was selected for promotion to major and asked General Hassan and I to promote him. He then explained how they did promotions in Iraq, which of course involved kissing and holding hands. I explained to him how we did promotions in the U. S. Army, and since we won the war, we would do it that way. I told him that in our army we were usually promoted by a senior officer and our spouse. I told him the senior officer stands to the right, and the spouse stands to the left. Even though Hassan was a general, I told him I would stand to his right and General Hassan would stand to his left. I explained that meant that he had to shake hands to the right, and remember the three second rule, and kiss to his left. I told him if he got either of those confused, I would shoot him.

We conducted the promotion my way, he briefly shook my hand, then he kissed General Hassan. He occasionally would screw with me at meetings and asked if he could kiss me, always knowing the answer. About a week before we left Iraq we had a joint farewell with the senior leadership in my brigade and the senior leadership of the Iraqi police. CNN was there. When it was my turn to present my farewell gift to Basim, I looked at the CNN reporter, Nic Robertson, and asked if the camera was rolling. He said it was. I said good, because you can now film me kissing my first, and last, Iraqi, Then I kissed Basim on national TV. The Iraqis went wild!

On another occasion, we were trying to mediate a dispute involving an Iraqi. He complained that he had just bought a car but the government had confiscated it because it had been a stolen government vehicle in the first place. The Iraqi wanted his car back. I was standing with General Jamal, who spoke great English, when the man approached me. Jamal stepped up and said he would translate. But General Jamal became so flustered at the man because of the way he was yelling at me, that he looked back at the man and repeated everything in English that I had just said.

Then, we both stopped, everyone looked at each other and started laughing.

"I could have done that, Jamal," I ribbed.

Sometimes, the soldiers closest to me would break the stress of combat, by using the Iraqi Police. During a trip to the police academy to check on the status of the first class of new Iraqi police recruits taking the first ever physical fitness test, my security team and I found the police recruits stripped down to only their underwear. Gym clothing was in short supply at the time and they told me they could run faster wearing only their shorts. My personal security detail convinced me we should have our picture made with the first class of recruits during their first physical training test so that we could record history in the making. Several days later as I sat in front of a computer at the brigade's tactical operations center, I couldn't believe what I saw on the screen infront of me.

"What in the shit is this?" I looked up from the computer and around the room.

Michael Prokop could hardly believe that I found the picture that he had cropped and placed on line for the brigade headquarters to see. Everyone else had been removed from the photograph taken in front of the Iraqi police recruits, leaving only me with a big smile, standing in front of a line of almost naked brand new Iraqi cops. It was the second time in a few months Prokop thought he might be fired.

"Thank God you have a sense of humor," Prokop breathed a sigh as we both started laughing.

Even General Dempsey and I had an occasional laugh. We conducted a grand opening of the Iraqi boat patrol in August. Dempsey and I both made a speech, followed by an offer by the police general running the boat patrol to take a quick patrol down the Tigress. Even though we had purchased the boats, I wasn't sure of the quality, a problem we always faced in nearly everything we purchased for the police. But when Dempsey agreed to the patrol, I had no choice. He and I got in the back of one of the boats, with the weight of our combat gear. One of my security members, my translator and the Iraqi police boat driver were also in the boat. We put the remaining security in another boat that would trail us and provide over-watch from possible gun fire from the bank of the river. As our driver took off the back of the boat went down to the top of the water. We were only an inch away from taking on water, with no life jackets. General Dempsey gave me the strangest look and I realized I was an inch away from drowning one of the senior military officers in Iraq. We laughed about it, once we were back on shore. This also means he was an inch away from not being the current Chairman of the Joint Chiefs of Staff.

If I wasn't convinced before we started the patrols and the reconstruction of the police academy, I grew increasingly confident that the strategy we had implemented to bring law and order to Iraq through the military police and the Iraqi police training efforts, were the only alternative to building a democratic Iraq in the aftermath of invasion and war. I found myself regretting that high level political and even some military decision makers had little understanding of police operations and missions. There were substantial cultural barriers to modern policing in Iraq and those combined with the reputation of the police under Saddam as corrupt, ruthless and incompetent, made it extremely difficult to build trust for the police within Iraqi communities. Having a viable police force, with visibility and professionalism, was the only way Iraqis would start to believe that a normalcy was returning to their lives. It was the only way a lasting peace could come to Iraq.

I knew what needed to be done to replace the tyrannical regime of Saddam and establish law and order, but far too often, the political leaders we in the military answered to, failed to understand the connection. Even many high ranking military leaders failed to grasp the importance of the military police role in a post-invasion Iraq. They were all from the combat arms side of the army and had a totally different philosophy of dealing with the public. They weren't trained as policemen, had never been policemen on the streets at home in America, and failed to understand the importance of having face to face contact with average Iraqis, and enlisting them to identify the criminals and terrorists living among them. Only if and when they got to know the American and Iraqi police, working side by side, would Iraqis develop the necessary faith to become involved and help with the mission.

I was frequently questioned about our strategy to patrol the night in an effort to halt the violence in Baghdad. Major General Martin Dempsey approached me on one occasion and asked whether I believed the enemy was specifically targeting the MPs since our police patrols seemed to be bearing the brunt of attacks.

"I do think the enemy is targeting my MPs. Many of the IEDs and ambushes have taken place along the routes to the police stations, so they knew we would be coming along and waited for us," was my response.

"Colonel, maybe we should be doing fewer patrols and staying inside the fire bases more," Dempsey questioned.

"In all due respect Sir, if we are going to hunker down then we should just leave Iraq because we wouldn't be contributing anything," I answered.

"Well, take a look at it anyway," Dempsey turned and walked away.

I called my battalion commanders together to discuss the exchange I had with Major General Dempsey. They all felt the same way—we couldn't surrender the streets, day or night, to the terrorists..

Ba'athists were not allowed to serve in Iraqi government institutions so Iraqi citizens with the education, leadership skills and experience necessary to move the country along were lacking in a number of important areas. Jamal Abdullah, the highly respected former Iraqi police official who had extensive experience in conducting police patrols of Iraq, had been my choice to be the new Chief of Police for Baghdad.

But Ambassador Bremer, with plenty of bad advice from Bernie Kerik, refused to listen to us and a less qualified candidate became the Iraqi police chief with inferior results. This decision, combined with the overall lack of experience of the U. S.Army's higher ranking officers about the role and use of our military police during 2003 and early 2004, sabotaged our efforts to establish trust with and rebuild the Iraqi police force after the invasion. For thousands of Iraqis and American soldiers in the ensuing years, the consequences were lethal.

CHAPTER NINE: NOTES
1 "Washington Post Foreign Service," July 1, 2003, "Frustrated Reservists See A Mission Impossible," by Anthony Shadad.

CHAPTER TEN

THE HIDDEN WEAKNESS OF THE
GEORGE W. BUSH COALITION
OF THE UNWILLING

The "coalition of the willing" was politics and not strategy, putting soldiers in danger. President George W. Bush frequently said on television that America and its allies in Iraq comprised the "coalition of the willing." More realistically, forty-nine countries, including the United States, represented the invasion force in the early months of the war. By the end of our first year in Iraq, there were still thirty-seven countries in the coalition, including the US. However, most Americans never heard that the majority of the other countries contributed less than fifty soldiers each to the "coalition of the willing."

As is usually the case, our best ally was the United Kingdom. They were brave fighters during the ground war, but after the ground war they were dealing with their political issues back home just as we were, I just never dreamed I would be dragged into it.

One day in the middle of May I was called by Wallace's staff and told to meet him in his personal office at midnight. I asked for, but wasn't given, the subject of the meeting. I was told I would find out when I got there. The midnight meeting was not a normal occurrence so my curiosity really peaked, but I couldn't find anyone on his staff that either knew about the meeting, or if they did, they weren't telling me why we were having it.

Once I arrived, there were only about five or six people in the room. One was theBritish Foreign Secretary Jack Straw, essentially the British equivalent of our Secretary of State. Another was the British Vice-Chief of Staff of the Army. I was absolutely stunned when the senior British officials started explaining their political dilemma backin the UK. The citizens of the UK were calling for the immediate redeployment of all of their military forces. Prime Minister Tony Blair was in the middle of trying to support President Bush, while protecting his own political career. They then explained that they wanted to move a UK Brigade from where it was currently deployed in Southern Iraq, up to Baghdad for about sixty days.

They felt this was a good compromise that would help support Bush, yet not alienate the British people. The brigade they were considering was the 16th Air Assault Brigade.

"But what did this have to do with me?" I thought.

Wallace explained that if the brigade came to Baghdad, they would work for me, but then I found out that their commander was our equivalent of a Brigadier General, one rank higher than me. When I expressed my concern, they told me not to worry about it. Wallace asked what my other concerns were.

I told him I needed to ensure that whatever mission I gave them, they would not create a void I couldn't fill once they departed. I could use them to help me rebuild and reopen the police academy, as well as training Iraqi police in other locations. That way, once they redeployed, I wouldn't have to back fill them with MP assets I didn't have. He liked the idea.

On May 18, I participated in two planning sessions on how we would receive and employ the UK Brigade. Major General Webster, from General Wallace's staff was there, along with Wallace. Representatives from the UK were there, along with Mr. Walt Slocombe from Ambassador Bremer's staff. Mr. Slocombe was a former Under Secretary of Defense for Policy from 1994-2001, but was currently serving as the Senior Advisor for Security and Defense to the CPA. I learned the British Air Assault Brigade would help me with training the Iraqi police and that they had Northern Ireland experience, which could assist us with some of our joint combat operations with the Iraqis. I also learned they would arrive the second week of June, but would depart the first week of August. The British Vice-Chief of Staff of the Army was at the meeting. He said they could also help screen new police hires and conduct training for the Iraqi police leaders.

The first session ended with General Wallace conducting a recap of the meeting: the UK brigade would help me with the police academy, police stations, jails, new police uniforms, communication equipment, vehicles, establish a course for basic security, a separate course for training the lower ranking policemen, a third course for training the police leaders, that would culminate with joint patrols and a practical exercise. After the meeting, I participated in a lower level meeting with the G3 planning section, where we finalized the details.

I left the meeting in Wallace's water palace for the short drive back to my Headquarters, wondering what I had gotten myself into. For the next ten days my staff feverishly planned for the reception of the UK brigade, while also doing their regular work, only to find out from me on May 28 that I had been told the deployment was off.

Prime Minister Blair had been unable to sell the idea politically back in the UK, so the 16th Air Assault Brigade was returning to the UK on their normal rotation, instead of joining us in Baghdad. This concluded my first, but not my last, lesson on the limits of the coalition of the willing. Politics and the media were going to bring the UK brigade to Baghdad, and it was politics and the media that determined they would not deploy to Baghdad. Since they never arrived, it only resulted in a lot of wasted planning time for me and my staff. Ironically Mr. Straw returned to Baghdad later and on July 3. I met with him at the Police Academy, where he was reviewing the training we were conducting for the Iraqi Police. There was no discussion on the 16th Air Assault Brigade.

The Polish Division, operating south of Baghdad, was another story. After the ground war, almost all of the countries serving in Iraq were under the command of the Polish Division. The largest American military unit in that division was assigned to me, the 716th Military Police Battalion. President Bush wouldn't allow American forces to be under the command of the coalition, a decision I wholeheartedly agreed with. Unfortunately, because I wasn't allowed to task them, I didn't really command the American military police within the Polish Division. I couldn't move them, stage them, or be the final arbiter of how they should be deployed tactically. This was the nature of the agreement governing the so-called "coalition of the willing."

When the fragmentary order, or "FRAGO," came out, I questioned the command and control relationship that CJTF7 was establishing between me and the 716th. Until this point they were assigned to the United States Marines, who really were part of our coalition of the willing. But once the Marines were redeployed back to the states the 716th had to go under an American brigade, and the 18th was the logical choice.

Once Sanchez' staff explained the relationship they wanted, I saw it more as an administrative control relationship, in that the 18th had all of the administrative responsibility, without the necessary control. I regret to this day that I didn't go stand on Sanchez' desk and complain about such an awkward relationship. Later, Major General Dempsey told me he had also questioned the weird relationship in the FRAGO and wished he had discussed it with me.

During training in peace time, most commanders have what we call "wake up"criteria which articulates the conditions under which we want to be notified of something during the night. I deployed to Iraq with one set of wake up criteria, but modified it several times during the early stages of the deployment. I originally wanted to be notified of any gun fights, but learned quickly that I would be awakened nearly every night.

So I modified my guidance to include only gunfights when one of my soldiers were shot, or we shot one of the bad guys. That still led me to be awakened during too many nights. I modified my guidance again to exclude being awakened when we shot bad guys. That could wait until my early morning update, which occurred each morning around 4 am.

But even this guidance led me to be awakened more than necessary, especially when I couldn't do anything but take the information and attempt to go back to sleep, which I seldom could. I modified my guidance yet again, to be awakened when one of my soldiers was seriously injured or killed. The little sleep I did get during the night seemed more the result of exhaustion than relaxation.

My security team occasionally harassed me about falling asleep during patrols, or during especially boring meetings with the senior Iraqi police generals who were trying to explain why they couldn't do something I was asking them to do. I had my wife mail me some no-doze that I could take before any extended meeting with Sanchez and the division commanders. I certainly didn't want Sanchez to make an example of me in front of the others if I nodded off while he was "mentoring" us during his periodic marathon meetings.

On one night in mid-October, I received some of the most painful news I had ever been awakened about. Some background is necessary before going further with my story.

Major Brian Feser was the Executive Officer of the 716th MP Battalion, under the command of Lt. Colonel Kim Orlando during our deployment to Iraq. It was mid-day, October 15, 2003 when Orlando and Feser, walked to the top of a hillside behind the headquarters of the 716th Military Police Battalion stationed in Babylon. They had made the walk many times before. Once on top, they sat across from each other at a picnic table someone had built there. The two men had known each other long before their Iraq deployment. They were good friends, as were their families back home in Fort Campbell, Kentucky, Their young children had already adapted to the sometimes harsh realities of having parents in the military.

On two occasions when Major Feser had to say agonizing goodbyes to his wife and their three children, ages three, five, and nine, as he left to catch a plane taking him to war, he had to return home again because the flights were cancelled and rescheduled for the next day. On the third try, one of his young sons, resilient but impacted by it all, looked up at his soldier/father and reminded him of his purpose.

"Dad, you're going to get the bad guys?"

Who wouldn't be okay with their dad going off to fight the "bad guys," Feser thought to himself as he reflected on his young son's words.

Orlando was born in Nashville, Tennessee. In 1982 he joined the army asan MP. By 1986 Orlando was commissioned through Officer Candidate School at Fort Benning, Georgia. Highly decorated and serving as a platoon leader and Deputy Provost Marshal prior to becoming a Battalion Commander, Orlando brought solid experience and integrity to every position he served. With a B.A. Degree in Political Science from Baylor University, Master's in Public Administration from Central Michigan University, he was a graduate of the FBI's National Academy for America's top police prospects. Lt.Colonel Orlando was the embodiment of America's rebuilt, modern, and professional "army of one."

With his trusted friend, Major Brian Feser, Orlando made

sure his soldiers performed their jobs with precision and honor. This was no simple task given their dispersion across Southern Iraq, and the monumental task of trying to support the Polish Division, who were fighting a different war than they were. In mid October, Orlando had a law and order detachment and the 194th MP Company with the 1st Brigade of the Polish Division in Karbala; his headquarters and headquarters detachment, along with the 442nd MP Company also with the Polish 1st Brigade in Al Hillah; the 977th MP Company in Ad Diwaniyah, with the Spanish 3rd Brigade, and the 988th in Najaf, also with the Spanish 3rd Brigade, totaling nearly 1000 soldiers.

The hilltop meetings helped bring his part of the army together. The meetings were an opportunity for Orlando and Feser to take a reflective break from war. Informal talks they had on top of the mountain allowed the two men to de-stress from the effects of daily battle, recharge their batteries and for the continuous building of their personal friendship. During the meetings, the two men could dream of the day when they would leave the war for good and return to their families. And on the hilltop they could pause, rest and smoke some of the hundreds of cigars sent from appreciative Americans back home.

The relationship Orlando had with Feser reminded me of the one between Deputy Commander Tom Evans and I. The personal chemistry Orlando and Feser developed helped solidify the example they set for their troops. They could disagree behind closed doors, where Feser was always respectful when he and Orlando had differing opinions or approaches. But once the doors opened, they briefed their men and women with consistency and unity.

Orlando and Feser constantly reminded the soldiers and commanders serving with them that the MP mission had to be carried out in an ethical and moral way. There was no gray area. Only if they maintained the highest standards of integrity and honor would they succeed in dealing with Iraqi citizens. They realized that their mission was to take prisoners, keep them safely and securely, and eventually pass them on—with no incidents and no torture. They were keenly aware that they would do no one any good if they lost their discipline in the middle of war.

We all found that it was easier said than done. Sitting down with a young platoon leader who had just suffered the loss of a soldier to tell him or her to go back out in front of their command and inspire them to return to battle the next day with the understanding that not every Iraqi out there is the "enemy," was no easy sell. But it had to be done. Lt. Colonel Orlando always said, "we have to take the high road."

Back in peace time, the 716th MP Battalion normally partnered with the 101st Airborne, its army parent division. They were co-located together at Ft. Campbell, Kentucky. But like so many other organizational changes implemented during Operation Iraqi Freedom, the battalion was tasked organized to the 1st Marine Division, training with them in the California desert prior to the invasion. Accompanying the Marines, they swept through Iraq, ending up responsible for the country's major cities south of Baghdad. One MP Company and a Marine Battalion were assigned to Karbala, al-Kut and Najaf. The 716th was headquartered in the Iraqi city of Babylon, about two hours south of Karbala. Two hours further south of Babylon was al-Kut with Najaf to the east. At least two surface roads ran between Karbala, al-Kut, and Najaf, forming a triangle with Babylon in the center. Passage among the cities was dangerous, with the road ways targeted by terrorists, common criminals, and a dozen other names for the people who took shots at soldiers of the U. S. Army.

By September, 2003, Muqtada al-Sadr in Najaf was causing so many problems for Iraqi citizens and the U. S. military that I was summoned to see Major General TomMiller, Sanchez' Operations Officer, to talk with him about a plan to deal with al-Sadr.

"Track him. Determine the patterns of his movements from his residence to hiswork place," I was told.

I knew al-Sadr would be more vulnerable to attack as he moved, just as I was. His residence and his work place were heavily fortified and protected, but there is always a limit to the protection you have during movement.

"Be prepared to capture him if we give you the order. If we give you the green light capture him alive if possible, but if he were to get killed while you were trying to capture him, that would be OK too," Miller summed it up for me.

Miller's spoken words were never put on paper but I clearly understood my orders. I passed the instructions to Lt. Colonel Orlando. He developed plans to shadow Al-Sadr and to be prepared to do what he had to do. The 716th was able to establish a pattern and on a couple of occasions they let me know they were ready to execute their plan when ordered. On one occasion Major General Miller gave me the green light, but then withdrew it before the 716th could implement their plan with the minimum number of casualties. Even though he did not say it directly, there is no doubt in my mind that the green light, then the red light, was being given from Washington, DC, a long way from the battle fields of Iraq. The capture never happened, and Al-Sadr is still causing trouble in Iraq today.

In Karbala, the in-fighting between al Sadr and the Grand Ayatollah Ali al-Sistani was creating dangerous situations for American soldiers and destabilizing Karbala and Najaf. Al-Sadr was highly influential with younger Iraqis and was stirring up thousands of followers to resist the Coalition Provisional Authority and the Iraqi Governing Council it had appointed. Al-Sistani was pushing Shia clerics to become more politically active after the U.S. invasion. His apparent motivation was the installation of a Shia dominated Iraqi government.

Late one night Evans answered the phone in our office. I

heard him tell the person at the other end of the field phone to hold on. Evans then told me that Sanchez wanted to talk to me. I grabbed the phone and was told, "Hold on for the CG." Sanchez then got on the phone.

Lt. General Sanchez conveyed a message to me that he wanted me to keep a field grade officer in the Karbala/Babylon region at all times for the immediate future because of what was going on between Sistani and Al-Sadr. Orlando had recently asked me for permission to allow him to move his headquarters to Karbala, because that's where they needed to be to best command and control his subordinates units. That was the right tactical decision for his battalion. But Orlando told me that the Polish Division Commander wouldn't allow him to move. I went to Sanchez' staff twice to fight that battle and lost. Sanchez didn't want to fight the "coalition of the willing" over what they thought was a minor issue. It wasn't minor to me or the 716th. Having lost this battle a couple of times, made the call from Lt. General Sanchez even harder to take.

"Sir, as you know I only have three field grade officers in that entire area of operations," I told Sanchez.

A battalion only has three field grade officers to begin with- the commander, who is a Lieutenant Colonel; and the two Majors, one who is the Executive Officer and the other who is the Operations Officer.

"I know how many field grades there are in a battalion," Sanchez was indignant.

I then told Sanchez that I had requested to move the 716th Headquarters to Karbala, the very city he was asking me to put a field grade in, but had been denied that request twice already.

"I'm not going to fight our allies over an MP Battalion," Sanchez ended the call.

I suspect if he would have needed to move a combat arms battalion there, it would have happened, but not a lowly MP battalion. Sanchez then told me that he would release me from this requirement as soon as possible. Unfortunately, I was never released from the requirement until the death of Lt. Colonel Orlando, Staff Sergeant Bellavia, and Corporal Sean Grilley.

Someone from Sanchez' staff later told me how the requirement came about. Sanchez received a briefing about the turmoil between Sistani and Al-Sadr that led to a fire fight between their factions in Karbala. Sanchez asked who the senior American was in Karbala and was told it was an MP captain. Orlando had a company stationed in Karbala, commanded by an MP captain. Once Sanchez learned that an MP Captain was the senior American he told someone from his staff, "Get Spain on the phone," Sanchez ordered me to put a field grade in Karbala. I called Orlando.

This was not my nature, but I explained to Lt. Colonel Orlando that this was one of those times I would just have to tell him what to do, knowing he wouldn't like it. I told him he could complain to me if he wanted to, but I was still going to give an order and he had to follow it. I gave the order. He complained, but followed the order. A few days after my talk with Orlando, I received another call from Lt. General Sanchez.

"Have the Battalion Commander meet me in Karbala on October 14," was his direct order.

During this same time the 988th MP company had reported there was a news crew and 18 vehicles at the suspected residence of Al-Sadr, one of three such suspected locations. We also had information from a police informant that Al-Sadr would conduct a news conference and announce he was taking over a government building and a cement factory and that his people had already taken over the Shahib Hotel in An Najaf. This was in the 3rd Spanish Brigade's area of operations, in a sector patrolled by powerhouse platoons from Honduras and El Salvador, so obviously it would be up to the 716th to conduct any real operations.

I was informed that the 82nd Airborne Division was prepared to send two battalions there if needed.

I called Orlando and set up the meeting between him and Sanchez, not knowing in my wildest nightmare that my friend and fellow soldier would be dead about forty-eight hours after the meeting with Sanchez.

In a nightly radio update to Major General Dempsey on October 14, I briefed him, "The 716th Commander linked up with Lieutenant General Sanchez in the Polish One Star's office and police station today."

Since Orlando, Majors Feser and Dolota were the only three field grade officers in the battalion, one or the other began patrols in Karbala each evening as the sun went down. Tensions were running high in Karbala with the two factions vying for influence bringing in large numbers of their fighters traveling on the back roads between the towns and their encampments. Karbala was a city waiting to explode. Everybody knew it and was trying to keep the city from a full blown civil war.

Patrolling Karbala meant that the potential enemy could be anyone or anywhere. Attacks against Americans supporting Iraqi police came from Iranians, followers of al Sistani or al Sadr, terrorists and criminals. Responding to these attacks and maintaining security of military compounds was complicated by the joint command aspect of the multi-national invasion force. In the southern area of Iraq, the American units took their directions from a Polish Division which was prohibited from engaging in any type of combat operation. The 716th MP Battalion was assigned to me, but fell under the control of the Polish. The multi-national forces were allowed to defend any military compound coming under attack, but could not assist the Americans engaging "shooters" in the cities.

Concerned about the safety of my soldiers within this command structure where the Polish were in the lead, I held a meeting with the Polish General in charge in the southern area. I explained my worries about the security of the 716th MP Battalion and the responsibility of the international contingent to protect it. The Polish General's response did nothing to satisfy my concerns or ease my worries.

He told me, in perfect English, that he was in Phase IV, which was what was supposed to be Post Hostility Operations. I found this interesting because the Americans were certainly not in Post Hostility Operations. I had visited both Bosnia and Kosovo in a previous assignment. Now, that was Post Hostility Operations. I had a battalion of soldiers in Kosovo when we invaded Iraq and their patrols were completely different than my Iraqi patrols. The Polish general told me that his country did not allow him to participate in combat operations. He ended our conversation by telling me he was being replaced in about 90 days, then he would go home and have sex with his wife.

I dismissed his sexual comments as a cultural difference between him and me, and decided to keep my thoughts about my wife to myself.

If additional help was needed for any significant problems, the Americans had to contact the army command in Baghdad and request helicopter support. While we grew to have a deep admiration for the 215 "fierce" fighters from the Fiji Islands, they could only be used to protect compounds and couldn't provide any other type of assistance. The remainder of the international contingent was largely irrelevant.

Combined with this command arrangement with our allies, a policy shift by the Coalition Provisional Authority (CPA) set the stage for a fatal clash between the MPs and a group of Iraqi "bad guys." At the outset of the invasion of Iraq, some military units allowed each Iraqi citizen of a certain age to keep one weapon for self defense. Unable to separate the average citizen from Iraqi soldiers who simply threw down their arms in the path of the invaders, the Americans faced smiling citizens by day.

After dark, some of the smiling Iraqis transformed into transplanted terrorists from Iran, or common criminals released into the population by Saddam Hussein just before the invasion began. The policy fed countless assaults on soldiers as the fighting continued after President Bush declared an end to hostilities.

The changing dynamics of what they could and couldn't do, combined with the CPA decision to dissolve the Iraqi Army, left the MPs highly vulnerable when law and order broke down around them. Iraqi citizens didn't trust many of the combat arms soldiers, who really didn't understand the differences between combat and police work. The volatile combination translated into mounting attacks on American forces trying to patrol Iraqi towns and cities. The MPs became one of the prime targets. When the MPs tried to rebuild the Iraqi police force, they could never be certain that the new recruits were not ex-Iraqi soldiers, ex-policemen still loyal to Saddam or terrorists.

Vetting new Iraqi police became increasingly difficult. When 2003 came to a close, Orlando's battalion was hit by 30-40 IED attacks. Nighttime patrols of Karbala rarely finished their shifts without experiencing four to five attacks. Seeing the Americans work side by side with the Iraqi police helped citizens feel more confident that Iraq would rebuild its government. At the same time America's soldiers were left more vulnerable. The Iraqi police, police stations and even the police academy increasingly became the focus of terrorist attacks. The terrorists realized that the average Iraqi would panic if they formed the impression that even their police were helpless to protect themselves from the growing violence in Iraq. It was classic bully behavior.

Major Feser described the difficulty of performing the MP doctrinal and a variety of other missions while consumed by what the Army Command and General Staff College taught was the "fog of war." What he had to say was applicable to what we all faced each and every day patrolling the streets of Iraq's towns and cities:

> "We never knew from day to day the identities of the people shooting at us or trying to kill us. It could have been one of the policemen we were training the day before. There was so much mission creep. We would work hard to rebuild a bridge blown up during the war, replace a dam and start water flowing again, or reopen a road that had-been impassable. The next day we would wake up to find the bridge blown up again, the dam destroyed, or the road obstructed. It was a hard thing to grasp. Things were made worse by the decisions of our own government authorities. In early September, 2003, we were told to turn in some of our special weapons such as Stingers because our government declared that combat operations were over and we didn't need to be using or showing such weapons. Of course there was more fighting after the cessation of hostilities than before. And we became more vulnerable."

This was the state of play as the three field grade officers of the 716th began alternating stints of night duty in Karbala. The two largest mosques were located in the middle of the city. Roads that looked like concentric circles traveled out from the mosques, leading to other parts of town. Karbala was dull, dirty, often overcast and the constant victim of blowing sand. Unlike al-Kut, which was green with vegetation, Karbala's nasty streets were laden with garbage and the entire city took on a grayish tan hue, barren against the sun. There was always a certain eeriness patrolling the narrow, winding streets that made their way through the city. The patrols became surreal as the convoys passed waving Iraqi children, smiling, giving the thumbs up and wanting candy.

Many times, the smiling children were standing next to their parents, who stared at the American army with contempt. Perhaps that explains why the soldiers developed a sixth sense, a quiet and intuitive feeling that something was about to happen. Maybe it was a car driving quickly by the convoy, sporadic gunfire, an all out ambush or IED attack. The MPs always tried to front the Iraqi police so that any arrests of Iraqis were made by Iraqis, with the hope that hot emotions could be cooled.

On the afternoon of October 15, Major Brian Feser's convoy left the protection of the gated army barracks in Babylon bound for Karbala. He had two security vehicles with him and planned on meeting up with the Iraqi police after the two hour trip north. Approaching the gate, preparing to exit through the checkpoint, the soldier cops put on their "game face." The gunners on top of the Humvees locked and loaded rounds in their M-60s, 50 cals, SAWS, and MK 19s with the distinctive click echoing as the bolt snapped forward, securing the rounds in the chamber. The weapon was ready to fire.

Individual soldiers did the same, loading their personal 9 MM automatic pistols, and their M4s, with the smaller weapons armed in unison creating a softer tenor chorus by comparison. Any time they left the protective curtain of the army compound, the MPs knew they may not come back. Subject to ambush and attack from rows of IEDs lining their routes, each of their routine missions was more like a major SWAT assault back inthe states. As they passed citizen Iraqis, they never knew whether the people staring tried to blow up an earlier convoy with a surprise mortar attack.

Karbala was especially tense on this mid-October day. Two weeks earlier, twenty people were killed and fifty injured at an explosion at a smaller mosque. The Iraqi police and American MPs still didn't know who was responsible. After their rendezvous at the police station, six vehicles sped out into the city, responding to a call that yet another mosque was under fire.

When they arrived, they could see ten or twelve men armed with AK-47s in the courtyard. The MPs were forbidden from entering the courtyard of the mosque unless fired upon. Some of the men exited the mosque through the rear and were arrested. The Iraqi police chief accompanying the convoy went into the courtyard and collected weapons. By the time the patrol shift ended, sixteen Iraqis were arrested and brought to the police station and thirty to forty weapons were seized.

After the successful day in Karbala, as Feser led his patrol back to Babylon, an IED exploded as his tiny column crossed over a bridge. Even away from Karbala, the danger was still present with every mile traveled. Once inside the safety of the gated checkpoint, Feser conducted a debrief of his evening, conveying information about everything from crowds to incidents to subtle changes he and his soldiers noticed during their shift.

Then, he met up with Lt. Colonel Orlando and the two recreated their ritual of walking up the hillside, lighting cigars, and looking out over the geography below them. On that particular day, they discussed the situation in Karbala, troop evaluations, rotations, and a laundry list of "administrative matters." Even in war time, they were responsible for so many pieces of "stuff," that didn't seem worthy of the energy they were expending to deal with it. As the hours wore on, it was time for Orlando to round up his security detail and make the move towards Karbala, alternating with Feser as he had done on previous nights. But Feser noticed one thing different as their meeting ended that afternoon.

Lt. Colonel Orlando got up from the table and hugged his friend and Deputy Commander.

"Brian, don't forget what I've taught you," Orlando said solemnly to Feser.

As Feser took it in, Orlando looked him in the eye and repeated what he had said once again. Then, Orlando descended the hillside to begin his sojourn to Karbala. Feser returned to his room to get a couple of hours of sleep. He didn't know that it was the last time he and his friend would climb the hill together.

After they arrived in Karbala, Orlando and his soldiers joined with their Iraqi police counterparts and started out to patrol the city. Following some of the same routes that Feser and his team had been on, they received a call that there was some sort of disturbance at the same mosque that had been problematic the previous evening. They drove down a roadway adjacent to the mosque, coming to a stop near a brick wall in an alley. Two armed Iraqis stood in front of the wall. Through Orlando's army interpreter, the two men were given a command.

"Hey, you've got to turn the weapons over."

"No, we're not going to do that," the men didn't budge, but instead defied a second command to put their weapons down.

Orlando and his soldiers were in Iraq as part of an invasion force to dethrone a brutal dictator, but they addressed the situation as any policeman would do on the streets of our own country. Disciplined, cautious, and giving the benefit of the doubt to the gun toting Iraqis, they withheld fire on the two men facing off in front of them, choosing diplomacy and discussion over shooting. Then a third armed Iraqi jumped from the shadows, waving his rifle in the air.

"Put your gun down now!" The order was firmer than the first, an indicator that the adrenaline was building, that survival instincts and the brain were computing the danger.

At first, the Iraqi leaned towards the ground and motioned that he was complying with the order to put the weapon down. Just as suddenly, and in one immediate motion he came up firing, but the gunner atop the Humvee had already sensed and then processed her suspicions. The M-60 simultaneously unleashed a volley of shots in his direction, killing the gunman instantly, leaving shreds of human flesh. Suddenly, as if on queue, shots poured from rooftops of the surrounding buildings and from both sides of the alley. All hell broke loose. Anyone that thinks females should not serve in combat should have been with me as General Petraeus pinned bronze stars with valor on several females because of their heroic actions during this firefight.

Lt. Colonel Orlando, who had been out in front of the Humvee with his interpreter was hit in the right shoulder. The rounds, fired from somewhere above him, were able to bypass his vest and traveled throughout his body. As the solidly built, 6,' 190 pound commander fell to the ground, his smaller driver, only 5'3" and weighing 120 pounds, pulled him towards the protection of the Humvee, while 28 year old Staff Sergeant Joseph Bellavia of Clarksville, Tennessee, provided cover fire. Married and scheduled to depart from Iraq in a few months, Bellavia's fire drew the attention of militants, who reined upon him grenades and bullets. Bellavia died from shrapnel wounds. He left Christina, his wife of almost four years and who he always referred to as "Princess." With a contagious smile and the spirit of an eternal optimist, Bellavia had been a military policeman since entering the United States Army in 1995.

Also providing protective fire, Corporal Sean R. Grilley, from San Bernadino,California, was killed in action on that mid-October evening in Karbala, leaving behindhis wife Luciana. Grilley joined the army in 2001 and had received word that he was being promoted to Sergeant. In a haunting memorial on the internet an "anonymous" author had these words to say about Grilley:

> "Sean, you were every sergeant's dream. You were a great NCO...Still remember trading DVD's with you. You haunt my dreams. I should have been the one to take that hit. You had so much to live for. I had and still have nothing other than pain in my life. You were the best of us Sean. When I now look at my own failed marriage and

daughter because of all this, I don't know why. It should have been me. I have nothing to live for. I'd gladly trade my life for yours. You were the best Sean." [1]

The convoy sped away, desperately seeking medical assistance, as the phones in the Tactical Operations Center in Babylon began ringing. The TOC rotation was occurring as it did every night. Some of the senior staff had left. MPs from the New York National Guard were on duty. Major Feser had been in the TOC until about 7:30pm, when he walked back to his room to get a Gatorade.

"Sir, the commander has been in a fire fight," was the message from the TOC.

"OK, I'll be over to the TOC in a minute." Feser was not treating the news lightly, but lived with the reality that he, Lt. Colonel Orlando and their military police teams had been involved in frequent firefights during their patrols. It had become almost routine.

When Captain Terrie Dorn made the next call, the tone of her voice more than herwords, delivered the terrible news.

"The Commander was hit," she uttered in disbelief.

Staff Sergeant Bellavia and Cpl. Grilley died at the scene from their wounds. Kim Orlando was evacuated to the camp hospital, where his wounds were treated by a Spanish physician, serving as part of the multi-national force. His wounds severe, the battalion commander died from the loss of too much blood. Feser was numbed, but his training and the knowledge that he was now responsible for the men and women of the 716th sprung to action.

After Orlando was killed, Feser knew that he was in charge. There were alerts to issue, the need to see and comfort the wounded, and sending platoons into Karbala to be ready for uprisings.

Feser called Major General Petraeaus and the 18th MP

Brigade TOC to tell us of Orlando's death. Then, breaking all the rules, he called Major Daryl Johnson back in the states, a mutual buddy of Feser and Orlando. If the chaplain was going to visit Orlando's wife, Sherry, Feser was determined that the chaplain would be accompanied by their family friend, called "DJ."

"DJ, the boss, is down. He's been killed." Feser still recalls Johnson's immediate reaction.

"You're lying," were the words from DJ, and then silence.

_____

As events were unfolding in Babylon and Karbala, at our 18th MP Brigade Headquarters TOC in Baghdad, the news of the firefight was fragmented by the confusion at the scene and the uncertainty of Lt. Colonel Orlando's condition once he was rushed into the hospital. When Gillian Boice woke me the first time, she was only able to tell me that Orlando was in the hospital. I was relieved by her words and recall clearly how it felt.

"He's fine. Go back to sleep."

Upon her return, the news had changed and confirmed my most intense worry. "Sir, Colonel Orlando is dead."

As Major Feser was having to do in Babylon, I relied on my soldier's training and responsibility for leadership to override my grief, allowing me to take the necessary steps to protect the entire command in the aftermath of this tragic turn.

"Get Major Feser on the phone," I instructed Boice.

"Brian, you're the commander of the 716th. You're not the acting commander, you're the commander. Do you understand that? I've got Major Tom Blair here. He'll come right down there and you should use him however you need to."

Violating all the rules, I telephoned Brigadier General Curry, the Commandant of the Military Police Corps at Ft. Leonard Wood, Missouri to let him know of Orlando's death in Karbala. I needed him to start the process of getting his replacement into

Iraq. I knew that the army had selected a replacement for Orlando, as part of the normal rotation among all army commanders. I already knew that I was being replaced by Colonel Jim Brown, even though we were ten months away from changing over. I had a tremendous guilt feeling calling Curry to replace Orlando, yet we were still in combat and the enemy was not going to give us a break. We were aware they would exploit our tragedy as a weakness if they could.

Curry's secretary got him on the phone.

"Sir, do you know who is slated to replace Lt. Colonel Orlando?" I asked

I knew the transition to a new leader had to occur as soon as possible in Iraq. Even during my own grieving, I had to focus on the soldiers who were still in battle. Orlando would have understood and wanted it that way.

"Ashton Hayes," was the Brigadier General's response.

"Do you know how I can get in touch with him?" I asked Curry.

"He just left the military police pre-command course here at Ft. Leonard Wood yesterday to go to Leavenworth for a pre-command course there," Curry knew that I had an immediate need for Hayes to get to Iraq.

"General Curry, we must keep this between you and I until I call you back and let you know that Mrs. Orlando has been notified. Then I'll need your help tracking down Lt. Colonel Hayes"

I called Curry back after confirming that Mrs. Orlando had receivedword of her husband's death.

"General Curry, Hayes is going to have to get from Leavenworth to Ft. Campbell, Kentucky, then onto Germany and Kuwait so he can make his way to Iraq. Will you help me get him from Leavenworth to Ft. Campbell?" Curry offered his assistance and the transition to a replacement for Lt. Colonel Orlando moved into high gear.

I called Brigadier General Helmick, stationed in northern Iraq as a deputy to Major General Petraeus. Helmick and I had served together when he was a lieutenant colonel in the 82nd in 1996 and 1997 along with General Petraeus.

"Can you help me get Hayes in-processed into Ft. Campbell and sent to Germanyas soon as possible?" I asked Helmick and of course he quickly agreed.

My final request was a matter of simply turning to Tom Evans, "Can you get Ashton Hayes in and out of Germany and into Kuwait and then Iraq as soon as you can?"

Evans went to work. About ten days after the death of Lt. Colonel Kim Orlando, his replacement, Ashton Hayes, arrived in Iraq. It was only after the sequence of calls that Boice and I dropped onto our chairs in the TOC in a state of shock. I had personally known Orlando for over 20 years, first meeting him when he was an army lieutenant. Boice had visited with Orlando and his battalion in Babylon only a week earlier. When she returned she expressed critical concerns about the security position of the 716th in southern Iraq. After my retirement, Boice recalled her assessment of the situation at the time of the tragedy:

"There wasn't a major combat arms unit there to provide back-up support to this battalion. All of the major combat US forces were supporting Baghdad, Tikrit or Mosulareas of operation and southern Iraq was left to non-US coalition forces. These coalition forces often operated under restricted Rules of Engagement and were super reluctant to engage in combat operations. We had reported this reluctance repeatedly. Lt. Colonel Orlando had discussed his concerns with Colonel Spain. Spain had told Orlando that he was to do whatever he had to do to secure his soldiers. Of course Orlando was doing that already. Orlando and Spain were not going to put the politics of the "coalition of the willing," over the safety of their soldiers. The situation was well known to the multi-national command leadership. Even though they agreed with our assessment, no adjustments were made. Certainly the mission for the 716th didn't go away when the combat U.S. forces were realigned across Iraq. It just meant they were less protected."

"There were many armed religious guards around local mosques to protect the religious leaders and their coffers. Some of these locations were used as weapons caches or areas to incite terrorist activity. The internal competition between religious leaders was also especially high in this region. Many of these religious guards were hard to distinguish in plain clothes, and many of them were also thugs of their communities. On this particular night the religious guards targeted our MPs with deadly results."

The army prepared for an all out assault in Karbala to identify and capture the terrorists responsible for the murders of Kim Orlando, Sean Grilley, and Joseph Bellavia. As he assumed temporary command of the 716th, Major Brian Feser took time to climb up the hill to the picnic table where he and Orlando had spent so many hours together thinking of their soldiers' welfare and of home.

Feser was accompanied by the officer stepping up to fill the position he was leaving behind. Before the trip, Feser had collected all of Kim Orlando's blood stained clothing from the doctors who tried valiantly to save his life. The two officers lit up cigars, started a fire in the trash can at the top of the hill and watched quietly as Orlando's clothes burned in the flames.

As the smoke lifted into the air, they saw Orlando's determined face, heard his commanding voice and felt his presence as their friend. They walked slowly back down the hill. They could feel the warmth of the smoke brushing behind them and were good with the thought that Lt. Colonel Kim Orlando was watching over them and would always have their backs. Their tribute complete, they soldiered on.

While I would never suggest that the politics of the "coalition of the willing" contributed to the deaths of these dedicated Americans, I will always maintain that I should have been allowed to position the 716th where it made the most tactical sense, as Lt. Colonel Orlando requested. I will never know where Orlando, Bellevia, and Grilley would be today if Kim would have been allowed to relocate the Battalion headquarters to Karbala. I will always be haunted by what could have been. I will always believe I should have fought much harder with Lt. General Sanchez and his staff over the issue. The pain that I felt throughout our efforts to deal with the death of Lt. Colonel Orlando and the brave men who were at his side will be with me forever. As for Lt. General Sanchez, he wasted little time fixing responsibility for what happened on that night in October, 2003.

At about 9:00 am, the day after Lt. Colonel Orlando had died, I was still fighting off the terrible fatigue that came from lack of sleep and constant grieving over my lost friend. General Sanchez called my office.

"Colonel Spain," Lieutenant General Sanchez began without any further formalities, "what intelligence did you have in your possession about al-Sadr and al-Sistani?"

As I tried to answer, Sanchez broke in abruptly, "Come over to my office in two hours and tell me what you knew."

Since operations against al-Sadr and al-Sistani were outside of my area of operations, I spent most of the next two hours trying to get the best briefings I could on the situation that had existed in Karbala, both prior to and after the ambush. Strained by the crisis at hand and the burden of the tedious brief, I showed up outside Lt. General Sanchez' office door as requested, just shy of two hours later.

"Come on in here," General Sanchez motioned as he spoke, and moved to shut the door behind me.

"Have you seen this?" Sanchez angrily thrust at me a stack of papers as we stood alone in his office.

I started to read the top page of the stack, trying to determine what the papers were about before I gave an answer to Sanchez. I was near exhaustion when Sanchez barked again about thirty seconds later.

"I asked you if you'd seen this!" He glared as he took the stack of papers from my hands.

"Based on what little I read before you took it out of my hands, Sir, I hadn't seen the document before," I tried to explain.

"Why not?" Sanchez focused an intent and punishing stare in my direction.

"Sir, certainly you know that you get intelligence I don't get," I tried to answer.

"You should have had this and been familiar with it," Sanchez continued to castan unfriendly gaze at me.

The situation was a losing one. There was nothing that I could say that Sanchez couldn't challenge as the wrong answer to the questions he was asking.

"General Sanchez, there is no way you can make me feel worse about losing a battalion commander than I already do. I don't remember every detail, but I was told before all of this happened that I could not task the 716th."

"Who told you that?" Sanchez barked.

"Your staff," I replied.

"You were told wrong, that was your battalion!" Sanchez sat in silence again, justwaiting for my response.

"Do you have anything else you want to say to me?" Sanchez broke the silence hehad started.

"No Sir, I did not ask to see you, you asked to see me," was my quiet and appropriate military retort.

"Colonel, you can get out of here now. I suggest you go visit the battalion," which is where I would have been, had he not called me earlier and wasted two hours of my time preparing for this guilt session.

Sanchez harshly dismissed me, clearly placing the blame for the loss of Orlando and his soldiers squarely on my shoulders.

When I returned to the detachment headquarters, my Deputy Commander Tom Evans was waiting for me at the door.

"General Sanchez implied I am to blame for Kim Orlando's death, Tom," I tried to speak calmly without any hint that I questioned Sanchez' conclusion. Evans attempted to reassure me but to little avail.

Major Gillian Boice was with me just before I went to see General Sanchez and was one of the first to see me after I returned. Upon my retirement, Boice had harsh words for the way Lt. General Sanchez handled the tragedy:

> "It was probably the most indecent action by a leader that I've ever witnessed in my 20 years of service. It was so unwarranted. I lost incredible respect for this commander. Several of his key staff did their best to ameliorate his poor leadership. But for Colonel Spain this was especially painful. Laying this type of unwarranted guilt on the heart of an already combat tattered brigade that sacrificed so much was unthinkable. It was extremely poor leadership on the part of General Sanchez. Instead of mentorship, he just doled out ill placed blame and anger."

But nothing changed with the coalition of the unwilling as a result of this tragedy. On October 23, I met with a key member of Major General Miller's staff, Lt. Colonel Sean McFarland, and reiterated that the Polish division didn't see their area of operations the same way that the 1st Armored Division did. I told him

I was still concerned about the safety of my MPs and I requested some type of armored company, either Abrams tanks, or Bradley fighting vehicles, to serve as a quick reaction force, because I couldn't count on the Polish Division. My request was denied.

Three days later, on October 26, I met personally with Major General Miller Sanchez' top operations officer. I requested the meeting because of the continuing confusion over my command and control status of the 716th. He reminded me that they were attached to me, but under the tactical control of the Polish Division. I knew that already, that's what I was trying to change. I briefed him on what missions they were performing, and since they were all Iraqi police related I thought they should be assigned to me, and under my complete command and control. When he pushed back on me I reminded him that the Polish saw themselves as peace keepers, but we didn't have peace yet to keep and again requested a quick reaction force because of my concern over the safety of my soldiers. I ended my brief by telling him I was still under the requirement to keep a field grade officer in Najaf or Karbala.

He didn't tell me what I wanted to hear. He said that Sanchez believed that military police presence was the key and wanted us to remain visible and not to lay low. He said that Karbala and Najaf were some of the hottest spots in Iraq and we needed to keep pressure on Al-Sadr, and especially stay visible in Najaf. He wouldn't relieve me of my field grade requirement until they were more comfortable with conditions and that it was probably for a short term. I had been told that before. He again denied my request to move the 716th Headquarters to Karbala.

He wanted me to continue providing intelligence on Al-Sadr. For example, he wanted to know what car al-Sadr traveled in. He said if the right conditions existed we would get him, but it must be a safe capture. He told me there was a murder warrant on al-Sadr, but he wanted the Iraqi police to make the arrest if possible.

He emphasized we would get al-Sadr with or without the police. He asked me to increase the force protection at the Najaf police stations.

When I visited one of the police stations with the company commander, I pointed out a great way for a suicide bomber to get in. That's exactly what happened a few weeks later, and even though several Iraqi police officers were killed, no MPs from the 716th were injured. Miller told me that if the 716th wanted to adjust their named areas of interest, that would be okay. We just needed to report them. He said the Polish Division would only get involved if the coalition forces were threatened. They would not participate in any arrests. He closed by saying that he wanted an officer from the 716th to attend all important meetings, not just someone from the Polish Division. I left the meeting no better off than when I entered his office. The situation never improved during our remaining time in Iraq.

I learned in war the only coalition that really mattered were the soldiers who stood by each other during every patrol, through every battle, and with every poor decision by a senior military commander or high-ranking civilian. When the shooting starts, soldiers fight for the soldier on their right and left. The only ones we could really trust were the ones who took the same oath we did, "To support and defend the Constitution of the United States against all enemies, foreign and domestic." I still believe that today, regardless of all the talk about the so-called "coalition of the willing."

CHAPTER TEN: NOTES
1   "American Heroes Memorial," to Sean Grilley, posted on the Internet, November 18, 2008.

Conclusion

When I left Iraq in February, 2004, I was frustrated and disappointed. I didn't accomplish my mission to the level that I should have. It didn't have to be that way. I realize there are millions of people who don't think we should have been in Iraq at all. Many of them feel that the politicians who led us there misrepresented the facts. The premise that Iraq posed an urgent threat to America's national security because it possessed and might use its weapons of mass destruction against us never really panned out to be true. My inner conflict about the war has nothing to do with whether there were any weapons of mass destruction ever found in Iraq. Saddam was a one man weapon of mass destruction.

For me, there were, and continue to remain, only two personal truths about Iraq. One, I was a soldier in the United States Army. Soldiers and armies do what their political leaders order them to do. Mission accomplishment is the focus of an army regardless of whether there are loud protests and debates back home about the political wisdom or not.

Second, soldiers deserve the best leadership possible. Soldiers who put their lives on the line have a right to know that their cause is just and the facts are on their side. They should be able to expect that the politicians who sent them off to war made solid decisions based in wisdom and truth.

Good leaders at all levels should mitigate the bad decisions they inherit to the best of their ability. Good leaders will also never forget that it is the soldier, and their families, that ultimately pay the price if they don't. Those families live with the consequences long after the soldiers leave the battlefield.

My family is but one of the hundreds of thousands of families that worry everyday their soldier is in harm's way. I asked my wife to never call me in Iraq unless it was an emergency. She only called me one time. The day the Lieutenant Colonel was killed at the Al Rasheed hotel during the assassination attempt on Paul Wolfowitz, the headline on the Armed Forces Network that alerted my wife to call was, "Colonel killed in Baghdad." She had no way of knowing if it was me, so she decided to call, just as I was sitting in a critical meeting with several Iraqi police generals. As soon as I answered the phone she said, "I just wanted to hear your voice," and hung up. At the time I was not aware of the death of the lieutenant colonel so I thought she had lost her mind. I called her later that night and she explained herself.

Neither my youngest son Josh, or my oldest son Chris have ever been much on watching the news. But R'ami said they were glued to the news while I was deployed. The constant fear of the unknown and the dreaded possible "knock at the door" have terrified countless families since 9/11.

I was speaking at a Memorial Day ceremony shortly after my retirement. As the city mayor was making his introductory remarks and preparing to introduce me he made reference to family members losing someone in combat. Josh, 15 years old at the time, looked at me and said, "I don't know what it's like to lose someone I love in combat, but I know what it's like to worry about losing someone I love in combat."

The impact of combat stays with the soldier and his or her loved ones forever.

If a politician writes a book, years after he or she made a decision based on a specific set of facts, the facts in the book should be the same as the set of facts they had when they made the decision. If the facts aren't the same, the politician is attempting to amend history for the sake of their own reputation. They aren't interested in a truthful dialogue that will assist those who face similar situations in the future to learn from the past. Real leaders are truthful. They are guided by what they feel in their heart. A true leader's heart is the best counter balance to the abuse of power. A real leader knows the truth, speaks up to power, and would never recklessly place the lives of soldiers under their command, in harm's way.

We invaded Iraq because we were ordered to do so. But, we weren't ready to invade Iraq on March 10, 2003, the first established target date for us to leave Kuwait and strike out across the desert. So we postponed launching the invasion until March 21, eleven days later. Even then, we didn't have sufficient numbers of soldiers and equipment to sustain the occupation. More significantly, we had no plan for transforming a post-invasion Iraq from a broken country to a people who could have hope for their future. Lacking such a plan, it was a given that Iraq would plunge into chaos almost a year after the invasion. There was little we could do on the ground to prevent this outcome.

As the U.S. Army colonel responsible for many of the military police in Iraq, I felt a solemn responsibility to use my MPs to rebuild the Iraqi police, their police stations and their policing philosophy, using the American style "rule of law," as my blueprint. Despite all of our hard work and effort, I believe I failed to make this happen. I don't mean this as a criticism of the military police who worked alongside of me. They did everything that I asked them to do and more. Thirteen of them gave their lives in combat to help carve the rule of law into the fabric of a new Iraqi system of political and social justice. I have reflected on Iraq ever since I left there nine years ago and no matter how I relive and rethink it, I believe I ultimately personally failed to bridge the gap of "politics trumping military tactics."

We wrote this book because we feel America will get involved in another armed conflict where a military policing situation seeks to transform a country's government after the invasion. We can't afford to make the same mistakes we did in Iraq. We can't tolerate having military leaders who take orders from a higher level and then just blindly do what they are told without questioning their political leaders. If we believe political decisions having a bearing on the lives of our soldiers in the field are the wrong decisions, we should speak out loud and clear against them, regardless of the consequences to our individual careers. As American politics become even more toxic and politicians even less trustworthy, military professionals have to become more entrenched in speaking the truth to power and avoiding potentially tragic outcomes if they don't. I tried to speak the truth to power in Iraq. I don't think I spoke loudly enough, strongly enough, or was persistent enough when they sent me out of the room. The ten decisions I have discussed in *Breaking Iraq*, illustrate how terribly wrong things can go if politics succeeds in trumping military tactics, when the wrong people are in charge of decision making. Consistently making the wrong decisions to please a political master to secure one's next promotion, rather than accomplishing a military objective, is a recipe for disaster. This is how Iraq turned bad for America between 2004 and 2007, and beyond.

The old saying that those who don't learn from history are doomed to repeat it is relevant if we're to answer the question of what happened to America in Iraq. If America repeats the same mistakes in the future as it did in Iraq, we will suffer the same tragic results. Instead of learning from our experiences in Bosnia, Haiti, Kosovo and Panama, we moved into Iraq as if those other deployments never happened. Listening to politicians talk today about substantial reductions to America's future military force while they brag about al-Qaeda's degraded capabilities, sounds to me like they are preparing to make some of the same bad decisions that have so harmed our political, social and economic standing in the world the past ten years. If they do what they say they are going to do, America is positioning itself for a very dangerous world indeed. If we lack the future military and economic strength to hold the world's bullies at bay, it won't much matter if we have a changed "will" about taking them on. As we found in the years after President Bill Clinton drastically slashed the size of the military, you can't just grow an army overnight.

America truly broke Iraq without having any plan to put it back together again. Leadership on the battlefield was the only answer to try and overcome the impact of poor decisions that took us to war. I learned that good leadership at all levels, could be the difference between mission success or failure. My soldiers and junior leaders knew great leadership when they saw it. They readily identified toxic leadership as well.

My philosophy is that a leader is seen four ways—through subordinates, peers, superiors, and his own eyes. I always believed that my leadership was validated by my subordinates, not my superiors. Sadly, I saw many army leaders gauge their effectiveness through a self-serving lens or by simply wishing to please their superiors. Soldiers immediately saw through leaders who displayed this behavior.

General Martin Dempsey, as the Chief of Staff of the Army, created a new personnel evaluation system that will allow for a 360 degree view of leadership. Critical in combat situations like Iraq, the new system recognizes that today's leaders cannot ask soldiers to do what their leader is unwilling to do. Most of my commanders and I traveled to the sound of the guns in Iraq, not away from them. I went on patrols every day and checked on Iraqi police stations in dangerous parts of Baghdad. It was the only way to try and compensate for so many poor decisions, to see first hand what was happening on the ground, and to try and rebuild Iraq under the rule of law. Most of my subordinate leaders did the same thing.

Dempsey recognized early in Iraq it was our only avenue to

success. I never expected my soldiers to do anything that I wouldn't do. I always demanded that they treat each other, and their enemies, with respect and dignity. I took the blame for things in war that didn't go right and gave the credit to my soldiers when things did. I spoke the truth to my military and civilian superiors when sometimes they didn't want to hear it. I never hesitated to paint an accurate portrait of life in the war zone to politicians of both parties, who all too often placed agendas before sacrifice.

I would never claim that I was a "born" leader or that all of my education, formal and in the field, were the key elements that enabled me to lead soldiers into war. There are certainly many things I would do differently if I could do it over. But there are no "do-overs" in life. I was just as afraid as they were of the consequences of mistaken judgments and the tragic results of poor cohesion and morale on the battlefield. I learned from the people who served with me that humility was the greatest preventative for bad decisions and the contagion of power. True leaders need to be guided by a humble spirit.

During our year in Iraq, nine MP Battalion Headquarters, one Infantry Battalion Headquarters, thirty-seven MP companies, three infantry companies, and two Law and Order detachments were assigned to the brigade. I had to reassign some to other units before they even left Kuwait and joined me in Iraq. Had they all been properly used, we would have seen greater success.

By the end of 2003, requirements for MPs throughout the army exceeded the force structure capability. It wasn't unusual for active component MP soldiers to return from a deployment with one unit, be reassigned to another post somewhere else in the world, only to be redeployed in less than twelve months. The situation impacted family stability, posed increased risk to the community law enforcement role played by the MPs at military installations and increased the probability of equipment shortages across the MP force.

I worked hard with my Deputy Commander, Lt. Colonel Tom Evans, to develop a flexible force plan that would allow for the rotation of MPs into and out of Iraq for the foreseeable future at the time. We were acutely aware of the MP shortage throughout the army, but our knowledge of the force structure made us feel confident that our plan would accomplish the required MP mission in Iraq. At the same time, it would provide maximum assistance to the Iraqis while they rebuilt their police, courts, and prison systems. When we presented our plan to Lt. General Ricardo Sanchez, he rejected its implementation.

In an article in the August 29, 2003 *Stars and Stripes*, Sanchez was quoted as saying, "Putting more soldiers on the ground is not going to solve the problem if I don't have the intelligence to act on." [1]

Sanchez explained to the military newspaper: "What was needed was an Iraqi civil defense force and more Iraqi police to establish linkages to the Iraqi people...to get the information that we need..." [2]

Our plan Lt. General Sanchez rejected would have strengthened the ability of the military police to accomplish our mission in Iraq. Having a continuous flow of military police in the postwar phase would have facilitated the training of Iraqi police in the ways of democratic police forces and facilitated the collection of intelligence from Iraq icitizens. The differences between a highly successful American war strategy and largely neglected and agreed upon postwar plan to build a foundation for the rule of law in Iraq, helped plant the seeds for the insurgency that began while I was there.

The Army's senior military leaders were focused on killing the bad guys because that was their comfort zone. They had trained their entire life for that, and were good at it. But we could never kill enough bad guys to win the war. I felt that every time an innocent family member was thrown down in their house during a raid, potential new enemies were created. My MPs knew how to deal with these situations, because of their law enforcement experiences. I tried repeatedly to convince my military superiors and civilian leaders that a key part of an Iraqi solution was to stand up a legitimate Iraqi police service so they could become the main component to restoring order in Iraq. Some American Army generals were too busy killing terrorists and trying to stand up a new Iraqi army to listen to concerns about the importance of policing. But it wasn't an either/or proposition. They could have placed the proper emphasis, without detracting from their missions.

I tried to convince my military superiors that while the U. S. Army was well trained in High Intensity Conflict, it had little understanding of transitioning to a policing environment after hostilities ceased. America owned Iraq after the invasion but didn't have a clear plan to begin its renovation to democracy. The Iraqi people needed to see a functioning police and prison system immediately if they were to feel secure in the aftermath of war.

Security was just as important as having food to eat and water to drink. But when criminals and terrorists rose up to intimidate the population, the Iraqi police and army had already been disbanded by the American civilian authority that administered postwar Iraq. Just as looting and rioting broke out on the streets of New Orleans after Hurricane Katrina, the lawless element of Iraq took advantage of the invasion to threaten the innocent and intimidate the unprotected. After all, this is what bullies and terrorists do. It is why they exist in the first place.

I realized that any successful policing operations in Iraq would depend upon establishing trust with Iraqi citizens. They would be the key to providing intelligence and information that identified the bad guys living and hiding among them. At great personal peril Iraqis did come forward, asking only for security in exchange for providing information. Many times they were not protected. The constant delays in establishing a viable police, court and prison system gave solace to the criminal mindset and created a restless and frightened population.

The Coalition Provisional Authority should have defined the desired endstate of the Iraqi police, courts and prison system, but never did. Bremer and Sanchez didn't appear to me to have a routine means of communication or ongoing liaison relationship which would have allowed them to effectively discuss Iraq's future and the role of its police and army in that future.

The tone is always set at the top of the food chain. The decisions being made by Lt. General Sanchez in Iraq were consistent with the tone coming from Washington D. C. in the summer of 2003.

In his book *Decision Points*, former President George W. Bush presents a mindset that explains why my troops and I were experiencing so much discomfort on the ground in Iraq in the early months of war:

> "...I raised the question of troops with Don Rumsfeld and the military leadership.
>
> They assured me we had enough...I accepted Don and the military's judgment...Jerry issued two orders after his arrival in Baghdad. One declared that certain members of Saddam's Baath party would not be eligible to serve in the new government in Iraq. The other formally disbanded the Iraqi army...I should have insisted on more debate on Jerry's orders...The security situation continued to deteriorate over the summer. Iraq was becoming a magnet for extremists. They shared an immediate goal: to drive America out of Iraq." [3]

In former Defense Secretary Donald Rumsfeld's, book, *Known and Unknown*, he provides his views on America's role in postwar Iraq. He offers an explanation as to why we had such a difficult time convincing Sanchez and other senior military officers on how best to use the MP force after the invasion. It's not at all surprising to me that Sanchez would never have made any decisions counter to the message Rumsfeld was giving him:

"When it came to the Administration's goals in Iraq, my views were straightforward...The aim was not to bestow...an American-style democracy, a capitalist economy, or a world-class military force.

"...I thought it important that we reduce the American military role in reconstruction and increase assistance from the United Nations and other willing coalition countries. Any U.S. troops remaining in Iraq would focus on capturing and killing terrorists and leftover supporters of the old regime that were still fighting."[4]

When Rumsfeld saw problems developing in Iraq after the invasion ended, he asked President Bush to authorize him to go to Iraq to organize America's postwar phase of operations. The President decided against the idea and today Rumsfeld wishes he had pressed harder on the issue. In his book, he writes:

"It was clearly important to establish order in Iraq after Saddam was gone—after coalition forces would end three decades of Ba'athist rule. We would have to fill the resulting political vacuum with a mechanism by which sectarian and ethnic groups could join to govern in a peaceful way. The tensions from State officials pulling in one direction, toward a more lengthy U. S. run occupation and the Defense Department in another direction, would have to be managed carefully. A top-level administration official in Baghdad might have made a difference in those early days. There would have been someone able to decide firmly in favor of one option over the other and extract additional guidance from Washington as required. I did not have a full understanding at the time, however, just how badly that was going to be needed."[5]

American policy makers should have learned a lesson from the invasions of Panama, Bosnia, Haiti and Kosovo, where the US successfully intervened to rescue civilian populations from tyrannical leaders. The military police played a substantial role in the post-invasion rebuilding of those countries and institutions. It is hard to imagine, with the spending of hundreds of billions of dollars on intelligence collection and analysis at the time of the second war with Iraq, that America's top leaders would later say they were not adequately prepared for the contingency of "lawlessness" after the invasion or that the goal was not to bestow "an American-style democracy." It is little wonder that the 18th MP Brigade found itself in the middle of a swamp, always slogging through the mud trying to find firmer ground that was constantly being washed away.

A recently completed assessment by the army of the MP role in Operation Iraqi Freedom incorporated my thoughts regarding the misuse of MPs in Iraq:

> "When MPs were in direct support of a maneuver commander, they sometimes misused MP assets by placing them to guard a bridge or secure a building… More times than not, maneuver commanders used combat forces to train Iraqi police instead of using MP forces. This created a rift between maneuver and MP Commanders…there was little concentration on law, investigations, evidence processing, reports, and interviews; all the necessary tools needed to be an effective and legitimate police force." [6]

On one level the breakdown in security in Iraq could be attributed to the obvious factors—not enough American soldiers, lack of cultural understanding, foreign interference from Iran, Syria and al-Qaeda, and conflicts among Iraq's own ethnic groups. On another level, the breakdown happened because there was a lack of leadership where it mattered. Lt. General Sanchez and Ambassador Paul Bremer were not working as a coordinated team. There was no military strategy from the top as to how trust could be developed within the Iraqi civilian population. There was no immediate CPA strategy to stand up an integrated system of police, courts and prisons to administer justice in Iraq and no one person or group of people to coordinate and implement such a system.

On January 4, 2004, I was interviewed in my office by a three star general incivilian clothes and who I had never heard of. He identified himself as Karl Eikenberry. He told me he had been sent by Secretary Rumsfeld to meet with senior military commanders that were about to re-deploy. His directions from Rumsfeld were to get our lessons learned and recommendations on what needed improvement.

I gave him lots of lessons learned, not knowing that almost exactly five years later he would be nominated by the newly elected President Obama to be the next Ambassador to Afghanistan. I've always wondered what he did with those lessons learned. They don't appear to have been used in Afghanistan.

I departed Iraq a month after my meeting with Eikenberry. For my remaining six months in the Army, we trained follow on forces to deploy to Iraq. I travelled to the MP School and talked to the students, including commanders that were about to go into battalion and brigade command, most which have now served in combat. I also spoke to many of my own soldiers who had been left back in Germany but were now preparing to deploy. I tried so hard to open up their heads and pour my experiences in, but it just doesn't work that way. Some of the ones I spoke to never returned home.

On July 21, 2004, I had a change of command and retirement ceremony all in one. I gave my final speech as an active duty soldier. Passages from that speech reinforce much of what we've said in this book:

About the people of Iraq, I said, "Regardless of how history looks at Operation Iraqi Freedom I know my soldiers, along with thousands of other soldiers, provided the Iraqi people with an opportunity for a better life. We will see what they do with that opportunity."

About my soldiers and leadership, I said, "They performed way above the level that I had the right to ask them to do. I have served with the best soldiers the Army has to offer, and they are being represented by the soldiers on the parade field today. They have courage to match anyone's courage and they deserve the very best leadership. I read the bottom of an e-mail I received from someone I didn't even know shortly after I returned from Iraq and it said if you can read, thank a teacher, if you can read in English, thank a soldier." I later said, "As I look back over the years I have been around lots of great units and one or two not so great units; it is always the leaders that make the difference."

On the family members I said, "I would also like to publicly thank the family members of our soldiers. We don't pay them and we often ask too much from them. We could not do what we do if they didn't do what they do. We drag them around the world; we bounce our children from school to school and from friend to friend."

I went on to say, "Lastly, I want to thank my best friend in life and my personal hero, my wife R'ami. She is the reason I am here today and she is responsible for whatever success I've enjoyed in the Army."

The impact of good leadership on morale and the ability to successfully accomplish a mission can't be understated. Sometimes it's hard to define and debate leadership, but you know a good leader when you see them in action. I experienced countless examples of good and poor leadership in Iraq and saw the tragic results of the latter. I have criticized some of the bad decisions I feel were made by President George W. Bush. To be fair, however, I watched him on Thanksgiving Day as he personified outstanding leadership in front of the troops.

As I left Iraq in February of 2004, the insurgency was growing and the situation out in the streets of Baghdad and other cities and towns was becoming more onerous. In April, 2004, photographs were distributed showing that Iraqi prisoners of war at Abu Ghraib prison had been abused by Americans. The disclosure did little to help build trust with Iraqi citizens. Lt. General Sanchez was removed from his position the following month by President Bush. He was replaced by General George W. Casey. Casey served as the Commanding General of the Multi-National force in Iraq until February, 2007, when he was replaced General David Petraeus.

Petraeus understood the importance of developing a connection with Iraq icitizens. The only way the insurgency could truly be stopped was to enlist the support of Iraqis. Law enforcement and intelligence collection would be the key to reversing the violence in Iraq. With a "surge" of over 20,000 additional troops provided by President Bush and the Congress, Petraeus went to work implementing his plan. It was more dependent upon leadership and looked very familiar in tone and substance to the work of the 18th MP Brigade years earlier. The similarities may not have been coincidental. Gillian Boice recalled the techniques the 18th had to use in Iraq and the fight we went through to employ them.

What bothered me was the lack of understanding that some

leaders had of our business as military police and law enforcement officers. We must actively patrol and enter into locations dominated by criminals and bad guys. We can't just visit these places infrequently. We have to get out of our vehicles, talk to local people, make contacts, gain information and be present to win our battles. Luckily, General Petraeus rose to high enough ranks to learn this mode of warfare."

In an article in July, 2010, Thomas E. Ricks, author and former *Washington Post* reporter, described the Petraeus approach to reversing course in Iraq:

> "...Petraeus' critical contribution in Iraq was one of leadership...after he tookover the No. 1 task for U.S. troops explicitly listed in the mission statement he issued, was to protect the Iraqi people.
>
> "...He worked tirelessly with his military subordinates...He issued letters to the troops explaining the new approach of living among the people and protecting them with small, vulnerable outposts...He walked the streets and talked to Iraqi's...He took a much more humble stance, in which Iraqis were not told what to do and how and when to do it, but were asked their advice about what to do and the best way to do it."[7]

Petraeus left Iraq in 2008 to take charge of the U. S. Central Command. In 2010 he was appointed as the Commander of U. S. Forces in Afghanistan, succeeding General Stanley A. McChrystal. Petraeus pursued strategies in Afghanistan similar to those that worked in Iraq. His first priority, as it was in Iraq, was to protect the Afghan people. He met with Afghanistan's President Karzai every day. He stationed troops in small frontier towns once controlled by the Taliban to reach out to and engage the population. He used his soldiers to remove Taliban fighters from safe havens while training Afghan security forces and local towns-men to protect themselves from any Taliban or al-Qaeda fighters wanting to return. He endorsed the idea of reconciliation with Taliban fighters who wish to give up the fight. Perhaps most important he brought together civilian and military authorities just as he did in Iraq to accomplish the objective of helping Afghanistan prepare to protect and defend itself when America ultimately leaves.

Testifying before a U. S. Senate Committee on June 29, 2010, General Petraeus spelled out exactly what he hoped to accomplish:

"We cannot allow al-Qaeda or other transnational ex-tremist elements to once again establish sanctuaries from which they can launch attacks on our homeland or on our allies. Achieving that objective, however, requires that we not only counter there surgent Taliban elements who allowed such sanctuaries in the past...we must also help our Afghan partners develop their security forces and governance capacity so that they can, over time, take on the tasks of securing their country and seeing to the needs of their people."

"The commitment to Afghanistan is necessarily, therefore, an enduring one, and neither the Taliban nor the Afghan and Pakistani partners should doubt that."[8]

Petraeus expressed confidence the strategy would work because it had worked in Iraq. The strategy worked because Petraeus was the spirit behind it. The strategy worked because Petraeus was the right leader at the right time. General Petraeus retired from the military and was the Director of the CIA for a short time. Even though many felt he fell from grace as he departed the CIA, I don't. His alleged indiscretions don't detract from his many accomplishments and his great service to our nation. His lifetime of outstanding military leadership will be his legacy.

Looking back at all that has happened since the 18th MP Brigade first entered Iraq in 2003, I feel that we did make some things work in Iraq in the summer and fall of 2003. In the absence of a consistent strategy to deal with postwar Iraq, most of my subordinate leaders understood the importance of providing solid and consistent leadership.

There is little doubt this led us to some success in establishing relationships and in building trust with Iraqi citizens. This is how we developed the substitute for a postwar plan the US government never had for Iraq in 2003. The principles sound simple, but their implementation is complex, dependent upon personality, a "never giveup" attitude, and an ability to win trust and be trusted. I am truly proud of the men and women of the 18th MP Brigade who never strayed from providing leadership throughout Iraq at all levels of interaction, despite the odds against them. As sad as it was, and is, to lose thirteen of my soldiers, I believe this approach saved the lives of many more.

I retired from the United States Army at the end of 2004. I now reside with my family in South Carolina, where I am responsible for tactical force operations at one of the country's pre-eminent special nuclear material storage areas. From the screened patio in the backyard of our suburban home my wife R'ami, a retired Military Police Lt. Colonel, and I often relax and look out on the forested woodlands forming a border around our lush green lawn. We both find comfort in the sights and smells of the trees and greenery on quiet summer evenings.

Although years have gone by since the Iraq war, I think every day about the soldiers I was given the honor to lead in combat. The wonderful life I enjoy today doesn't overcome the memories from the battlefield. My wife understands because she understands me. For twenty-seven years, my life was one of service to our country and to the men and women who became war-time family. The bond we formed was special and impossible to describe to anyone who hasn't experienced it.

The words of the soldiers who came home from Iraq with me have helped me cope every day of my life as I think about the heroic men and women we left behind. Gillian Boice retired from the army and recently shared with me some of her thoughts about our days in Iraq, "I have real comfort in knowing what we did during Operation Iraqi Freedom was miraculous in many ways."

Bennie Yousif, my ever present interpreter in the middle of the war zone, has served subsequent tours in Iraq, providing translation services for a private corporation. He has never forgotten his service as a linguist. He told me, "Working for you was a great experience. I looked forward to every mission we went on. Each one was more exciting than the one before it. I learned many things from you about the military, about respect, and about discipline."

For his part, Bennie still maintains contact with his friend and my former Humvee driver, Buchmeier, now a policeman outside the city of Chicago. Both share a passion for vintage cars, a hobby that has drawn them together in the days since they met during their war time lives. Both have continued their contacts with me since retirement.

Sgt. Buchmeier can't hide his disappointment over the politics of invading Iraq. He stated, "President Clinton deployed me to the Balkans where people were being killed for their ethnicity or religious beliefs. There were no precious resources to plunder. It was simply the right thing to intervene. I served proudly then. This time I became very disillusioned that political and bureaucratic leaders sent American kids to die for a premise based completely on knowingly fabricated intelligence. After I came home I felt ashamed when people thanked me for my service. I would tell them that I wish I reall ycould have done something to truly make the world a safer place. All that mattered to most of us in Iraq was each other."

Sgt. Jordan, who while laughing to himself, always tried to keep me on time for his meetings in Iraq, still serves in the army. He has been on multiple deployments since his days in Iraq.

My young communications expert from Milwaukee, Wisconsin, Michael Prokop, has since left the Army but touched me deeply with comments he made about the experiences we had together. He believes they changed his life and personified what leadership is about:

> "I never felt like Colonel Spain was doing anything out of vanity. The colonel's decisions were based on the welfare of his troops and what was best for the effort at hand. I have the greatest respect for Colonel Spain and appreciate him for how well he treated everyone. We spent so many of our days just helping people that the transition out of Iraq was like handing off a child to someone else. All of the MPs loved the colonel to death for what he taught us and for who he was."

I also have strong feelings about the great Americans who took time from their busy schedules to visit our soldiers on the front lines of battle, to lift their spirits. There were too many to mention here but two especially stand out. David Letterman spent time with us on Christmas Eve, and even held the American flag while we re-enlisted a soldier. And then there was Vince McMahon and the wrestlers of the World Wrestling Entertainment—the WWE. The soldiers almost lost their minds as the wrestlers circulated among my soldiers under Saddam's arches. I was so impressed by the sincerity of those amazing athletes, many of which were the heroes of my soldiers. What was so great about the event, was the wrestlers treated my soldiers like the heroes they were. To this day, the soldiers that I occasionally run into speak of the fond memories they have from that visit. For just a few minutes their minds were taken away from the daily horror of combat.

"My soldiers were more damned excited when they heard you were coming than when the President came," I jokingly told McMahon.

Lacking any post-war plan to fix Iraq after the invasion, the cumulative impact of the ten decisions discussed in this book, prolonged the war and put soldiers' lives at risk. America will face other wars similar in nature, as well as differing kinds of national crises. Understanding the nature of leadership in the decision making process will go a way towards ensuring the right outcome.

General Colin Powell, one of my personal models of leadership, may have said it best:

"Leadership is the art of accomplishing more than the science of management says is possible."

On September 22, 2009, I had the honor of being inducted into the United States Army Military Police Regimental Hall of Fame, at a ceremony held at Fort Leonard Wood, Missouri. Colonel Pat Lowery described the selection process as highly competitive, underscoring, "the significance of...many contributions to the Military Police Corps, the Army and the Nation."

Lt. Colonel Tom Evans stood beside me at the ceremony, as he did during our time in Iraq as my Brigade Deputy Commander. In fact, he wrote the submission that garnered me the high honor in Missouri. Evans went on to realize his greatest dream-command the 18th MP Brigade. He recently retired and now does similar work as me at another Department of Energy site.

Evans and I remain close friends. Evans spends a great deal of time these days mentoring others in the greatest tradition of the American military, the tradition of leadership. Evans recognizes, as I did, it is the only tradition that can make a difference between success and failure. Sometimes, it's difficult to be a real leader. But it's never been difficult to know one when you see them in action. , Hopefully General Dempsey's efforts to establish a better personnel evaluation system in the Army will help us locate those leaders of the future.

CONCLUSION: NOTES
1 "Stars and Stripes," August 29, 2003, interview of Lt. General Ricardo Sanchez.
2 Ibid, End Note #1.
3 "Decision Points," George W. Bush, 2010, Crown Publishers.
4 "Known and Unknown, a Memoir," Donald Rumsfeld, 2011, Sentinel Publishing.
5 Ibid, End Note #4.
6 United States Army MP Assessment
7 "Washington Post," June 27, 2010, "In Afghanistan, Petraeus Will have Difficulty Replicating His Iraq Success," by Tom Ricks.
8 June 29, 2010 Testimony of General Petraeus Before the United States Senate .
9 General Colin Powell, Chairman (Ret), Joint Chiefs of Staff, "A Leadership Primer."

Glossary

2 ACR	2nd Armored Cavalry Regiment
BN	Battalion
CAPT	Captain
CENTCOM	Central Command
CFLCC	Coalition Forces Land Component Command
CIA	Central Intelligence Agency
CJTF-7	Combined Joint Task Force
COL	Colonel
CPA	Coalition Provisional Authority
CPL	Corporal
DECK OF 55	High Value Detainees of Saddam's Inner Circle on Playing Cards
EPW	Enemy Prisoner of War
FBI	Federal Bureau of Investigation
FRAGO	Fragmentary Order
GEN	General
3 ID	Third Infantry Division
ILO	In Lieu Of
JAG	Judge Advocate General
Lt C	Lieutenant Colonel
Lt	Lieutenant
MKT	Mobile Kitchen Trailer
MOI	Iraq Provisional Ministry of Interior
MP	Military Police
MRE	Meals Ready to Eat
OPFOR	Opposing Forces
ORHA	Office for Reconstruction and Humanitarian Assistance

PFC	Private First Class
PLUGGER	U.S. Army Version of the GPS
RPG	Rocket Propelled Grenade
SAW	Squad Automatic Weapon
SGT	Sergeant
SPC	Specialist
SSG	Staff Sergeant
TACON	Tactical Control
TPFFD	Time-Phased Force and Deployment Data Maintenance
UH-60	Black Hawk Helicopter
V CORPS	Victory Corps (U.S. Army)
1-41 or 1/41	1st Battalion, 41st Mechanized Infantry Division

Index